SAP™ R/3™ Reporting and eBusiness Intelligence

ISBN 0-13-022615-7

9 780130 226150

90000

Prentice Hall PTR
Enterprise Software Series

Thomas A. Curran, Series Editor

SAP™ R/3™ Reporting and eBusiness Intelligence

Curran / Ladd / Ladd

SAP™ R/3™ Business Blueprint:
Understanding Enterprise Supply Chain Management, Second Edition

Curran / Ladd

PeopleSoft HRMS Reporting

Bromwich

Acquiring Enterprise Software: Beating the Vendors at Their Own Game

Verville / Halingten

SAP™ R/3 Reporting and eBusiness Intelligence

Thomas A. Curran
Andrew Ladd
Dennis Ladd

Prentice Hall PTR, Upper Saddle River, NJ 07458
www.phptr.com

Library of Congress Cataloging-in-Publication Data

Curran, Thomas (Thomas Aidan)
    SAP R/3 reporting and e-business intelligence / Thomas A. Curran, Andrew Ladd, Dennis Ladd.
        p.   cm.
    Includes index.
    ISBN 0-13-022615-7 (pbk. : alk. paper)
        1. SAP R/3.   2. Business enterprises--Computer networks--Management.
    3. Client/server computing.   4. Management information systems.   I. Ladd, Andrew.
    II. Ladd, Dennis   III. Title
    HF5548.4.R2 C874 2000
    651.7'8'028553769--dc21   00-029829

Editorial/Production Supervision: Patti Guerrieri
Acquisitions Editor: Tim Moore
Editorial Assistant: Julie Okulicz
Marketing Manager: Bryan Gambrel
Buyer: Maura Goldstaub
Cover Design: Anthony Gemmellaro
Cover Design Direction: Jerry Votta
Art Director: Gail Cocker-Bogusz
Interior Series Design: Meg VanArsdale

© 2000 Thomas Curran, Andrew Ladd, Dennis Ladd
Published by Prentice Hall PTR
Prentice-Hall, Inc.
Upper Saddle River, NJ 07458

Prentice Hall books are widely used by corporations and government agencies for training, marketing, and resale.

The publisher offers discounts on this book when ordered in bulk quantities.
For more information, contact
Corporate Sales Department
Phone: 800-382-3419; FAX: 201-236-7141
E-mail (Internet): corpsales@prenhall.com
or write:
Prentice Hall PTR
Corp. Sales Dept.
One Lake Street
Upper Saddle River, NJ 07458

SAP is a registered trademark of SAP Aktiengesellschaft, Systems, Applications and Products in Data Processing, Neurottstrasse 16, 69190 Walldorf, Germany. The publisher gratefully acknowledges SAP's kind permission to use its trademark in this publication. SAP AG is not the publisher of this book and is not responsible for it under any aspect of press law.

Printed in the United States of America

10 9 8 7 6 5 4 3 2 1

ISBN 0-13-022615-7

Prentice-Hall International (UK) Limited, London
Prentice-Hall of Australia Pty. Limited, Sydney
Prentice-Hall Canada Inc., Toronto
Prentice-Hall Hispanoamericana, S.A., Mexico
Prentice-Hall of India Private Limited, New Delhi
Prentice-Hall of Japan, Inc., Tokyo
Pearson Education Asia Pte. Ltd.
Editora Prentice-Hall do Brasil, Ltda., Rio de Janeiro

Contents

Section 2 *Business-to-Business Sales*

Chapter 4

Understanding R/3 Sales Information

Chapter 5

Analyzing R/3 Sales Information

Chapter 8
Putting It All Together: Creating an R/3-based Sales Reporting System Using the MAPP Method 133

Section 3   *Business-to-Business Procurement*

Chapter 9
Understanding R/3 Procurement Information

Chapter 10
Analyzing R/3 Procurement Information

Section 4 *Financial Accounting* 244

Chapter 14

Understanding R/3 Financial Accounting Information 247

Chapter 15

Analyzing R/3 Financial Accounting Information 255

Chapter 16

Chapter 17

Preface

This book is intended for the wide range of business professionals who want to learn more about using R/3™ for reporting across the enterprise. It provides an overview of SAP™'s value chain processes and a roadmap for solving business problems using a wide range of reporting strategies.

A guide to the R/3™ system, this book is written for business executives, senior decision makers, business engineers, members of R/3™ evaluation and/or implementation teams, along with students and academicians devoted to understanding corporate information delivery. We have attempted to make the book specific enough to satisfy the expert, but general enough to provide a good overview for the intelligent newcomer. Our main objectives are to:

- Help senior decision makers understand the business benefits of reporting in R/3™
- Provide detailed descriptions of key business process scenarios so that business professionals can determine if a particular scenario applies to their business and, if so, how it applies
- Describe the features and tools available for the evaluation and implementation of R/3™
- Help decision makers improve R/3™ information delivery throughout their organization
- Provide the reader with an easy method of reporting in R/3™ using Microsoft® Office

For business leaders either currently or about to be involved in new business design, this book will explain SAP™'s information structures. To that end, we have labored to explain information in R/3™ clearly, keeping the big picture in mind, especially for those who do not want to get too bogged down in technical detail. The first section details a reporting methodology—the MAPP method—designed by the authors. It also provides detailed information about reporting and reporting tools in the R/3™ system.

Sections 2 through 5 will be of special interest to business users working in the fields of sales, procurement, controlling, and finance. These sections structure the type of information in R/3™, and takes the reader through common types and uses of reporting in R/3™. Each section concludes with a case study that illustrates all stages of the reporting process of a fictional company.

Throughout this book, we show how R/3™ information can be simplified and organized in Microsoft Excel. The reader will learn how to access the vast data resources of SAP™ R/3™ quickly and easily, without having R/3™ expertise. Using an Excel add-in contained in the complementary software CD, R/3™ users will learn how to retrieve up-to-date R/3™ operational and financial information. The reader will learn how to get easier and broader access to R/3™ data, to simplify the reporting process, and to make more informed management decisions. They will learn to use the Excel tool for:

- Decision support for management reporting
- Financial statement reports
- Pivot tables for companies and groups
- Ad hoc queries applied to R/3™ Information Systems
- Routine tasks like printing, e-mailing a report, or making a graph
- Reports using other Microsoft Office products and tools

On one hand, this book provides a comprehensive overview for those who are currently considering SAP™ as a solution for its business reengineering problems. On the other, for those who are already familiar with R/3™ and would like to know more, we offer a holistic approach to explaining how information is structured in the R/3™ system. Ultimately, we hope to satisfy in part the growing need in the current business community to know more about solving typical business problems with R/3™.

The authors would like to thank a number of individuals who contributed to the production and content of this book. They are: Bonnie Burns for her writing, editing, and insightful comments; the development team at Component Software: Sam Gerstein, Hendrik Mager, Frank Wittmann, Steve Abramson, Dave Shih, and especially Kirill Shklovsky for his work in creating the software that is contained in this book; Nathaniel Bruce for his marketing expertise; and the kind people at Prentice Hall who patiently guided this book to press: Patti Guerrieri and especially Tim Moore. Thanks to all!

Copyright and Trademark Acknowledgments

All R/3 Reference Model diagrams and R/3 system screen shots © SAP AG. Reproduced with permission.

Microsoft, Microsoft Exchange, ActiveX, MS Word, PowerPoint, Visual Basic, LAN Manager, Windows and/or other Microsoft products are either registered trademarks or trademarks of Microsoft Corporation in the United States and/or other countries. MS Excel and MS-Net are registered trademarks of Microsoft Corporation. Windows is a registered trademark and NT is a trademark of Microsoft Corporation.

1-2-3 and Lotus are trademarks of the Lotus Development Corporation. Adabas D is a trademark of Software AG. Java is a trademark of Sun Microsystems, Inc. Oracle is a registered trademark of the Oracle Corporation. Power-Builder is a trademark of Powersoft, Inc. AIX, DB2, DB2 6000, and OS/2 are registered trademarks of IBM. Apple is a registered trademark and Macintosh, Mac, Mac OS are trademarks of Apple Computer, Inc. UNIX is a registered trademark in the United States and other countries licensed exclusively through X/Open Company Ltd. LiveModel is a trademark and Intellicorp is a registered trademark of IntelliCorp., Inc. Visio is a registered trademark and Visio Business Modeler is a trademark of Visio Corporation. Novell is a registered trademark and NetWare is a trademark of Novell, Inc. Informix is a registered trademark, and Informix-Online is a trademark of Informix Software, Inc. EnTIS and ActiveSheets are trademarks of Component Software Inc.

Other brand, product, or company names mentioned herein are trademarks, registered trademarks, or trade names of their respective owners.

Note: Because we have endeavored to cooperate with SAP policies, every reference to SAP and R/3 have been trademarked and copyrighted throughout this book. We apologize if this in any way provides a hindrance to the reader.

Introduction

The new Internet economy has radically altered the business landscape, transforming how businesses interact with customers, conduct core business processes, and support knowledge management across the organization. In the past, crucial reports about the health of a company were generated by analysts who gathered information, put it in usable form, distributed it across the organization and then, in the next quarter, started all over again. The introduction of Enterprise Resource Planning (ERP) systems dramatically improved how businesses integrated, consolidated, accessed, and managed information from all parts of an organization. Business functions such as human resources, accounting, manufacturing, sales, and customer management were integrated into one cross-functional database system that could respond to business needs with a degree of sophistication never before achieved. ERP's built-in business processes such as standard order handling, make-to-order production, procurement of stock material, customer processing, budgeting, and field service gave management a standardized framework for process level reporting with the aim of optimization or focusing the business.

Because of this sophistication, however, ERP systems have proven to be incredibly complex. While real-time information delivery is commonplace in the open Internet marketplace, it remains a challenge for most organizations. Despite the billions of dollars invested in ERP, most of the corporate world lives in the week-to-week, end-of-the-month reporting style of the post-punch card industrial era. Many Chief Information Officers still struggle to get the information locked up inside ERP systems out to constituents across the organization, even though this data can often have a tremendous impact on a company's bottom line.

1

While working at SAP™ AG in Germany in the late 90's, the authors of this book undertook extensive research of R/3™'s penetration in the client site. One of the truly amazing statistics that came out of that research is that roughly 7% of business users have access to the corporate information locked away in enterprise software applications from vendors like SAP™ AG, PeopleSoft, J.D. Edwards, and Baan. Most of the 7% will be involved in some kind of data input or transaction processing. The challenge, therefore, is to harvest the fruits of ERP and distribute them to the people who can make a difference. The fact is, these people are more likely to be accustomed to data processing with MS Excel or the Internet than with R/3™.

Today, the ubiquity, speed, and flexibility of the Internet drive bold new initiatives in ebusiness, transforming how business users think about proprietary, expensive, and arcane enterprise technologies. More than ever before, businesses need new structures for information delivery—different ways of accessing, analyzing, and distributing data that can better exploit business opportunities as they arise. Automating transactions is no longer enough. To conduct e-commerce on the Web, companies need to be able to create real-time collaborative environments for business users, customers, supply chain constituents, and partners. A sales manager, for instance, might need to view incoming sales orders via a wireless device. A customer might want to check on the progress of her order over the Internet. Suppliers might need to be notified by pager or fax that their last shipment has been received. Partners often require a remote demonstration of a particular product or service. In the next generation enterprise, all of these tasks need to happen effortlessly and in real time.

The introduction of initiatives such as SAP™'s mySAP.com suggests that enterprise software vendors understand that the Internet, which connects over 100 million individuals and businesses globally, has radically transformed how businesses work. The server-based architecture of the Internet and its unique ability to deliver on demand such desktop application components as data charting or travel and expense tracking, now drives the development and deployment of enterprise software. If in the last decade ERP systems integrated business processes within the enterprise, in the next generation the Internet and other pervasive computing applications will continue to drive ebusiness intelligence, that is, business-to-business integration and cross-enterprise collaboration.

Market sources indicate that the enterprise application market will continue to grow at a rate of 32 percent over the next five years to $66.6 billion by 2003, fueled primarily by the desire for analytic applications that optimize business processes. To remain competitive, companies will continue to push key decision-making processes down to employees and out to partners. These economic drivers place new demands on enterprise reporting as companies seek complete reporting solutions in easy-to-use formats.

In today's enterprise reporting environment, business managers want to bring real-time information to a wide constituency. As more and more businesses adopt open and collaborative systems for information exchange, however, business managers have discovered that getting the right information to the right people and getting it to them quickly remain very real challenges. Improving customer relations, reaching new markets, and reducing the costs of bringing products and services to market are all potential benefits of ebusiness, but these benefits can only be realized if corporate information can be used to define clear business goals and to determine appropriate measures for determining success.

Because enterprise applications have traditionally focused on automating processes and not on delivering information to key decision makers, the overall value of enterprise applications has yet to be unlocked. Today, new initiatives in personalization, collaboration, and remote delivery have revolutionized the process of data acquisition. Germane to this is SAP™'s New Dimension Suite™, which is a set of specialized R/3™ applications targeting more sophisticated transaction processing (APO), front office interaction (CRM), and analytic applications (BW). In many ways, the possibilities for enterprise reporting seem almost limitless. A corporate executive can deliver a boardroom quality report from the back seat of a taxicab using a Nokia Communicator™, Psion™, or PalmPilot™, or access the latest metrics about the health of the organization using a 2-way pager. More and more, good enterprise reporting requires information that is timely, relevant, and accurate. But if enterprise reporting is to fulfill its mission of supporting the analytic requirements of key decision makers throughout the organization, it also requires sophisticated business intelligence. With initiatives like mySAP.com, enterprise reporting can now preserve the best business practices embedded in an information architecture like R/3™, while exploiting the connectivity of the Internet and other pervasive computing applications.

In *SAP™ R/3™ Reporting and eBusiness Intelligence*, we explain how to unlock the data in R/3™ and access the information in your system in a way that makes good business sense. Unlike previous reporting books that simply guide readers through the reporting tools of a particular enterprise software system, *SAP™ R/3™ Reporting and eBusiness Intelligence* will help you create reports with a proven method of analysis, respond to the business needs of an organization, and understand the what, where, and how of enterprise system information.

To help both new and experienced users better manipulate R/3™ data for reporting across the enterprise, this book explains how information is stored and delivered in the R/3™ system and demonstrates some useful methods for retrieving data from the R/3™ system. Before we turn to the information within the R/3™ system, we should first outline some basic information about SAP™ and the R/3™ system. If this is familiar territory for you, feel free to skip to the first chapter.

What Is R/3™?

Initially, SAP™ made the move from mainframes to open systems in the late 1980's with R/2™, a monolithic, mainframe legacy solution. As early as 1988, however, SAP™ chose to move toward client/server technology and began developing R/3™. In 1992, SAP™ unveiled R/3™ just as client/server and its potential were beginning to be fully realized in the business world. R/3™'s success is largely due to its ability to provide a highly integrated environment that can fully exploit the potential of client/server computing, and its razor-sharp focus on selling the standard solution to the high echelons of corporate computing.

R/3™'s advantages lie in its flexibility, scalability, and expandability. It can be used in client/server architectures with 30 seats or in installations with 3,000 end-users. This scalability ensures that R/3™ can provide support for current business operations and still adapt to change and progress. Designed as a total system, but also suitable for modular use, R/3™ is expandable in stages, making it adaptable to the specific requirements of individual businesses. R/3™ can run on the hardware platforms of leading international manufacturers and can integrate with customers' in-house applications. It is also open to interoperability with third-party solutions and services. Experts in such scaleable software as Microsoft, IBM™, and Apple™ have all deployed SAP™ as their enterprise solution.

As we go to press with this book, SAP™ is busy repositioning the company from enterprise software to business Internet computing. The customers' desire for real-time business information has never been greater. More and more business users now expect personalized and synchronous data that can be delivered anywhere and at any time; in the next generation enterprise, systems that aren't flexible enough to serve the needs of end users will eventually founder. While the marketing literature seems to skim over the fact that R/3™ is the core of this outward push, the value that many customers have to gain has less to do with the Internet, and more to do with the basic client/server infrastructure to which R/3™ contributes.

mySAP.com

In 1999, SAP™ introduced mySAP.com, a comprehensive Internet-based initiative that promised to facilitate collaboration, personalize the work environment, and provide end-to-end integration of SAP™ and non-SAP™ software solutions. In the 1980's SAP™ revolutionized business computing by delivering an integrated view of the enterprise; by the 1990's, spurred by the possibilities of the Internet, SAP™ aspired to provide an equally integrated view of entire markets.

mySAP.com offers the following components:

- mySAP.com Marketplace—a business-to-business Internet site that brings together over 12,000 companies. By connecting buyers and sellers, creating new marketplace opportunities, and reducing transaction costs, mySAP.com Marketplace provides a better infrastructure for companies to conduct business.
- mySAP.com Workplace—an enterprise portal that provides SAP™ users with a personalized, Web-based work environment. It features an open and flexible infrastructure that delivers resources according to each user's role in the company. In addition, users can employ a Web browser to access intranet and extranet applications, front- and back-office systems, and legacy applications.
- mySAP.com business scenarios—a series of business-to-business and business-to-consumer solutions derived from over 25 years of industry experience. Business scenarios integrate business processes with industry-specific knowledge and services. The business logic intrinsic to these business scenarios helps companies design new business processes, increase productivity, enhance decision support, and improve customer service.
- Web-based application hosting, a cost-effective way for companies to access the full range of mySAP.com solutions.

The concept behind mySAP.com is to enable companies to "push" the business logic embedded in R/3™ outward, transforming operations into ebusinesses that can take full advantage of the Internet. Transactions are completed more swiftly because standard Web functions can be integrated with back-office systems. Businesses can more easily find and collaborate with suppliers and partners from around the world. Individuals have better access to services created specifically for them.

mySAP.com aims to deliver a total business process integration that begins with the customer and extends throughout the business operation. Combined with real-time collaboration among participants, it will have a tremendous impact on how information is managed and delivered in the next decade. Fulfilling the vision of "virtual integration" across industries and communities requires sophisticated business intelligence that can be delivered quickly and easily to key decision makers.

How Is R/3™ Designed?

The architecture of SAP™'s R/3™ system is a three-tier design of presentation, application, and database servers. SAP™ pioneered the client/server software design, which is used in much of today's enterprise software and enables the system to be distributed among PCs, workstations and midrange computers. This design allows a functional split to be made between front-end presentation servers and back-end database servers, with application servers operating between.

1. Presentation Server—This is the presentation tier of the client/server system that allows human-to-computer interaction using the keyboard, mouse, and monitor. System users deal directly with this first level only. The software includes a user-friendly graphical user interface (GUI) that takes requests from the user and passes them on to the application server.

2. Application Server—These servers act as the intermediary or the second tier of the client/server system. Using UNIX® or Windows NT® they can run on one or more computers. Application servers prepare, format, and process incoming data. Sometimes, application servers connect with databases and on-line services to provide information users request or to make changes to the database. Typically, the application server is dedicated to a large group of users, such as a department.

3. Database Server—Databases and other applications constitute the third tier of the client/server system. Briefly, this third tier stores information that servers can use. The software on the database server, or central computer, controls database management and batch processing. The software retrieves the data from the database and contains all the programs downloaded to the appropriate application servers.

The three-tier approach to the design of client/server systems takes advantage of local workplace computers and the computing power of central systems. R/3™ architecture ensures that the system is sufficiently flexible to expand with a company's needs and enables individual computers to reach their maximum performance capability. It also helps companies optimize business processes by integrating data and making it available on-line and in real time to every user and workplace.

In addition, the R/3™ architecture includes Business Application Programming Interfaces (BAPIs), which comprise an essential architectural layer for interacting on a peer-to-peer basis with a client/server system. For example, Microsoft Excel is used as an interactive presentation-level BAPI for balance sheet consolidation. Without ever leaving Excel, the user triggers consolidation between it and other servers running on the R/3™ system.

Besides the benefits offered by utilizing relational databases for data storage and the open BAPIs for incorporating third-party products, R/3™ is also oriented around a number of central "business objects." Before client/server technology, business software was designed in a formalistic, data schema-driven fashion. It performed individual business functions such as purchasing, inventory management, or financial accounting in response to functional requirements. In many companies, such functionally oriented applications gave rise to an unmanageably complex maze of data models and system components. Interfaces had to be hard programmed to link the applications together. Once instituted, function-oriented structures could not be transformed into process-oriented structures. Companies sacrificed flexibility and the ability to respond quickly to changing business needs.

By contrast, R/3™ is a process-based system geared toward business objects. Business objects such as "order," "goods receipt document," or "financial accounting document" can assume different guises and attributes within the R/3™ architecture. An order, for example, can take many forms depending on its context: standard order, delivery schedule, or outline agreement. It can also refer to a purchase requisition or be assigned to an account.

The flexibility of R/3™ allows the parameterization of such business objects and makes it possible to use the same system to model quite different processes. R/3™ architecture is such that the most important business objects are encapsulated along with the required methods. Business objects can also be freely invoked, permitting context-sensitive integration at any point along a company's business process chain.

What Is the R/3™ Business Blueprint?

SAP™ has packaged 25 years of best business practices in many different industries into a "blueprint" called the R/3™ Reference Model. The Reference Model, SAP™'s Business Blueprint, guides companies from the beginning phases of engineering, including evaluation and analysis, to the final stages of implementation. It is the definitive description of R/3™, providing a comprehensive view of all the processes and business solutions available in the system. Technical details, however, are "hidden" so that the business user can focus solely on business process issues. In other words, the Business Blueprint is written in the language of the business user.

The Business Blueprint is often the starting point for business engineering and software implementation project efforts. To date, few companies have been able to provide a comprehensive process-oriented description of a business that fits into almost any industry. The Business Blueprint is a means of streamlining processes and implementing R/3™ without having to start from scratch.

The Business Blueprint concentrates on four key areas necessary for understanding business: events, tasks or functions, organization, and communication. This model defines who must do what, when, and how. Events are the driving force behind a business process, prompting one or more activities to one place. This is the essence of SAP™'s Event-driven Process Chain (EPC) Methodology.

In Release 4.5, SAP™ offered roughly 800 predefined business processes, with variants, that generally correspond to different industries and corporations. These are illustrated with the EPC graphical method. By connecting events and tasks, even very complex business processes are modeled and analyzed. An EPC model can show where breaks in the chain of tasks and responsibilities hurt the ability of a company to optimize its processes. Graphical models help users select and understand the software, visualizing how data flows through business areas and showing how various functions interact with each other. The EPC model is the central, process-oriented view. Other models show function, process, information flow, and organization views.

The Business Blueprint can be viewed and analyzed with the help of the R/3™ Business Engineer. A set of integrated tools for configuring R/3™, the Business Engineer has graphical browsing facilities for displaying the Business Blueprint directly from the R/3™ Repository (which contains all the data definitions and structures required by ABAP/4 programs). The Business Engineer also includes customizing components that allow a user to adapt or modify the system to meet the user's own specific needs.

If you'd like to learn more about the R/3™ Reference Model and supply chain management in R/3™, read our first SAP™ book, *SAP™ R/3™ Business Blueprint*, second edition (Prentice Hall PTR, 1999).

Who Uses R/3™?

R/3™ is the accepted standard in such key industries as software, oil, chemicals, consumer packaged goods, and high-tech electronics. Other industries include automotive, building and heavy construction, communication services, consulting (software), financial services, furniture, healthcare and hospitals, pharmaceuticals, public sector, raw materials, retail, services, steel, tourism, transportation, and utilities.

Table I-1 is a partial list of R/3™ users.

Table I–1   R/3™ Users

Industry	Company
Automotive	ITT Automotive Europe
	Yamaha
	Audi
	General Motors
	Chrysler
	BMW
	Subaru
	Toyota
	Volkswagen
Building and Heavy Construction	ABB Industrietechnik AG
	Gebauer
	Kawasaki Heavy Industries
	ADtranz ABB Daimler-Benz
	Babcock Prozess Automation GmbH
	CEGELEC AEG Anlagen und GESOBAU GAG
	Dover Elevator International, Inc.
	Dürkopp Adler AG
	E. Heitkamp GmbH
	Eldim B.V.
	Frequentis
Chemicals	Bayer
	Ciba Geigy
	Procter & Gamble
	CCPL
	Degussa
	Henkel
	Kemira
	Lever Europe
	Pirelli Pneumatici S.P.A
	Reichhold
	Sasol Alpha Olefins
	Schülke & Mayr
	Wintershall, Wingas, Kali und Salz
	Zeneca

Table I–1   R/3™ Users (Continued)

Industry	Company
Communication Services, Media	Random House Simon & Schuster, Inc. IPSOA Editore S.R.L. Optus Vision Ringier AG Seattle Times SFR Telecom PTT
Computer Software	Apple 3com Corporation Autodesk Inc. Fujitsu Microelectronics Fujitsu Network Communications, Inc. Hewlett-Packard IBM Samsung Wang Intersolv Legend QDI Ltd. Logistix MicrografxMicrosoft Micro Software Group Visio
Consumer Products: Food	Alfred Ritter GmbH & Co. KG Anheuser-Busch Companies Boston Beer Colgate-Palmolive Cameo, S.P.A. Guinness Hardenberg'sche Firmengruppe Heinecken Italia S.P.A. Imperial Tobacco Nestlé Keebler Company
Consumer Products: Non-Food	Braun AG Colgate-Palmolive Hans Schwarzkopf GmbH Heissner Unilever Italia S.P.A.-Divisione Lever

Table I–1 R/3™ Users (Continued)

Industry	Company
Financial Services, Banks, Insurance	ABB Holding Ltd. (CN)
	Allied Irish Banks plc (IE)
	BMW Bank GmbH (DE)
	BMW Finance Ltd (GB)
	Banca D'Italia (IT)
	Banco De Portugal Det Dep. Emissão E Tesouraria (PT)
	Banco Itau S.A. (BR)
	Bank of Canada (CA)
	Bank of Slovenia (SI)
	Bayerische Landesbank (DE)
	Bayerische Vereinsbank (DE)
	Commerzbank AG (DE)
	Countrywide Banking Corporation Limited (NZ)
	Credit Suisse (CH)
	Deutsche Bank AG (DE)
	First Chicago NBD Corporation (US)
	First National Building Society (IE)
	Jyske Bank A/S (DK)
	LGT Bank in Liechtenstein (LI)
	Lloyds TSB Group plc (GB)
	Mercedes Benz Finance Ltd (GB)
	National Westminster Bank plc (GB)
	PARIBAS BANQUE France
	PT Bank Bali (ID)
	Putnam Company (US)
	The Bank of N.T. Butterfield & Son Ltd. (BM)
	The Government Savings Bank (TH)
	The Nomura Securities Company (JP)
	Toyota Finance (AU)
	UBS Schweiz. Bankgesellschaft (CH)
	Volkswagen Financial Services (DE)
	Volkswagen Leasing Polska SP. Z (PL)
	WestLB Westdeutsche Landesbank (DE)
	Zürcher Kantonalbank (CH)
	LBS Bayerische Landesbausparkasse
	Mercedes-Benz Lease Finanz
	Sega
	Victoria

Table I–1   R/3™ Users (Continued)

Industry	Company
Industrial and Commercial Machinery	Fiat Avio Gurtec GmbH Kapp Mann & Hummel Metabo Sulzer Electronics
Oil and Gas	British Gas Chevron Conoco Shell Exxon Mobil Petromidia
Pharmaceuticals	Boehringer Mannheim Italia S.P.A. Ciba-Geigy Degussa AG FRESENIUS AG Warner Lambert Merck Weimer Pharma Zeneca Plc.
Primary Metal, Metal Products, Steel	Carnaud Metalbox Degussa AG EBG/Thyssen
Retail	Diethelm Holdings Grofa GmbH Prisma-Aspri STANDA S.P.A. CompUSA Fleming Florsheim Home Depot Kerr Drugs Maxim Group Office Max PetsMart Reebok Shoe Show Woolworth

Table I-1   R/3™ Users (Continued)

Industry	Company
Transportation Services, Tourism	Condor Flugdienst GmbH Copenhagen Airport A/S
Utilities	British Gas GEA AG Industrielle Betriebe Aarau New York Power Authority Pacific Gas and Electric STEWEAG Energie Westcoast Energy
Wood and Paper	Gizen GmbH Papierfabrik August Köhler AG SCP

Conclusion

Changing market dynamics driven by the rise of ebusiness are compelling many enterprises to rethink both their organizational structure and use of technology. In the past, economies of scale produced benefits by offering standardized products to stable, large consumer markets. Technology was used to optimize well-defined, discretely functioning areas within the enterprise. Information specialists created and maintained application software to automate certain business functions. The systems were designed to take snapshots of the business. Each snapshot provided data for hierarchical control, local decision-making, and financial accounting.

Today, the new Internet economy is prompting companies to once again adapt their business processes by adding new applications for employees and developing outward-facing business systems that will support customers, suppliers, and partners. Companies are seeking applications and services that can reduce internal costs and improve margins through self-service applications such as human resources, travel and expense management, recruiting, and procurement. To compete in the ebusiness economy, companies will need to increase customer retention and loyalty by using customer relationship management, supply chain management, order management and fulfillment, and customer and supplier collaboration applications. SAP™ R/3™ and companion initiatives such as mySAP.com provide comprehensive solutions to help companies compete successfully in this new business environment. In combination, the

Internet and SAP™ R/3™ are highly flexible means for delivering business information across the enterprise.

The challenge remains: How to get the information to the right people in a timely and convenient manner.

Throughout this book, we will continue to draw from real business experiences and practices to illustrate basic principles of enterprise reporting. We have attempted to provide examples from a wide variety of industries so that the reader can intuit the many possibilities inherent in the R/3™ system.

Focusing on the producers and consumers of enterprise reports, *SAP™ R/3™ Reporting and eBusiness Intelligence* teaches you how to organize, create, and deploy reports in your company using a simple four-step formula: Manage, Analyze, Present, and Publish (MAPP). The MAPP technique allows any business user to create a logical way to organize, analyze, present, and deliver data so that the people who need the information the most can make decisions that matter. Because the most common transaction and presentation systems in business today are SAP™ R/3™, Microsoft Office, and the Internet, we center our attention on R/3™ and Microsoft Excel, the tools that provide the best approach to understanding enterprise reporting. We clearly articulate the goals of enterprise reporting and demonstrate how to achieve dynamic reports linked to the live data in your enterprise system.

SAP™ R/3™ Reporting and eBusiness Intelligence also explains how reports can be most effectively published to a corporate Intranet using tools such as Microsoft Outlook®/Exchange, personalized business information, data delivery subscription services, as well as analytical tools such as ActiveSolutions™, which combines business logic with real-time information delivery to give organizations the competitive advantage they need to make critical decisions about strategic planning, customer analysis, asset management, and product analysis.

While our main focus is reporting and information delivery in R/3™, we have tried to explain as much of the R/3™ system and its variants as possible. We understand that different parts of this book will interest different readers, and for that reason we have tried in this Introduction to steer readers toward their areas of interest. Generally speaking, the best strategy for readers with specific areas of interest is to follow these option paths.

- Readers who are most interested in the business logic of the R/3™ system should begin with Part 1, Information Delivery in R/3™.

- Those readers who know about the business side of R/3™ and would like to know more about R/3™ reporting functionality should begin with Chapter 3, R/3™ Reporting
- Readers who would like to examine specific business processes and their reporting content that are available in R/3™ should begin with the section that best fits their areas of interest: Section 2, Business-to-Business Sales, Section 3, Business-to-Business Procurement, or Section 4, Business-to-Business Financials.

Finally, the software that accompanies this book is specially designed to help both new and experienced users better manipulate and use R/3™ data for reporting across the enterprise.

SECTION 1

Reporting Basics: A MAPP for Enterprise Reporting

In this section we examine the fundamentals of enterprise reporting. Chapter 1 takes a look at the basic assumptions behind our approach and lays out the key terms and concepts that we'll be covering in the book. Chapter 2 embarks upon the methodology that we use, what we call the MAPP method for enterprise reporting. This chapter gives you a system for creating and executing ERP (Enterprise Resource Planning) reports in your organization. In the last chapter of the section, we cover the basics of reporting with SAP™ R/3™, the primary business information engine used for this book. We also provide a quick guide to creating Excel-based reporting solutions with R/3™.

The following topics are covered in this section:

- Enterprise reporting basics
- Enterprise reporting with SAP™ R/3™
- SAP™ R/3™ business objects and processes
- Enterprise reporting with Microsoft® Excel
- Fundamentals of good reporting
- Goals of the MAPP method
- MAPP method in detail
- Scenarios for each phase of the MAPP method
- SAP™ R/3™ reporting basics
- SAP™ R/3™ business logic
- SAP™ R/3™ reporting tools
- SAP™ R/3™ information systems
- Creating reports in SAP™ R/3™
- Creating Excel-based reports with ActiveSheets
- ActiveSheets templates

1

Enterprise Reporting

The primary responsibility of a CEO's staff is to produce reports about the health of the company. Not that long ago the Chief Financial Officers of companies sent out armies of reporting analysts at regular intervals to gather financial information for the organization. These analysts would determine content, put it in a usable form, and then distribute it for such diverse purposes as management, performance analysis, budgeting, and so forth. In large companies forty to fifty people would be needed to deliver this service to the organization. Enterprise Resource Planning (ERP) software systems took hold in companies across the world precisely because they not only could reduce the need for such heavy-handed and resource-intensive procedures, but they could localize all that information into a fully integrated business system. With ERP systems like SAP™'s R/3™, the crucial numbers in an organization have become readily available. Now management can spend time analyzing those numbers rather than simply gathering basic data and verifying its authenticity. In other words, ERP systems enable management to spend less time on harvesting information and more on determining what the numbers mean.

And yet, even with the vast improvements ERP systems have made possible, they remain difficult to understand and use, especially for the occasional end user, high-level management, and others who simply aren't involved in ERP data entry, implementation, data warehousing, or system administration. For these people, systems like R/3™ are incredibly complex. They know the information is there, but they don't understand how to get at it. Indeed, even expert R/3™ users tend to know only a fraction of the system, relying on what they already know to conduct day-to-day business. Consequently, managers still spend too much time ascertaining where and what their business information is rather than analyzing what the information means. Moreover, the delivery of the information to the end user remains caught up in a slow, antiquated process that does not utilize the full potential of the business information system. To use SAP™'s metaphor, companies are behind the wheel of a Ferrari, but they rarely take it over 30 mph. Corporate business people have an incredibly sophisticated business engine, yet information remains as difficult as ever to drive. The expected revolution of empowered end users, who have accurate, mission-critical data at their fingertips and are able to create and analyze the data most pertinent to their individual needs, has yet to reach the starting line.

The reasons for this failure in ERP systems are complicated. Some have to do with the carryover from old processes, antiquated legacy systems, and the general resistance to any change in the way things are done. Some have to do with the difficulty of understanding ERP systems such as R/3™. Also, end users tend to prefer the software they know best. Part of the problem has to do with the fact that companies are unique and that no two R/3™ implementations are exactly alike. As a result there is no real standard, no real solution for companies to adopt. Finally, there is no systematic approach to solving a company's reporting needs that both understands the business needs and goals of an organization *and* knows how to match those requirements to the ERP system. In other words, there's no publication out there that explains how to get at the information in an ERP system in a systematic way, makes good business sense, and still makes full use of the business software system.

These are the goals of this book. There are many ways to explain how to perform enterprise reporting. In the pages that follow, we don't just explain the tools of a particular ERP system. Instead, we help you create and understand reports by providing a method for analysis that is both generic to the reporting needs of an organization *and* explains the what, where, and how of the ERP system. The most common transaction and presentation systems in business today are SAP™ R/3™, Microsoft Office, and the Internet. To our minds, these tools offer the best way to deliver and present information to end users and so provide the best approach to understanding enterprise reporting. While our approach is applicable to other ERP systems, our focus will remain on R/3™ and Excel throughout the book.

1.1   REPORTING WITHIN THE ENTERPRISE

The stock market boom has made most Americans aware of the power of real-time information. In today's enterprise reporting environment, management wants to bring real-time information to end users. They also want to be aware of trends in business when possible. To that end, this book focuses on two primary groups that deal the most with enterprise reporting, groups we refer to as producers and consumers.

Producers are the business professionals who go about planning, designing, and creating company reports. Producers tend to be:

- Project team members
- Reporting analysts
- Implementation teams
- Upper level management

This book is not just for producers of information, however. We also want to reach the consumers, the end users who actually put the report information to work. Consumers typically consist of management and business end users in sales, financials, procurement, and operations.

Before moving on, we should make very clear what this book will and will not do. This book will help you develop a high level of understanding of enterprise reporting. However, even though we drill down as far as we can and present data models, we will not be spending a lot of time on tools, programs, and fields in the R/3™ system.

This book will also help you get an understanding of how to get information out of R/3™. You will learn how to use R/3™ to understand how your business works, but this book won't teach you how everything in R/3™ works. In other words, this is neither a book about R/3™ menu screens nor a step-by-step guide to the R/3™ system. We cover all the R/3™ basics, such as creating Advanced Business Application Programming (ABAP) reports, using R/3™ information systems, and using reporting tools such as Report Writer™ and Report Painter™, but we do not spend a great deal of time on R/3™ tools. Nor is this a book about how to create R/3™ programs to make reports. The reasons for these omissions are quite simple. For one, it is our opinion that SAP™'s tools and programs are part of the problem; that is, they are precisely what make SAP™ R/3™ reporting difficult. For another, other documents can take you through the screens and options that help create SAP™ reports. For example, an SAP™ department, the R/3™ Simplification Group, has just recently published a very thorough documentation of R/3™ standard reports and tools (http://207.105.30.51/simpweb/index.html).

Our book takes an "outside-in" approach, teaching you how to organize, create, and deploy reports in your company. However, this book neither describes a data warehousing model nor the transformation rules for the data. In short, this is not a data warehousing book. Other books focus entirely on data warehousing and data warehousing approaches to information. We touch upon these areas, but instead of trying to teach you what happens to information on a systems level, we focus on organizing, analyzing, and presenting information to end users.

Finally, if you are looking for an introduction to R/3™ systems and processes, this is not the book for you. We recommend our R/3™ best seller, *SAP*™ *R/3*™ *Business Blueprint: Understanding Supply Chain Management,* for the basic business logic behind the SAP™ R/3™ system.

Now that we have covered what this book is about, let's examine some of the basic assumptions behind our approach for understanding enterprise reporting.

1.2   *THE MAIN ACTIVITIES OF ENTERPRISE REPORTING*

In R/3™, a report can be many things: a program, a list, a predefined set of data, and so on. Indeed, some of the confusion about R/3™ reporting is simply due to the fact that the term is used to cover so many different areas of the systems. We prefer a utilitarian definition that makes the most business sense: a report is simply a way of organizing, analyzing, presenting, and delivering information to end users.

First, reports organize information. In a company, information is dynamic. A report is a snapshot of a specific business area at a certain point in time. These pictures enable the user to manage and analyze the crucial numbers of the business more effectively. Reports draw together all the significant questions that a business needs to answer, such as:

- What do the reports currently analyze?
- How important is the information?
- Who needs to see it and when?
- What are the time periods covered in the report?

These questions help focus a report into something useful for the organization. Second, reports analyze information. Reports are a collection of data capable of multiple purposes and perspectives that address the business needs of many end users. They are specific in that they address a specific need, but they are open-ended enough so that they can meet the requirements of the person using the report. To that end, the end user needs to know what kinds of information can be analyzed. For instance, what categories of information, what organizations, and what characteristics, key figures, and performances are being measured?

Third, reports present information. This is more than just formatting, although the appearance of a report and its form often determine how its content will be used. The form of the report should facilitate its use. If a report is going to be sent to many different users, the report should be in a form that is accessible to all end users, in Excel for example.

Finally, reports deliver information. Getting the report to end users where and when they need it is crucial to an organization. Reports sent to end users provide the latest, most up-to-date information on which they can base their decisions. To facilitate delivery, the report must be scheduled, tracked, and routed. Regular training must be conducted so that the end user understands and knows how to use the report. Rollouts need to be devised. In each case, the main objective is to get the report to the end user when they need it.

1.3   *SAP™: THE FOUNDATION FOR ENTERPRISE REPORTING*

There are many ERP systems that we could have chosen to explicate enterprise reporting. The fact remains, however, that SAP™ R/3™ is the foremost enterprise software system and is the one used by most Fortune 1000 companies.

Founded in 1972 in Walldorf, Germany, SAP™ (Systems, Applications and Products in Data Processing) commands a significant share of the worldwide client/server enterprise application software market. SAP™ is the number one vendor of standard business application software and is the fourth largest independent software supplier in the world. More than 6,000 companies in over 50 countries use SAP™ software. Prominent SAP™ company facts include:

- Pioneer of inter-enterprise marketplace
- Leading client/server business software company
- Leading vendor of standard business application software
- Worldwide market share of 33%
- Fourth-largest independent software supplier in the world
- Availability in 14 languages
- 34% of customer base under $200 million
- 10 out of the top 10 US companies with highest market value use SAP™
- 8 of the top 10 largest US corporations use SAP™
- 8 of the top 10 highest profit US companies use SAP™
- More than 7,500 customers in over 90 countries

Due to its collection of standard business processes, SAP™ R/3™ has become the de facto standard for business information systems. But SAP™ R/3™'s popularity is only one reason for our choice. Indeed, the main reason for our choice lies in its rich sources of business content.

SAP™ R/3™ business content is based on streamlined business processes. During implementation R/3™ is used to describe, simulate, and model organizations and to consider how changes made to the organizations affect processes. The organizational structures of the business processes—representing the actual business transactions and communications conducted by the company—are mapped into the architecture of the information systems. The system thus includes a working description of how things are done in the company, including the flow of information and communications as well as information about the company's tasks and functional structure. A well-integrated system not only improves overall business operations but also makes it easier for the company to identify areas for further improvement.

The best aspects of the R/3™ information management system lie in the ability to integrate all business processes and areas into a coherent and well-structured supply chain. Supply chain management involves the planning and control of all tasks along the business value chain—from production planning to capital asset management. The goal of supply chain management is to reduce inventory levels, costs, and time to market, and ultimately to provide better customer service and satisfaction. In the past, companies tended to isolate each of their operations and analyze them without any consideration of their interdependence. By introducing the supply chain, companies have a more comprehensive understanding of everything that effects the delivery of goods and materials from the original supplier to the customer.

From sales and distribution to production planning, R/3™ incorporates logistical and operational areas into an integrated workflow of value chains. The R/3™ system automatically links together logistically and operationally related areas, eliminating the need to repeat time- and resource-intensive procedures. By integrating such important value activity areas as finance or human resources, businesses make themselves more effective and efficient. R/3™ stores invaluable information that pertains to every aspect of the enterprise.

1.4 ENTERPRISE REPORTING WITH BUSINESS OBJECTS

Any discussion of R/3™ integration and business information must consider business objects and how they are used in R/3™. Business objects expose standard interfaces to R/3™, otherwise known as Business Application Programming Interfaces (BAPIs). The business object interface consists of transactional methods and a data interface. The transactional methods allow an external application to automate selected functions within R/3™. The data interface exposes the structure of the information in R/3™ from a business logic perspective.

An example of an SAP™ business object is a sales order. A sales order refers to other business objects, such as sales organization, purchase order, or customer. It also is associated with business processes as defined in the SAP™ Reference Model, such as "Standard Order Handling." In this way, the business object view provides both a higher level of understanding of business processes and the ability to specialize business objects, making them reusable in productive parts of system planning.

Starting with R/3™ Release 4, SAP™ has made an effort to reduce the complexity of its software and to use business objects to show integration and interrelationships on a business level, not only on a technical level.

1.5 *BUSINESS PROCESSES AND ENTERPRISE REPORTING*

The last R/3™ issue we need to discuss is why we talk about business processes here in this book, a topic which may seem out of place to some readers. We describe certain business processes in the book to provide a context for the information contained in R/3™. As discussed earlier, the logical structure of the business content is based on information flows that travel up and down the business supply chain.

The SAP™ strategy is to integrate all business operations in an overall system for planning, controlling, and monitoring a given business. This integration allows companies to restructure business activities along the supply chain and thereby help seize their competitive advantage. To help facilitate the restructuring of company processes along the supply chain, SAP™ has included over 800 best-business practices or scenarios in the Business Blueprint. These scenarios provide logical models for the optimization of specific business processes and can be modeled around primary and support value activities. For example, SAP™ provides detailed scenarios of such primary activities as materials management, sales and logistics, purchasing, and the like. Support activities include human resources management, business planning and controlling, capital asset management, and so forth.

Knowing how a business process actually functions in a company is an invaluable asset for reengineering purposes; it is also key to getting the right information out of R/3™. Getting that information leads to informed decisions, and informed decisions tend to be good decisions. Thus, we use the process models to orient the reader to the specific area in the supply chain that is being reported. Moreover, the process models themselves contain invaluable data for reporting purposes. But more of this later.

1.6 ENTERPRISE REPORTING WITH MICROSOFT EXCEL

In deciding to implement an ERP system, the world's largest companies have devoted hundreds of hours and billions of dollars working to align their information systems with key business processes. The result has been a more streamlined organization and an improved, integrated information system. That, at least, has been one of the more positive results. The ERP movement has produced some failures as well. In particular, the difficulty in understanding ERP systems has produced a generation of business professionals who have been alienated from critical business data.

Although the organization has been streamlined and R/3™ contains most of the enterprise's mission-critical data, users have had trouble getting the information. The data sits unused in the massive R/3™ database.

Despite SAP™'s many efforts to the contrary, reporting in R/3™ remains difficult. For this reason, third-party integration solutions promise to deliver, finally, the ease of use and comprehensibility that has eluded SAP™ R/3™ in the past. For example, the ability to use Excel to present R/3™ data has great possibilities for enhancing reporting across the enterprise. Excel is implemented on 98% of user desktops and is the application of choice for over 91% of reporting analysts.

The problem of poor information delivery in SAP™ R/3™ continues to be a sore subject for SAP™ customers. In fact, SAP™'s SAPPHIRE™ '98 focused squarely on the need to solve this problem for the R/3™ end user. In a nutshell, the R/3™ system is overly complex, especially for occasional users. Because of R/3™'s complexity, tasks such as reporting in R/3™ present the non-expert with several barriers to information, for example: an unwieldy graphical user interface, a confusing notation system, and an esoteric language in ABAP/4. Thus, the current R/3™ system prevents users from easily being able to access mission-critical data.

US software manufacturers have promised simpler links to complex systems for years. Allowing common connections between software systems means that users require less training and need less expertise in fewer software packages. Currently 97% of the computer literate know and use Microsoft Office products. Many experts see these products as a plausible gateway to accessing more complex technologies. The new wave of Desktop ERP products is solving the usability problems of ERP applications by integrating them into the Microsoft Office desktop. The first wave of these integrated desktop ERP applications has been engineered to solve the reporting problems in ERP applications, whose complexity and specialized language and functions make it difficult for non-expert users to understand and use ERP data for reporting purposes. Indeed, end users often must rely on SAP™ consultants and ABAP/4 programmers just to create a report in R/3™.

The initial entry into the Desktop ERP market is a product called ActiveSheets™. ActiveSheets effectively integrates Microsoft Excel and SAP™ R/3™. ActiveSheets essentially allows the user to create live reports in R/3™ using Excel as its front end. The application works differently than simply downloading SAP™ data into Excel (which R/3™ users already do regularly) because it gives users live numbers to work with—crucial, active data. If they have ActiveSheets, they have live data as well. Every time they open the Excel workbook, the report is refreshed with the live data.

Once the report is created users can send it to colleagues or publish it on a corporate Web page and still retain the fidelity of the original document. Products such as ActiveSheets greatly improve information delivery in R/3™. In sales departments, for instance, typically only a few power users are competent R/3™ users. They are responsible for disseminating reports with R/3™ data to other sales people and to management. Unfortunately, with this system, the range of reports is necessarily limited and the data is "old" by the time it gets into the hands of decision-makers. ActiveSheets can give the entire sales force the ability to create their own reports, and decision-makers have up-to-date data each and every time they open their Excel workbooks. The bottom line is, if the user knows how to use Excel, they can use ActiveSheets.

1.7   CONCLUSION

Enterprise reporting is not only a complex endeavor, it is infinitely individualistic as well. No two companies produce the same kind of reports, no matter what system they are using.

For this reason, we have had to impose a few standards and criteria to our reporting method. We will use the R/3™ system as the source for discussing business information and Excel as the main presentation and delivery strategy. These two tools are not only the most common in business today, they provide good standards for approaching enterprise reporting.

R/3™ is a vast, complicated system, and there are many ways to explain reporting. We have chosen not to focus on applications and tools, but rather to use the strategy behind reporting in R/3™ to help define a reporting system that is applicable to any organization.

Enough qualification. The next two chapters lay down the fundamental approaches to enterprise reporting. In Chapter 2, we will examine our method in detail. After this is established, we will explore the heart of R/3™ reporting.

2

MAPPing Reports

MAPP is our mnemonic for a method of enterprise reporting. It stands for Manage, Analyze, Present, and Publish, the four basic areas of our approach. In Chapter 1 we covered the main assumptions behind this approach. Now we examine the framework itself.

To begin, we must think like producers of reports. That is, we need to consider the entire process of creating a report for end users and examine in detail what goes into making an enterprise report. While as users of reports we tend to think only of our area of concern, as producers we must think about all phases of the reporting cycle, from research to design, analysis, presentation, and delivery. This approach will not only help us understand the entire flow of the reporting process, it will help us access and use information in the R/3™ system more efficiently. If R/3™ is not your main area of concern, the method is applicable to other ERP systems as well. Remember, the main object here is to improve information delivery in your company using an ERP system as the source of information.

2.1   THE CYCLE OF INFORMATION DELIVERY

Regardless of the information system, a good process for enterprise reporting follows a typical cycle—if not in theory, then at least in practice. There are four general stages to this process, which are illustrated in Figure 2–1.

When they are created and delivered, all good reports will feature these four main processes.

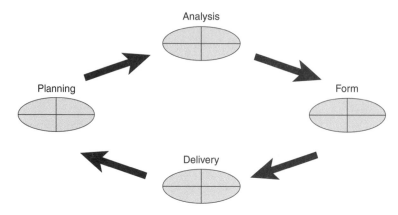

▶ **Figure 2–1** Cycle of Information Delivery

Planning

In creating a new report, the initial stage always involves some form of planning. Often, it can be a very simple plan that is driven by a particular business
need. Or, it may involve a more complex consideration of the entire enterprise's
needs, as well as the most important business drivers in the organization. The
planning process may entail examining reports that have already been created to
see if they fit current demands. Information flows, approval cycles, and documentation procedures will also have to be planned out. In enterprise reporting,
the planning process also involves finding out where the right information is
within the software system and getting it to the users. Due to the complexity of
ERP systems, this is not always as easy as one would like.

Analysis

The next phase of reporting considers the content of the report in greater detail.
It takes into consideration the business needs and drivers of the planning phase
and matches them to what is available in the ERP system. Thus, analysis typically is a process of matching available information to current or future business
needs. For enterprise reporting, the analysis phase will consider the key figures,
characteristics, and ratios that are being measured in the report. Analysis will
typically examine which organizations are affected by the report and how the
information contained in the report will be used by end users.

Format

Once its content is determined, the presentation of the report needs to be considered. How a report is presented to an end user is a critical aspect of the enterprise reporting process. Indeed, the form of the report will largely determine how effectively it conveys information. Moreover, the software program chosen to deliver the report will have an enormous impact on how the report will be used in the organization. For example, if the report is used for business analysis, Microsoft Excel might prove to be the best presentation application.

Delivery

Like the form of the report, delivery most affects those who use the reports. Delivery considers time, routing procedures, permissions (if applicable), and so forth. This phase is usually an administrative procedure; that is, it is typically an administrator's responsibility that the right reports get to the right users at the right time. This responsibility may also entail feedback, training, and the like.

2.2   THE MAPP METHOD

The MAPP method takes the preceding processes into consideration and structures them into four discrete areas of responsibility. Building on the cycle of information delivery, we have devised these four main areas:

- Manage
- Analyze
- Present
- Publish

Figure 2–2 outlines the core features of our MAPP framework.

While we will be examining each piece of the process in detail, it is important to remember that the entire system is a dynamic, fluid, living process of knowledge transfer. We must think of the entire flow of information as an evolving process. The cycle of the enterprise reporting process repeats itself, reexamines itself, and ultimately changes as the needs of the company, the needs of the end users, and the needs of customers change. For example, there is always an ongoing process of feedback, testing, validation, and documentation running behind all processes. Moreover, each phase refers forward and

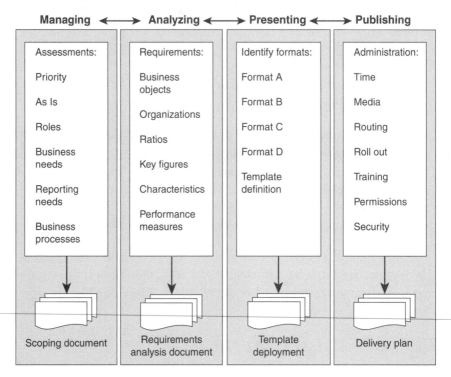

▶ **Figure 2–2**   The MAPP Framework

backward to its predecessor. A change in one area will impact any number of other areas of responsibility.

Let's first examine the four main goals of each area. As you can see from Figure 2–2, each phase concludes with a task that will carry over to the next phase of the report's development.

Goals for Managing

The goal of the managing phase is to create a plan, or scoping document, for report requirements. This document will consider the overall goals of the report. It will consider users, business needs, priorities, schedules, and so forth. The scoping document will outline how the report will be used and what it is supposed to accomplish.

Goals for Analyzing

In this phase, the goal is to create a requirements analysis document for the report. This document will outline the performance measures and ratios reflected in the report, the organizations affected, and the "to be" state of the report. It will also define the main data points reflected in the report. The goal of this phase is to match up the business needs defined in the last stage with what is available in the business information system.

Goals for Presenting

The goal for the presentation phase is to design a finished report, including formats, the order of the headings, and so forth. Essentially, at the end of the presentation phase we will have devised a template, a proto-report containing the basic information and structure of the report.

Goals for Publishing

In the last phase, we devise a plan for propagating the report within the organization. This plan will take into account all administration issues, permissions, routing, media, etc. Also, we will need to take into account user training, documentation, and anything else that will aid in the successful transmission and communication of the report within the organization. The publishing plan will also have a good feedback system so that the creators of the report can gauge the successes or failures of the report.

2.3 THE MAPP METHOD IN DETAIL

The following sections explore the main areas of the MAPP method. It is not necessary that you master every detail at this point, but rather that you begin to understand the logic driving the process.

At the end of each section we provide an example of the kind of documents that would be created at that stage of the reporting process. The examples that follow begin with the higher-level managing view and progressively drill down to the other areas.

Manage

It is a truism of business management that you cannot manage what you cannot measure. In the managing phase, we identify what needs to be measured by looking at the hard *data* that is available for the report. Management includes assessing the following business information:

Assign priority

To effectively manage reporting, it is important from the start to judge the value of each report. By establishing it in an orderly hierarchy, you ultimately assess the real value of the report to the organization. Assigning a priority to the report includes assessing when the report is needed and how often it will be used.

Assess the "as is" state

The "as is" assessment is crucial to enterprise reporting. The real struggle in enterprise reporting is not creating new reports, but determining what reports already exist, assessing what value they have, and deciding what modifications need to be made, if any. The "as is" assessment should include a healthy dose of skepticism and managers should be willing to discard what's not working. It is very common for companies new to ERP systems to carry over their legacy reports rather than delete those that could be done better in the new system.

Determine business needs

The most basic question to ask of any report is: What are the business needs or drivers behind the report? The answer to this question should always be the starting point in designing any new report. Moreover, the needs assessment will help target those reports that no longer serve a business purpose.

Identify audience

Related to the needs assessment is identifying the precise audience of the report. The questions to ask here are: Who will benefit from the report? What purpose will this report serve? Again, such questions not only will help identify the key business issues at stake in the report, they will also help to flag reports that have no real audience.

Identify business processes

The last area we need to consider is where the report exists in the overall flow of information. To do so, we need to identify what part of the business process is being depicted in the report. Once we have done so, we can uncover the business content of the report. Identifying business processes will help us not only define the business areas and organizations covered in the report, but will help us cover the "who, what, where, and when" issues of the report.

Once this information has been organized and researched, it is possible to define a scoping document for requirements analysis. This document will initiate a validation and review process from management.

Managing Scenario

The spreadsheet list shown in Table 2–1 is the sort of analysis that would come out of the management phase of the process. The analysis would form the basis of a scoping document, which, as you remember, is the goal of this area.

▶ **Table 2–1**   Managing Spreadsheet

Priority	Report	Business Need	For Whom	Source
1	Stock Levels	Review inventory on hand	Buyer	R/3™ standard
1	Open Purchase Orders	Identify incoming purchase orders (to be delivered)	Clerk	R/3™ standard
1	Requisitions	Identify materials to order	Secretary	R/3™ standard
2	Vendor Evaluation	Rate vendors	Buyer	R/3™ standard
2	Buyer's Negotiation Sheet	Tool for negotiating with vendor	Buyer	New
2	Range of Coverage	Identify possible stockouts	Buyer	New
3	ABC Analysis/Material	Identify material with most value	Manager	R/3™ standard
3	ABC Analysis/Vendor	Identify vendors with highest order value	Manager	R/3™ standard
3	Purchase Order Value by Purchasing Department	Monitor open-to-buy position for each buyer in a department	Manager	R/3™ standard

This analysis measures a typical purchasing report scenario. The leftmost column assigns a priority to the reports based on need and other business drivers. The second column lists the reports that have been identified as necessary to the organization in the "as is" assessment. The next column represents the business needs of the company (the likely starting point of the management stage).

The next column lists the audience. Note that the audience will consist of three main groups: a purchasing manager, a buying agent, and a purchasing clerk, and so will give the report at least three levels of need. The manager and purchasing agent will need to see the raw data of the report, while the clerk who handles the data every day will need visibility and drilldown capability and likely will need to work on the report in R/3™. The last column indicates the source of the report. Here, we see that some of the reports will come from R/3™, while others will need to be created. We could also have located the business processes that will be affected by the report. This example follows the purchase orders for stock materials business process scenario in R/3™. In the end, this spreadsheet will help managers visualize what will be needed in the process of creating the report.

Analyze

In the analysis phase of reporting, it is important to identify all the relevant information available for the report. One of the main objects of this process is to match up the business needs identified in the previous phase with the requirements of the ERP system. This will entail an analysis of the business information contained in the system, including knowledge of tools used to measure performance, organizational dimensions used, and the source data required from the underlying On-Line Transaction Processing (OLTP) system.

The following are the main points of analysis:

Business objects

As discussed earlier, business objects help identify the main data points of the report that lie in the transaction system. By definition, a business object is an integrated set of business data, transactions, and events within R/3™. For reporting purposes, a business object will tell you the main fields and columns that can be used in the report, the organizations involved, and most important, all relevant data pertaining to the business object that is stored in the R/3™ system. A business object can be a valuable source of information for understanding the business information contained in your R/3™ system.

Time

Here, we will decide what time periods need to be covered in the report and what are actually available in the system. We may find, for example, that there are no weekly numbers available in the system for a given transaction, and thus we may have to switch to a monthly analysis for our report.

Organizations

This area of analysis considers which organizations or organizational views need to be shown in the report. An R/3™ sales organization, for example, structures the company according to its sales requirements. For reporting purposes, this "view" will provide a summary of ordering activities and customer transactions by sales organization.

Characteristics, key figures, and ratios

These form the real business content of the report because they actually tell us what is being analyzed in the report and how it is being measured. In R/3™, characteristics are the objects you report on, such as customer or material. Key figures are the statistical values used to forecast or measure performance, such as "invoiced sales." Key figures are usually expressed as a value or quantity. Ratios combine a characteristic and associated key figure that can be used as a performance measure. For example "Sales per employee" is a performance measure composed of a key figure (sales or sales value) and a characteristic (employee).

At the completion of the analysis phase, we will need to create a requirements analysis document (Table 2–2) that will help finalize the content of the report and prepare it for use in the next two stages.

▶ **Table 2–2** Analysis Spreadsheet

For Whom	Organization	Business Object	Time	Ratio/Key Figure
Manager	Purchasing Department/Plant	Material	Monthly/ Quarterly	Material quantity/ Material value
Manager	Purchasing Department/Plant	Vendor	Monthly/ Quarterly	Vendor order value
Manager	Purchasing Department/ Company/Plant	Purchase Order/ Contracts/Purchasing Organization/ Purchasing Group	Monthly/ Quarterly	Total order value
Buyer	Purchasing Department/ Company/Plant/ Purchasing Group	Vendor	Monthly	Price score/ Delivery score/ Quality score
Buyer	Purchasing Department/ Company/Plant/ Purchasing Group	Vendor/Material/ Material Group	Monthly	Price history/ Vendor price/ Market price
Buyer	Purchasing Department/ Company/Plant/ Purchasing Group	Material/ Material Group	Monthly/ Weekly	Material quantity/ Material usage/ Projected coverage in days
Buyer	Purchasing Department/ Company/Plant/ Purchasing Group	Material	Daily	Unrestricted quantities on hand
Clerk	Purchasing Department/ Company/Plant/ Purchasing Group	Purchase Orders/ Vendor	Daily	Quantity ordered/ Quantity delivered/ Quantity received
Secretary	Purchasing Department/ Company/Plant/ Purchasing Group	Purchase Requisition/ Material/Cost Center	Daily	Quantity to order/ Material value

Analysis Scenario

In the management phase, we defined what types of purchasing reports are necessary and the audience that will use them. In the analysis phase, we drill down a little bit further to match these needs with what is in the ERP system.

The audience that was defined in the previous stage now defines three levels of need for buyer, manager, and clerk. These are represented in the first column. In the next column we have identified which purchasing organizational units are affected in the report. The third column identifies which purchasing objects match the business objects in R/3™, such as vendor material, purchase order, and so on. Next, we define the time. In this report time is a consequence of the audience: the manager needs to have an aggregation by the quarter or month, the buyer needs figures by the month, and the purchasing clerk needs the data down to the day. In the last column we have the performance measures, which are especially important for managers. The key figures are going to be types of data that we want to measure, such as the values, total order value, total order quantity, and so on.

In the end, we have documented in this table the basic requirements that will need to be in the report. We have extended the managing document to include the ERP data that will go into the report. Now we're ready to move on to the presentation of the report.

Present

In the presentation phase of building the report, we are concerned most with transferring knowledge to other users. Practically speaking, this process will entail a decision on the most effective form for the report to take to be clearly transmitted to end users. Here, we will define the following:

Template
The template is actually the end result of our presentation phase, but first we need to define its basic components, such as design, application, and information structure.

Query
In defining the structure of information in the report, you will need to make sure that the right amount of data is returned to the user, not too much or too little. This is where queries come in. In R/3™, queries are programs used to constrain the amount of information delivered from the R/3™ system. For example, you might not want all of last year's sales data from sales organization A. Instead, you might want to construct a query so that the desired time period would be returned in the report, say from June to December.

Formats

Determining the best format takes into consideration the uses of the report and the form that will be most effective in making the report a success. Here we need to ask ourselves which format will best suit the uses of the report in the organization. For example, if appearance and printing are important, then PDF would be a likely format. If on-line capabilities are important, then HTML would make sense. Lastly, if analysis is the most important use of the report, then Excel would likely provide the best format.

At the end of the presentation phase, a template will have been created and you will be ready to deploy the report in the organization.

Presenting Scenario

For this phase of our scenario, we can carry over much of the information that we identified earlier in the managing phase. The priority, report, and audience have been clearly defined for us, and are shown in the first three columns of Table 2–3.

▶ **Table 2–3**   Presentation Spreadsheet

Priority	Report	For Whom	Query	Format
Department: Raw Material Procurement (Purchasing Organization 2000)				
1	Stock Levels	Buyer	"All or any materials for Purchasing Organization 2000"	ABAP
1	Open Purchase Orders	Clerk	"All or any purchase orders for any vendor or material in Purchasing Organization 2000"	ABAP
1	Requisitions	Secretary	"All or any requisition for any material in Purchasing Organization 2000"	Excel
2	Vendor Evaluation	Buyer	"All or any vendors for Purchasing Organization 2000"	PURC HIS
2	Buyer's Negotiation Sheet	Buyer	"All or any vendors for Purchasing Organization 2000"	PURC HIS
2	Range of Coverage	Buyer	"All or any materials for Purchasing Organization 2000"	PURC HIS

▶ **Table 2–3**   Presentation Spreadsheet (Continued)

Priority	Report	For Whom	Query	Format
3	ABC Analysis/Material	Manager	"All or any materials for Purchasing Organization 2000"	Excel
3	ABC Analysis/Vendor	Manager	"All or any vendors for Purchasing Organization 2000"	Excel
3	Purchase Order Value by Purchasing Department	Manager	"All or any materials for Purchasing Organization 2000"	Excel
Department: MRO Procurement (Purchasing Organization 3000)				
1	Stock Levels	Buyer	"All or any materials for Purchasing Organization 3000"	ABAP
1	Open Purchase Orders	Clerk	"All or any purchase orders for any vendor or material in Purchasing Organization 3000"	ABAP
2	Vendor Evaluation	Buyer	"All or any vendors for Purchasing Organization 3000"	PURC HIS
2	Buyer's Negotiation Sheet	Buyer	"All or any vendors for Purchasing Organization 3000"	PURC HIS
2	Range of Coverage	Buyer	"All or any materials for Purchasing Organization 3000"	PURC HIS
3	ABC Analysis/Material	Manager	"All or any materials for Purchasing Organization 3000"	Excel
3	ABC Analysis/Vendor	Manager	"All or any vendors for Purchasing Organization 3000"	Excel
3	Purchase Order Value by Purchasing Department	Manager	"All or any materials for Purchasing Organization 3000"	Excel
Company North America (Company Code 1000)				
1	Requisitions	Secretary	"All or any materials in Company Code 1000"	HTML Self Service

The next two columns help us define the layout of the report and the chosen formats. In column four, we have defined the "query" parameters of the report. In R/3™ a query defines the data that will be returned from the R/3™ system when generating the report. In this example, the query will return all the data in the purchasing organization for the manager, while the buyer will query everything for the purchasing group. As a practical matter, the query will largely define the columns and rows that constitute the report. In the last column, we have a number of format options: Excel for managers because it is best for analyzing data; a purchasing Information System report and a custom ABAP report for the buyer; and finally, an HTML report or an SAP™ Self Service Application for the purchasing clerk.

Publish

We need to think of the publishing process as the report's return on investment. How can we get the most out of the data we've assembled? To that end, we will need to answer the following kinds of questions:

Permissions
What information can go to which users?
Who needs what authorizations?

Time
When must the report be delivered?
What is the routing schedule?

Media
Are there special media concerns?
What is the most effective medium, given the audience and the uses of the report?

Routing
In what order will it be received?
Is there a hierarchy for the report that needs to be followed?

Rollout
What's the process for the rollout?
What is the training schedule?
Who needs to be involved in the rollout?

Training
What training materials must be created?
What is the plan for training new end users?
How will changes to the report be transferred?

After considering the answers to these questions, we can deliver a publishing plan for the report to management. Then, we should be ready to take on implementation, rollout, and so forth.

Publishing Scenario

In the last stage of our MAPPing scenario, we define the publishing needs of the report as shown in Table 2–4.

▶ **Table 2–4**   Publishing Spreadsheet

For Whom	Permission (R/3™ Profile)	Report	Rollout Group	Training
Department: Raw Material Procurement (Purchasing Organization 2000)				
Joe Lasser	Manager	ABC Analysis/Material	Group C	Hands on
Joe Lasser	Manager	ABC Analysis/Vendor	Group C	Hands on
Mary Johnson	Manager	ABC Analysis/Vendor	Group C	Hands on
Mary Johnson	Manager	Purchase Order Value by Purchasing Department	Group C	Hands on
Joe Smith	Purchasing Group 001	Vendor Evaluation	Group B	SAP™ CBT/Video
Ron Giraldi	Purchasing Group 002	Buyer's Negotiation Sheet	Group B	SAP™ CBT/Video
Wendy Fillmore	Purchasing Group 003	Range of Coverage	Group B	SAP™ CBT /Video
Betty Sardis	Purchasing Group 004	Stock Levels	Group B	SAP™ CBT /Video
Rashid Rama	Purchasing Group 004	Open Purchase Orders	Group A	Hands on
Secretary	Secretary	Requisitions	Group A	Online

As you can see, we have drilled down now from the loft planning stages and performance measures to deal with the practical methods of delivery to particular users. They are defined in the first column. In the next column we have indicated a plausible permissions scenario for each user. The third column identifies the specific report. The next column offers a schedule grouping and the last identifies the method of training for each particular user, as well as for future managers, purchasing agents, and clerks who join the company after the rollout.

The end result of this spreadsheet is that we now have the basic data for creating a publishing plan that can be distributed, verified, and approved.

2.4 *MOVING ON*

By now you should have a basic understanding of the MAPP process for building, creating, and delivering enterprise reports. Since every business is different, we cannot possibly begin to account for all the possibilities that lie in building specific reports for your company. Thus, we need to shift the discussion almost entirely to the business engine, if for no other reason than to provide a common standard for discussing key areas of reporting.

Before we can adequately discuss these areas, we will need to know the fundamentals of reporting in the R/3™ system, a subject to which we now turn.

3

R/3™ Reporting Basics

R/3™ helps manage business processes and contains invaluable information that touches upon every aspect of the company. With R/3™, users have the information they need to conduct business analyses and make informed decisions. R/3™ also has extensive reporting capabilities that help users access and deliver that information. However, without a proper understanding of what a report is in R/3™ or how those reports are used, it is very difficult to get the necessary information out of R/3™, let alone make good decisions about that information. Fortunately, knowing a few things about R/3™ can make it easier for you to know where to find the data you need. Although reporting in R/3™ remains a challenge, it is not that difficult if you understand the basic reporting tools and principles.

To that end, we need to cover some of the fundamentals of R/3™ reporting. In this chapter, we have endeavored to give you the most essential information about the R/3™ system. And even if you already know a lot about R/3™, this chapter may still prove useful simply because it explains R/3™ primarily from the point of view of reporting.

We begin with the "theory" behind the organization of R/3™ information. Here, we'll address R/3™ business basics, such as information systems, business processes, and value chains. These sections will help you understand the basic information flow in the R/3™ system. They will also help you use various tools that can make locating information in R/3™ easier.

Next, we'll take a look at the "practice" of R/3™ reporting. We'll examine the fundamentals of R/3™ usage, such as logging on and off, R/3™ menu screens, the main reporting tools, and how to run a report.

Finally, we'll take a look at some Excel-based reporting options. Because there is no one tool in R/3™ that can access information across applications in R/3™, we provide an easy-to-use software solution to tackle this problem.

3.1   *R/3™ Information Organization*

The R/3™ system is organized in many different ways, and because of this fact there are a lot of different ways to describe it. If you have read the literature on R/3™, you know very well that there are as many views of the system as there are books. For reporting purposes, we find the "value chain" view to be the best descriptive model for understanding data organization in R/3™. We'll begin with this value chain concept, which will not only provide us with the primary business logic behind R/3™, but will give us a bird's eye view of the system as well. We'll then drill down to different levels of organization, all of which provide more detailed views of how information is structured in R/3™.

Value Chain Principle

The concept of the value chain was popularized by Harvard Business School professor Michael E. Porter, who describes the value chain as a tool for ascertaining a company's competitive advantage. According to Porter, every firm can be understood as a collection of activities that involve the design, marketing, delivery, and support of a product. The value chain breaks these activities down to strategically relevant categories "in order to understand the behavior of cost and the existing and potential sources of differentiation" By considering each activity within a company in terms of the value chain, a firm can isolate potential sources of competitive advantage.

The best aspects of the R/3™ information management system lie in its ability to integrate all business processes and areas into a coherent and well-structured value chain. From sales and distribution to production planning, R/3™ incorporates logistical and operational areas into an integrated workflow of business events. The R/3™ system automatically links together logistically and operationally related areas, eliminating the need to repeat time- and resource-intensive procedures. By integrating such important value activity areas as finance or human resources, businesses make themselves more effective and efficient.

Business Blueprint View

The best tool for understanding the entire value chain in an organization is the R/3™ Business Blueprint, or Reference Model, the main source for business information in R/3™. SAP™ has packaged 25 years of best business practices in many different industries in the form of a "blueprint" called the R/3™ Reference Model. The Reference Model, also known as SAP™'s Business Blueprint, guides companies from the beginning phases of engineering, including evaluation and analysis, to the final stages of implementation. It is the definitive description of R/3™, providing a comprehensive view of all the processes and business solutions available in the system. Technical details, however, are "hidden" so that the business user may focus solely on business process issues. Thus, the Business Blueprint is written in the language of the business user. In Release 3.0, SAP™ offered roughly 800 predefined business processes, with variants, that generally correspond to different industries and corporations.

The Business Blueprint can be viewed and analyzed with the help of the R/3™ Business Engineer, as illustrated in Figure 3–1. The Business Engineer helps users work their way through R/3™ with clear business language, rather than with technical jargon. The Business Engineer also employs on-line graphics to map the processes, configurations, and variations in R/3™. The tool's versatility

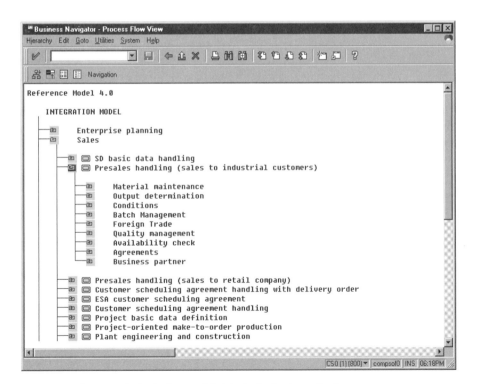

▶ **Figure 3–1**   Reference Model via the Business Engineer

provides a key ingredient in customizing R/3™ into a powerful information technology system. By selecting and adjusting the model data, a user can determine the scope and content of the actions to be performed within a chosen process. The ability to navigate through the variety of model types and collect information about the process design are essential for understanding the business models behind R/3™.

If you'd like to learn more about the R/3™ Reference Model and supply chain management in R/3™, please see our *SAP™ R/3™ Business Blueprint* (Prentice Hall, 1999).

Application Component View

The Business Engineer centers on application components and broad business process value chains, which consist of application areas or business modules. The application components act as consistent aids to navigation, describing all logical parts with uniform terminology. In the application component view, multiple levels describe the complete R/3™ application, as shown in Figure 3–2. For example, the application components can permit navigation down to "purchase requisition creation" to see which processes, object models, and data models are involved in the procedure.

As Figure 3–2 illustrates, application components provide a structural view of the enterprise application. In other words, you can find and isolate the part of the application that is related to your current scope of interest. For example, in the area of financial accounting, the decision maker can use the component legal consolidation to locate associated processes. From the process model, the decision maker can then see the organizational data and business object views available in the component.

Although most users do not want to change the underlying data, they can drill down directly from the object deeper into the system. Navigating from the business object view to the data model of that business object enables users to see and understand the underlying tables, fields, and data elements. From this point, a user can also navigate into the particular elements that use this data across the system.

R/3™ Value Chain and Business Process View

In an ERP system, it is important to understand how information flows within and between the business process transactions, not merely its static state in the database. This is best understood through the business process and business process scenario models within the R/3™ system. These models can be used to identify the business objects and organizational dimensions for decision support in particular and reporting in general.

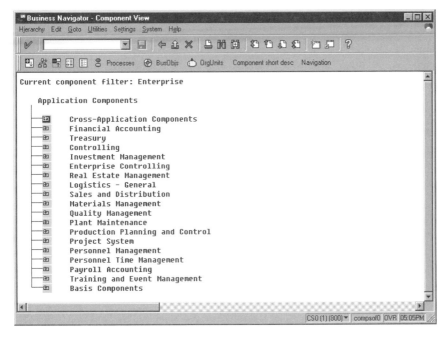

▶ **Figure 3–2**   Application Component View

All operational business processes are summarized in R/3™ via the value chain. A value chain ties together related business process scenarios and depicts the informational flow at a high level. For sales, we could go into the Business Engineer and view the following value chain to identify the main business processes contained in the system (Figure 3–3).

Beneath the value chain, the R/3™ Business Process Repository reveals the underlying business processes, business objects and their associated data models, the data associated with each business object, and the organizational dimensions related to each business process.

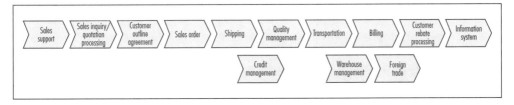

▶ **Figure 3–3**   Direct Sale to Business Customer: Value Chain

Business Process Scenario View

Using the Business Engineer, customers have access to the Business Blueprint and its set of predefined processes, which serve as a model for a company's business transactions. The Business Blueprint is designed to illustrate and describe the existing business processes in R/3™. The Blueprint helps users understand business processes of SAP™ applications—such as finance and accounting, logistics, and human resources—with the help of graphic models.

Included in the Business Blueprint as a foundation for the customer's application are over 800 process models. They are configured and populated with company data through the use of Business Engineer tools. The Business Blueprint is actively linked to the R/3™ application being installed. For example, a customer can use the Business Engineer to select a certain function within a purchasing model and see the associated transaction live.

The more than 800 predefined business processes in the Business Engineer were created using the EPC process description language, a unique methodology for graphically defining and displaying business systems, illustrated in Figure 3–4.

Users work in an understandable graphical environment to add their own company-specific details to the predefined processes. Graphical portrayals of business processes help users understand the data flow through business areas and also demonstrate how various company functions interact with each other.

Business Object View

Business objects expose standard interfaces to R/3™, otherwise known as "BAPIs" or Business Application Programming Interfaces. Business objects and their associated BAPIs consist of transactional methods and a data interface. The transactional methods allow an external application to automate selected functions within R/3™. For reporting purposes, business objects help explain different tasks, process models, and data models within the SAP™ system.

An example of an SAP™ business object is a sales order. A sales order refers to other business objects, such as sales organization, purchase order, or customer. It is also associated with business processes as defined in the SAP™ Reference Model, such as "Standard Order Handling." Another example of an SAP™ business object is a purchase order, which refers to other business objects from sales, such as purchasing, customer, and order type.

As illustrated in Figure 3–5, a business object view permits users to locate particular areas where the focus of their analysis can be improved by capturing functionality and data in the Business Blueprint. Business objects provide a higher level of understanding of business processes.

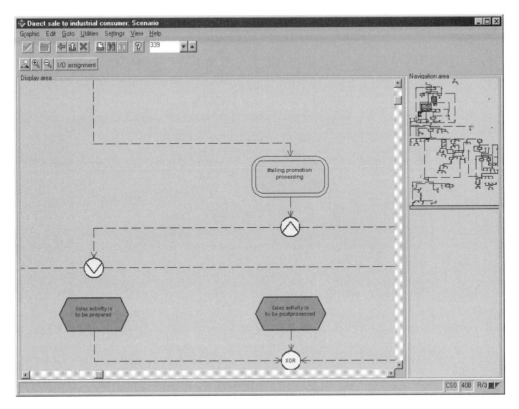

▶ **Figure 3–4**   Business Process Scenario View

R/3™ contains more than 170 different SAP™ Business Objects documented in the Business Object Repository. Their associated BAPIs have various uses; for example, they are the foundation of SAP™'s Internet strategy because they provide high-level interfaces to R/3™'s standard functionality making initiatives such as MYSAP.com possible. In the future, BAPIs will contribute to the realization of component software by enabling object-oriented communication among R/3™ components.

SAP™ decided to introduce business objects in R/3™ that have key business meanings and that describe integrated business aspects of the system. The inherent complexity of business is made manageable by introducing business encapsulation. Business Objects not only describe the business at a more abstract level but also introduce the behavior into the description. From the 4,000 data objects of the Enterprise Data Model, SAP™ identified the core SAP™ Business Objects that represent the central business logic of R/3™. Inasmuch as business objects should represent the world as the SAP™ user sees it, common Business Objects take the form of purchase orders, material, vendor, price condition, and so on.

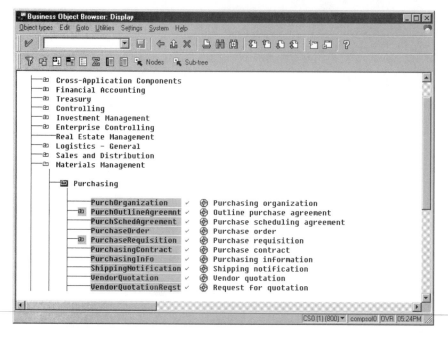

▶ **Figure 3–5**   Business Object View

Information Systems

As you can see in the value chain of Figure 3–3, a value chain usually concludes with a link to an information system. R/3™ information systems are a collection of data that have been gathered for a particular application area or business process. Info systems are repositories of information based on transactions made in the system. These systems are used as the basis for creating certain kinds of reports in R/3™. There is no one overall information system, however, that will aggregate the information. Instead, there are numerous information systems that have been created and that have evolved over time. They include Logistics, Executive Information System, Accounting, Human Resources, and Project Management. These may contain information systems within the information system as well. For example, the Logistics Information System (LIS) is made up of the following information systems:

- Sales Information System
- Purchasing Information System
- Inventory Controlling
- Shop Floor Information System

- Plant Maintenance Information System
- Quality Management Information System
- Retail Information System (RIS)

Perhaps one of the most difficult aspects of R/3™ reporting is realizing that there are a variety of sources of information in R/3™. The effect of this is that in a standard R/3™ system, reporting may be implemented with a different tool for financials or with the Info systems for logistics. More of this later.

Business Warehouse

Before we examine the specific tools for reporting in R/3™, we need to examine one last "view" of the system, which is SAP™'s latest and greatest attempt at organizing R/3™ data. This initiative is called the SAP™ Business Warehouse, which is a special purpose application that summarizes data from R/3™ applications and external data sources and supports retrieval and analysis of enterprise business data. This new application aims to improve R/3™'s lack of Online Analytical Processing (OLAP) capabilities, and signifies a major shift from transaction processing to business analysis.

Because it promises to have a great impact on enterprise reporting, it is necessary that we touch upon SAP™'s latest data warehousing product, the SAP™ Business Information Warehouse (BW). The BW represents a new reporting tool for SAP™ customers. It is fundamentally, however, a data warehousing solution, a subject which is outside the scope of this book. Without getting bogged down with too much detail, we'll discuss the general concept of data warehouses and then talk broadly about SAP™'s BW approach. This approach should familiarize you with the tool from a user's standpoint and help you to understand generally what your organization is doing when it implements a data warehouse solution.

First, what is a data warehouse? According to Ralph Kimball, a leading expert on data warehouses, a data warehouse is the "queryable presentation resource for an enterprise's data." A data warehouse is a collection of "data marts," single or multiple business processes that are targeted toward a specific group of business users. In short, a data warehouse is a method of organization of enterprise data geared toward distinct business processes, areas, and groups. Enterprises implement data warehouse solutions for reasons that include:

- Improved presentation
- Better organization

- Better decision-making
- Improved security
- Better adaptability

On the presentation level, data warehouses improve navigation capabilities and generally make data more accessible to users. Such improvements help users understand the data contained within the system, which leads to better decision-making within the organization. On the data level, information is better organized, typically around business processes or a set of business activities. The organization makes the data more consistent and better focused for analysis and decision support.

The basic process of a data warehousing begins with the extraction of data from some source system, such as legacy systems or the like. Next, the extracted data is stored in a "data staging area," where data is essentially "cleaned," removing redundancies, old or useless data, and combining useful elements together in logical aggregations of information. From here we enter the data warehouse proper. The information is collected and organized into as many data marts as needed. This is the data that will be accessed by the end users, using whatever tool is needed (report writer or query tools, for examples) to query the information in the data mart. These are the basic elements of data warehouse solutions.

The SAP™ BW contains the same basic elements. Data can be extracted from a number of sources: different R/3™ versions, R/2™, legacy systems, an outside provider, and so on. The data is stored and managed via InfoSources, InfoObjects, and InfoCubes—essentially data model summaries or structures that logically bring together different data areas based on different business needs from the underlying source system. With SAP™ BW Release 1.2, SAP™ has included more than 45 InfoCubes (subsets of InfoSources), over 100 key performance indicators, and more than 180 predefined reports. These are set up, administered, and maintained by means of the Business Administrator Workbench.

Reporting is done on "top" of the InfoSources. In other words, BW reports access and analyze the data in the InfoSources. The presentation application for these reports is the Business Explorer (Figure 3–6). The Business Explorer allows navigation and visualization of the InfoSources contained in the data warehouse server.

The advantage of the BW is that the data is easier to manage for reporting purposes, and it has more "present and publish" options. The SAP™ BW offers more flexible management options and the ability to "slice and dice" information. It is also SAP™'s recognition at long last of the importance of Excel for enterprise reporting, as Figure 3–7 illustrates.

We should note that the MAPP method fits in just as well in the BW environment. You still need to perform management assessments. While SAP™ provides

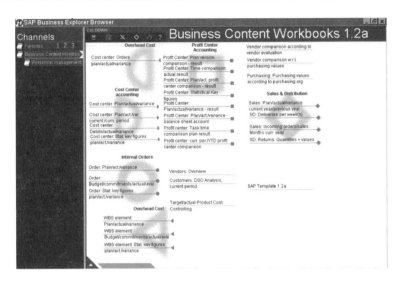

▶ **Figure 3–6** Business Explorer

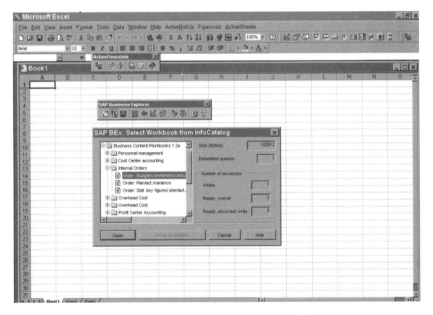

▶ **Figure 3–7** Excel Reporting With ActiveSheets and the SAP^{TM} BW

more "as is" reports to make your life easier, you still need to analyze the data. SAP™ makes this easier with InfoSources and the InfoWorkbench, but you still need to do the "present and publish" activities. These are made easier with the BW InfoWorkbench tools and the Business Explorer. Essentially the BW offers MAPPers more support for producing reports for users.

3.2 BASIC R/3™ REPORTING TOOLS

There are a variety of ways of doing a report in R/3™. You can load reports from the SAP™ Info systems, run standard Report Painter reports that are typically attached to the Report Tree, or create a new report using ABAP Query. The end result is that reporting is implemented in several different ways in the R/3™ system. There are a number of tools that you will need to be aware of to get the most out of the system. Be that as it may, this section is designed to get you up to speed as quickly as possible. We cover the following R/3™ reporting basics:

- Logging on/off
- Navigating the menus
- Finding reports
- Using reporting tools
- Creating and running reports
- Getting help

Logging On/Off

To establish a live connection to an R/3™ system, you must first log on to R/3™.

To log on to R/3™:

1. From the start menu, select SAP™ Front-end version X, and click on the SAP™ Logon button.

   The Logon dialog opens.

2. Select an R/3™ system from the list and click Logon.

NOTE If no systems appear in the list, consult your system administrator to obtain the correct settings for your specific implementation.

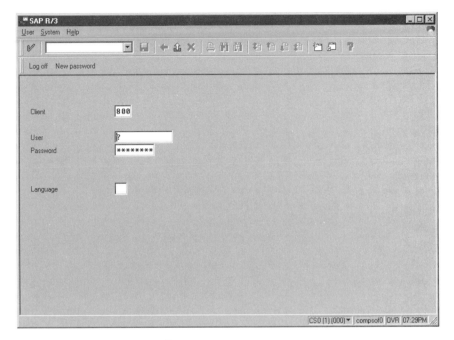

▶ **Figure 3–8** R/3™ Logon Screen

    3. Enter the client, your user name, password, and the language (Figure 3–8).

> **NOTE** Your system administrator needs the preceding information for pur-
> poses of maintaining security, adding new users, configuring the sys-
> tem for efficient use, and granting authorizations. Contact your system
> administrator if you have problems logging on.

    4. Click the green check mark (Enter) to log on to the R/3™ system.

    R/3™ establishes a live connection to your system.

Navigating R/3™ Menus

Now that you're logged on, let's do a quick tour of the main R/3™ menu
screen—what we affectionately refer to as the Toaster (Figure 3–9). Under the
Office menu, you have selections for running SAP™ office functions, such as
mail, running SAP™ workflow, and so forth.

    Under the Logistics menu, you have all the functions for a logistics application
such as materials management, including purchasing and inventory control, sales
and production, service management, logistics, controlling, and classification.

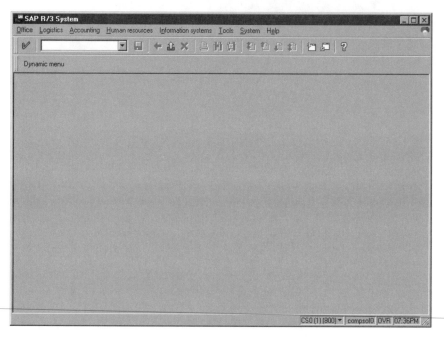

▶ **Figure 3–9**   The R/3™ Toaster: The Main Menu Screen

Within the Accounting menu you will find application areas from basic financial accounting, enterprise controlling, treasury and cash management, and real estate management. Under Human resources, you'll see the information for personnel management, payroll, and travel expense management.

The next menu is Information systems. Here you'll find a number of reporting tools, but not all of them from R/3™. These include the Executive Information system, Logistics IS, and the Accounting and Human resources Info systems. Here you'll also find reporting tools such as the SAP™ Report Painter.

Finding Reports with the General Report Selection Tool

When you select General report selection from the Information systems menu, you get a variety of links to reports within a tree of application areas.

| TIP | Rather than scrolling through menus, you may also enter in a transaction number to quickly navigate to the screen you want. For the General report selection tree, type in /nsart in the text box and click the green arrow to execute. |

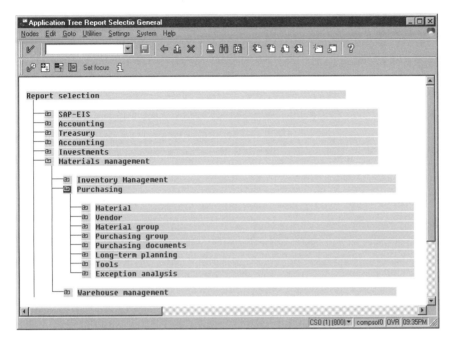

▶ **Figure 3–10**   General Selection Report Tree

For example, select materials management, and then purchasing. You'll see preconfigured reports for material (inventory) and vendors as well as a variety of ad hoc reports for vendor deliveries, goods receipt, and inventory (Figure 3–10).

Each of the folders can be expanded until reports are reached. From the Settings menu, you can select Technical names on/off, which will give you program names or transaction codes for reports. There are also search capabilities that will help you locate a report by its title.

The advantage of the report tree is that it gives a common view for all types of reports in SAP™ and organizes them usefully by application area. Thus, the General report selection tree gives you "one stop shopping" for all your R/3™ reports. The only thing you need to remember is that the handling of the reports will be different depending on the technology used for implementing the report. In other words, how you run each of the reports will be slightly different, depending on whether the report selected is an R/3™ standard report or is built with the SAP™ Information systems.

Reporting Tools

Let's now take a look at three of the most common forms of reports you will get in R/3™, Report Painter reports, ABAP reports, and Information System reports.

Report Painter Reports

Typically, financial reports in R/3™ are implemented with the Report Painter. This tool allows you to draw data from multiple applications to create such reports as financial statements, inventory, or sales reports.

With the Report Painter you can:

- Create a report based on standard report layouts
- Assign the report to a library and format the data in list form
- Assign combinations of characteristics to rows and columns of the report
- Edit and reformat the report by applying headers and footers, changing the text, etc.
- Perform ad hoc reporting

Let's take a look at a typical Report Painter report. From the General report selection tree select Accounting > Cost centers > Planned/actual comparisons > Actual/plan/variance. You will enter in a query that will return you a typical Report Painter report (Figure 3–11).

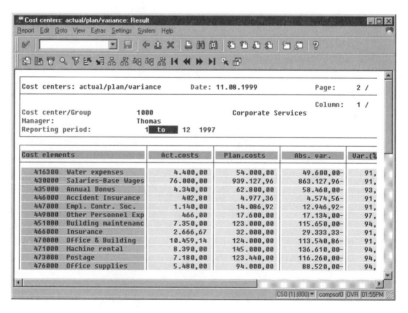

▶ **Figure 3–11**   Report Painter Report

As you can see, there are a number of options for drill down as well as graphics. You can set the levels on which a report is summoned, for example, setting a report variation level. This will allow you to traverse a hierarchy of values. A Report Painter report can also link to other reports based on other values you select. For example, if you've traversed across groups of cost centers to a cost center value, and you want to run another report based on a particular cost center, you can do it right from the Report Painter report.

As you run these reports, you access live data from the R/3™ system. Once the data is in, you can save it in a variety of formats, for instance, as a list, in one of the Office folders, or to a local file.

> **TIP** You can also save the completed report in your report tree (providing you have the right authorizations).

When you save the data as a file, you no longer have live data, but the report will be available the next time you open it. This is especially useful if the data is not likely to change significantly. It is important to remember that in the R/3™ system, you always get live R/3™ data when you run a report; however, saving always breaks the link. If you save the report as a list, the data is saved in the database. If you save it in the report tree, it is saved as a link to the query, which will preserve your live data. Lastly, if you save it to a file, then you could also place the report in an Excel format.

Report Painter reports also have fair layout capabilities. By selecting Layout from the Settings menu in a Report Painter report, you can change various layouts, such as how the page breaks, how graphics are displayed, or where the totals are set up.

The downside to Report Painter reports is that they tend to be difficult to configure, and do not allow for much variation in the report. Also, you have to create another report to maintain it. While this is better than maintaining R/3™ code, it still requires an overhead cost involved in its maintenance.

ABAP Reports

ABAP reports have much of the same look and feel as Report Painter reports. However, they do not have the layout capabilities that Report Painter reports have. ABAP reports are created by an ABAP programmer or by using the ABAP/Query tool. The ABAP report tends to be more free form than the others. These reports usually are part of a rollout for a certain type of report, one that is special to the needs of the organization. Thus, there's significantly more freedom in the data that is written into the report program. However, the report itself is limited to what the developer of the ABAP report presents to the user.

```
▓ Purchasing Documents for Vendor                                    _ □ ×
List  Edit  Goto  Environment  System  Help

  ✔  |            ▼ |  🖫  |  ⇐ ⬆ ✕  |  🖺 🖩 🖽 |  🖫 🖫 🖫 🖫 |  🖫 🖫 |  🖫
                                                         Help  F1
  🔍  🗐 PO history  🗐 Changes  🗐 Deliv. schedule  🗐 Services

┌──────────────────────────────────────────────────────────────────────┐
│ PO        Type Vendor    Name                        PGp Order date    │
│  Item  Material          Short text                      Mat. group    │
│  D I A Plnt SLoc             Order qty.   Un    Net Price Curr.  per Un │
│                                                                         │
│   L   K 1000 0001                  10  PC      300,00 DEM      1 PC     │
│       Still to be delivered         0  PC        0,00 DEM    0,00 %     │
│       Still to be invoiced          0  PC        0,00 DEM    0,00 %     │
│ 4500000019 NB   1000     C.E.B Berlin               001 25.11.1994     │
│  00010 100-300           Welle                          001            │
│        1000 0001                   10  PC      300,00 DEM      1 PC     │
│       Still to be delivered         0  PC        0,00 DEM    0,00 %     │
│       Still to be invoiced          0  PC        0,00 DEM    0,00 %     │
│ 4500000022 NB   1000     C.E.B Berlin               001 28.11.1994     │
│  00010 99-130            Sechskantschraube M10 (Konsi TEST)    001     │
│   K   1000 0001                   100  PC                              │
│   In stockkeeping unit            100  PC                              │
│   Contract release order 4600000002 Item 00010                        │
│       Still to be delivered         0  PC        0,00 DEM    0,00 %     │
│       Still to be invoiced          0  PC        0,00 DEM    0,00 %     │
│ 4500000036 NB   1000     C.E.B Berlin               003 28.11.1994     │
│  00010 99-100            Schmieröl                      010            │
│   K 1000                           10  L         2,00 DEM      1 L      │
└──────────────────────────────────────────────────────────────────────┘
◄                                                                     ►
                                      CS0 (3) (800) ▼  compsof0  OVR  01:57PM
```

▶ **Figure 3–12**   ABAP Report

Through the use of screens that have the same look and feel as the rest of the SAP™ GUI environment, the ABAP Query tool enables users to create more complex reports without having to write ABAP code. The result is a useful query screen that is actually converted into ABAP code based upon your selection criteria. The selection criteria screen is similar to that of the Report Painter. The report itself, however, is different from other reports. Figure 3–12 illustrates a typical ABAP report.

Here we see there are subtle differences. For one, you don't have all the running totals as before, nor do you have as many selections. You do have drilldown capability, but this is limited as well. For example, if you save the query as an extract (one of the Save As options) the report assignment used for drilldown reporting is not available from the extract.

The output options for an ABAP report are:

• Display on screen in a table format
• Display on screen using SAP™ graphics
• Download to an Excel spreadsheet
• Download to a flat file

Information System Reports

To close the loop, let's now compare the others with an Information System report. Similar to the process in other reports, you generate an Information System report by running the query after inputting your selection criteria. When the report is generated, you'll see that it has a different presentation and functionality as well. While similar to the Report Painter interface, the layout concept is quite different, as illustrated in Figure 3–13.

Here we have a report from the Logistics Information System, the prototypical Information System report. The LIS report doesn't have the layout concept or the print concept of the Report Painter reports. In general, Report Painter reports are better for printing and layout. There is, however, greater functionality in these LIS reports for performing such tasks as drilldowns and displaying graphics.

Creating and Running Reports

As you've seen from the preceding sections on reporting tools, when you select a report from the Report Tree, there is a screen common to all that asks for basic information. This basic information is called selection criteria. Selection criteria

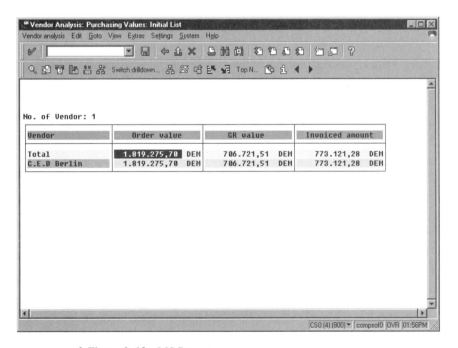

▶ **Figure 3–13**   LIS Report

constrains the amount of data that the R/3™ system will return to you in your report. When you enter in selection criteria and hit Execute, you are creating a query. A query asks the R/3™ system for the data you've requested in your selection criteria and then generates the report. This process is the standard for running R/3™ reports.

Let's take a look at a sample R/3™ ABAP selection criteria screen to create a report.

To call up an ABAP selection screen:

1. From the Settings Menu, select General selection report.
   The General selection Report Tree displays.
2. Open the Materials Management branch, then proceed through the following paths: Purchasing > Purchasing Documents > By Vendor.
   The Purchase Orders by Vendor report displays.
3. Double click on the Purchase Orders by Vendor report.
4. The ABAP Selection Criteria screen displays.

What we have before us is a typical selection criteria screen. Now we need to formulate our query by entering in certain selection criteria parameters. Remember, selection criteria are nothing more than characteristics by which you can select your report. The selection criteria for this report will be by vendor and purchasing organization. We will take a look at all the vendors for a particular purchasing organization that delivered material after the first of the year.

To formulate an ABAP query:

1. Click next to the purchasing organization text box.
   A downward pointing arrow displays.
2. Click the arrow.
   A "hit list" of possible selection criteria in your R/3™ system displays.
3. Click on 3000.
   3000 displays in the purchase organization text box.
4. Enter the following date in the Delivery date text box: `01011996`
5. Enter the following date in the Deliver date "to" text box: `01011998`
6. Click on the Execute arrow or select F8.
   R/3™ returns the results of your query. (Figure 3–14)

What have we done? We entered in some very basic selection criteria, executed a query, and now we have generated a report that tells us all the vendors

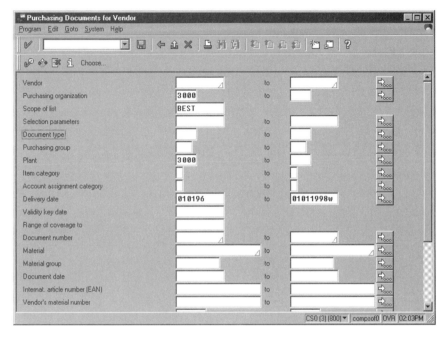

▶ **Figure 3–14** Selection Criteria Screen

who have supplied materials to a particular plant (plant 3000) from the fiscal year Jan. 1, 1996 to Jan. 1, 1998.

Of course, you can have much more complex criteria. If, for example, you didn't want to see all the vendors for that time period, you could further constrain the report by using the Multiple Selection dialog (Figure 3–15). You access this screen by selecting the right arrow next to the line item.

To use this tool, you will need to know what the possible ranges are. In our IDES system, we know that there are vendors identified in the thousands. If we wanted to select a range from 1000 to 3000, we would enter in single values (i.e., 1, 2, and 3) or enter 1000, 2000, and 3000 in the single values screen. We can also set a range (5000–6000) for our report. In this way, you can preselect the selection criteria that you need.

Let us suppose that you have executed a report that you need and now you want to save it in such a way that you will not have to keep typing in selection criteria every time you want to see the report. To do this in R/3™ you can save a report as a variant. Variants allow you to save a query so that you don't have to

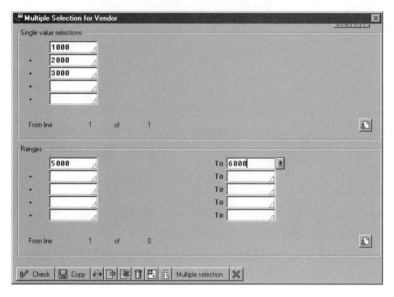

▶ **Figure 3–15**   Multiple Selection Dialog

run it again. Also, some other user can use the query that you've set up. When you're making a report template, you would save it here as a query.

To save a report as a variant

1. From the ABAP Selection Criteria screen, select Go to > Variants > Save as Variants…
   The Save as Variant screen displays (Figure 3–16).
2. Enter a variant name.
3. Check desired features of the variant.
4. Hit F11 or select the open folder icon.
   The variant is saved.

Getting Help

You can get basic information about many reports. The basic process for accessing help within a report is to choose Help from the menu bar, then select Extended help.

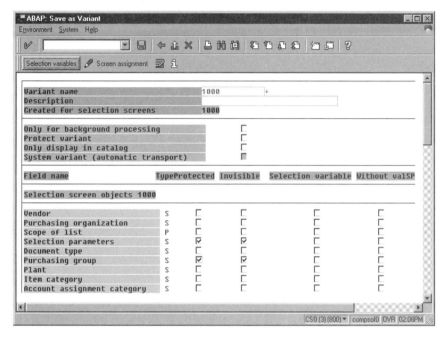

▶ **Figure 3–16**   Save as Variant Screen

To get help on a report within the selection criteria screen

1. Call a report from the General selection Report Tree (see "Finding
   Reports with the General Report Selection Tool" on page 58).
   The Selection Criteria screen displays.
2. From the Help menu, select Extended help.
   General information about the report displays.

3.3   EXCEL-BASED R/3™ REPORTING WITH ACTIVESHEETS

As you've seen from the above, there is some difficulty in using R/3™ Reporting
tools. First, there are many different ways of doing reporting, and there is no one
single tool to perform reporting across the enterprise. Also, live data can be pre-

sented only while running reports, which makes it difficult to exchange real-time information within the organization. Moreover, the tools are difficult to work with and the layout capabilities are not as complete as with an application such as Excel. Indeed, from our work in the industry, we have found that most business users would much prefer to work in Excel and access R/3™ data. For all these reasons, we have designed ActiveSheets, an easy-to-use software application that facilitates Excel-based R/3™ reporting.

ActiveSheets lets you use Microsoft Excel to access financial and management information in SAP™'s R/3™ system. Functioning as an application component in the Microsoft Windows environment, ActiveSheets delivers tremendous functionality for all R/3™ users. With ActiveSheets you can build your own reports or drag and drop reports from the R/3™ system directly into Excel. ActiveSheets gives you instant access to the latest information in R/3™.

ActiveSheets gives your Excel Workbooks an "active" connection to R/3™. Once you choose what to put in the report, that's it. The next time you edit the workbook in Excel, ActiveSheets automatically updates the data from R/3™.

For decision support, ActiveSheets makes it easier for management to access and manipulate R/3™ data contained in various SAP™ information systems and selected Business Application Interfaces (BAPIs). ActiveSheets components help you build queries and answer them even if you aren't familiar with the access paths involved in the R/3™ system. Without knowing R/3™ tables, programs, or reports, you can create a worksheet containing values from R/3™.

To try out the steps in this section, you will first need to load the software. This is an easy process—just follow the instructions as you load it. Then start Excel and begin working. You may access your current R/3™ system, or you may use the SAP™ International Demonstration and Education System (IDES). This chapter gives you a quick overview to:

- Getting Started
- The ActiveSheets Wizard
- Report Gallery

3.4   GETTING STARTED

To establish a live connection to an R/3™ system, you must first log on to R/3™.

To log on and off R/3™:

1. Click on the Logon button on the ActiveSheets toolbar.
   The Logon dialog opens.
2. Click the system you want to log on to.

NOTE If no systems appear in the list, click Add to specify one. Enter a description, the IP address or host name of the Application Server, any applicable Router String, and the System Number. Consult your system administrator to obtain the correct settings for your specific implementation.

3. Enter the client, your user name, password, and "E" for the language.

NOTE You must have a valid logon in the target R/3™ system.

4. Click OK to log on.
   ActiveSheets establishes a live connection to the R/3™ system.
5. Click on the Logoff button on the ActiveSheets toolbar.
   A dialog box opens, asking you if you want to log off from the R/3™ system.
6. Click Yes to confirm that you want to log off.

3.5   *THE ACTIVESHEETS WIZARD*

The ActiveSheets Wizard gives you access to management reporting in R/3™. The ActiveSheets Wizard uses the R/3™ Information Warehouse to extract reporting data from all SAP™ application areas—from financials to logistics. By referencing the data sources in your information catalog, you can use the ActiveSheets Wizard to build a report with speed, accuracy, and flexibility.

To create a report using the ActiveSheets Wizard:

1. Click the ActiveSheets Wizard button on the ActiveSheets toolbar.
   The Logon dialog opens.
2. Double-click the system you want to log on to.
3. Enter the client, your user name, password, and language.
4. Click OK to log on.

The first page of the ActiveSheets Wizard displays, as well as its Office Assistant (if you have enabled the Assistant).

NOTE If you have not previously refreshed your Local information catalog, ActiveSheets will prompt you to do so.

5. Click Next.

   The next page of the Wizard displays (Figure 3–17).

TIP The ActiveSheets Wizard provides you with a browser that helps you find the data source you need. Select the view that you would like to use for exploring the Information catalog.

6. Open the Sales and Distribution folder.

   Subjects related to Sales and Distribution display.

7. Open the Sales Organization subject (indicated by a circular object).

   Data sources related to Sales Organization display.

8. Select the Sales organization data source.

9. Click Next.

   The next page of the Wizard displays.

10. Select Distribution channel Text from the Available Fields column (click on the item once).

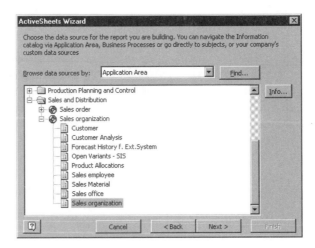

▶ **Figure 3–17**   ActiveSheets Browser

NOTE Each SAP™ data source contains a number of fields. The ActiveSheets Wizard displays a list of all Available Fields in the selected data source. Select the fields that you want to insert as columns into your worksheet.

11. Click on the Info button.

    The Info button provides you with additional information on the chosen field.

12. Close the Information window.

13. Click on the Add Column button.

    The field is moved to the Selected Field column.

14. Select the Net orders 1 and Sold-to party Text fields and click on the Add Column button for each.

15. Select the Sold-to party Text in the Columns area, then click the Move Up button twice.

    The field moves to the top of the list and now will be the first column in the worksheet.

16. Click Next.

    The next page of the Wizard displays.

17. Select the Sales organization ID criteria and click on the Add Column button.

NOTE The Available selection criteria listbox lists the criteria available to be used as a constraining factor for your report. The Required and chosen selection criteria lists both the required selection criteria that are essential to the report and the criteria that you define for limiting the data you want to retrieve. A question mark next to criteria (in the Required and chosen selection criteria area) indicates that the criteria have not been fully defined, and that you need to set the criteria properties. To edit criteria properties, click on the criteria item and then click Properties, or double-click the criteria item.

    The Sales Organization Criteria Properties dialog opens. Here you can specify the criteria placement and value properties.

18. Click cell B2 on your worksheet.

    The cell you selected is recorded in the Location text box.

19. Click in the Value text box and enter a value range. (Enter * to select all values, or, if you're using the IDES system, enter 1000 for the value.)

	A	B	C	D	E	F
1						
2	Sales organization ID	1000		**Sold-to party Text**	**Distribution channel Text**	**Net orders 1**
3				Becker Berlin	Final customer sales	3357500
4				Lampen-Markt GmbH	Sold for resale	740044
5				Omega Soft-Hardware Markt	Sold for resale	530478
6				Autohaus Franzl GmbH	Sold for resale	103920
7				Institut für Umweltforschung	Final customer sales	968820
8				Karsson High Tech Markt	Sold for resale	804722
9				Hitech AG	Final customer sales	274802.1
10				Hitech AG	Service	0
11				CBD Computer Based Design	Final customer sales	735732.44
12				CBD Computer Based Design	Service	0
13				Motomarkt Stuttgart GmbH	Sold for resale	330000
14				Elektromarkt Bamby	Sold for resale	1127125
15				Computer Competence Center AG	Service	0
16				Minerva Energieversorgung GmbH	Final customer sales	555500
17				Christal Clear	Sold for resale	2058975
18				Becker Köln	Final customer sales	97600
19				Becker Stuttgart	Final customer sales	1490940
20				NSM Pumpentechnik AG	Final customer sales	5500

▶ **Figure 3–18**   Completed ActiveSheets Report (IDES Values)

20. Click OK.

The sales organization ID is listed with a green check mark, indicating that its properties have been specified. The ActiveSheets Wizard places the criteria on your worksheet.

21. Click Next.

The final page of the Wizard displays.

TIP   To give a more polished look to your worksheet, select any of ActiveSheets's built-in formats. The Preview area displays each format.

22. Select any format from the list and click Finish.

The Select Results Area dialog displays.

23. Click OK to accept the default values.

The ActiveSheets Wizard places the report into your worksheet and then reformats the data to fit properly in the columns (Figure 3–18).

3.6   ACTIVESHEETS REPORT GALLERY

The ActiveSheets Report Gallery provides built-in templates for both new and experienced users. These templates work with the SAP™ IDES system. The Report Gallery is an easy way to start using ActiveSheets without having to build individual reports. It also demonstrates what kinds of reports ActiveSheets is capable of producing, and what you can do with reports you create yourself.

Each of the reports in the Report Gallery takes data from R/3™ and brings it into Excel. You can then use Excel's powerful pivot table and graphing functions to view and manipulate the data.

NOTE Each report in the Report Gallery contains macros. In order for the reports to function properly, Excel must be configured to enable these macros.

To use the Report Gallery:

1. From the File menu select Open. Find the ActiveSheets Report Gallery folder and then select the Cost Center Variance.xlt Excel template.

NOTE During installation, ActiveSheets placed the ActiveSheets Report Gallery folder in your Microsoft Office templates directory.

The Microsoft Excel dialog opens and asks you whether you want to enable macros.
2. Click Enable macros.
The EntIS for R/3™ logon dialog box displays.
3. Log on to R/3™ as before.
ActiveSheets displays the raw data retrieved from R/3™ (Figure 3–19).
4. On the left side of the worksheet, under Select Query Parameters, choose a different currency from the drop-down menu.
ActiveSheets recalculates the cells.

NOTE Under Select Query Parameters, you can change what data you use. For example, you might select a different fiscal year, or display monetary values using a different currency.

5. Under the Select Output Option, choose Graph.
ActiveSheets displays the sales performance data in a graph format (Figure 3–20).

TIP In addition to viewing a regular report, you can also view data in a pivot table or a graph (except for the Trial Balance report).

6. Under the Select Output Option, choose Pivot Table.
ActiveSheets displays the sales performance data in a pivot table format (Figure 3–21).

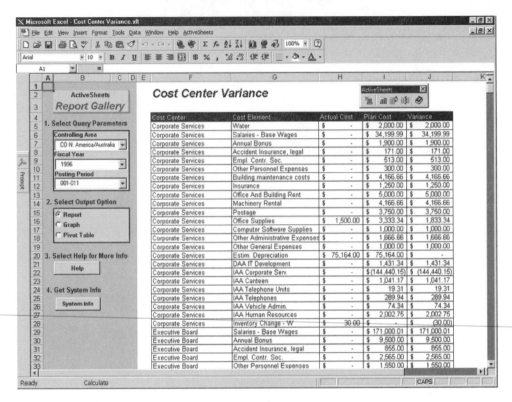

▶ **Figure 3–19**   Cost Center Variance Report (IDES Values)

NOTE The pivot table for each report is directly related to the report's graph.
ActiveSheets will automatically generate a graph based on the criteria
you select in the report's pivot table.

7. Under Select Help for More Info, click on the Help button.
   The Help button provides you with a brief description of the report.
8. Under Get System Info, click on the System Info button.
   The System Info button provides you with R/3™ connection information.

That's all there is to it. As you can see, you can create a variety of R/3™
reports using many different methods and accessing a wide range of R/3™ information—and you don't have to have R/3™ expertise. You can use a wizard to get
standard reports or open a prebuilt template—all from your Excel worksheets.
In fact, you can bring data from any R/3™ report into any Office application.

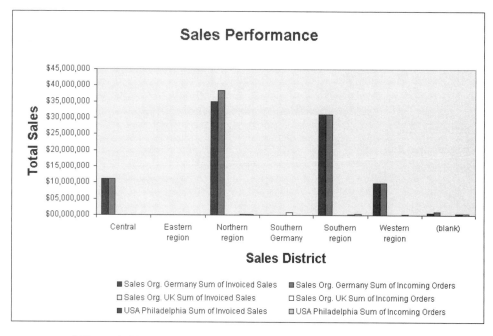

▶ **Figure 3–20** Sales Performance Analysis Graph

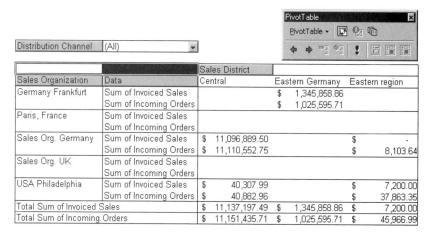

Distribution Channel	(All)				

		Sales District			
Sales Organization	Data	Central		Eastern Germany	Eastern region
Germany Frankfurt	Sum of Invoiced Sales			$ 1,345,858.86	
	Sum of Incoming Orders			$ 1,025,595.71	
Paris, France	Sum of Invoiced Sales				
	Sum of Incoming Orders				
Sales Org. Germany	Sum of Invoiced Sales	$ 11,096,889.50			$ -
	Sum of Incoming Orders	$ 11,110,552.75			$ 8,103.64
Sales Org. UK	Sum of Invoiced Sales				
	Sum of Incoming Orders				
USA Philadelphia	Sum of Invoiced Sales	$ 40,307.99			$ 7,200.00
	Sum of Incoming Orders	$ 40,882.96			$ 37,863.35
Total Sum of Invoiced Sales		$ 11,137,197.49	$ 1,345,858.86	$ 7,200.00	
Total Sum of Incoming Orders		$ 11,151,435.71	$ 1,025,595.71	$ 45,966.99	

▶ **Figure 3–21** Sales Performance Analysis Pivot Table

SECTION 2

Business-to-Business Sales

In this section, we will examine the management of business information according to its sales requirements. We follow the MAPP method to do so, focusing on the Managing, Analyzing, Presenting, and Publishing of R/3™ sales information.

The goal for Business-to-Business Sales is to describe typical reporting requirements for sales and marketing. We define the scope of the decision support tools used and the data required from the R/3™ system. We also describe the key business drivers for sales and distribution, including the typical questions that a sales report would need to answer, as well as the following key areas of R/3™ sales information:

- The business process (transaction) view
- Common business drivers used
- Sales and marketing tools used to measure performance
- A detailed description of the organizational dimensions used
- Analysis of standard R/3™ reports available
- Description of common R/3™ sales business objects
- Breakdown of characteristics, key figures, and ratios used
- Analysis of Sales Information System reports

The section concludes with a case study that exemplifies how to create an R/3™ sales reporting system utilizing the MAPP method.

4

Understanding R/3™ Sales Information

 As you recall from Chapter 2, the management stage of the reporting process entails identifying what needs to be measured to produce a successful report. That includes providing the following types of management assessments:

- Business drivers
- "As Is" assessment
- Business processes
- Audience (company specific)[1]
- Priority (company specific)

In this chapter, we examine these business background and decision support requirements from a sales and marketing perspective. We take a look at the data that is available for sales reporting in the R/3™ system and map out the key areas for managing sales activities. These areas include:

- Business drivers analysis
- Business needs assessment
- "As Is" assessment
- Value chain analysis
- Business process analysis
- Tasks and activities analysis

---

1. Both the audience and priority will be specific to your company's needs, usage, and requirements. Thus, they cannot be dealt with adequately here.

4.1 TYPICAL BUSINESS DRIVERS IN SALES

A large portion of the managing phase has to do with assessing reporting needs. Understanding the business drivers behind the report will help you determine what those needs are and will help you define the necessary content of the report.

The following list categorizes the key business requirements that drive sales and distribution in the SAP™ R/3™ system. It also includes cross-references for these business drivers and some of the typical questions that a user of a sales decision/support application might ask. This questioning method is useful for ensuring that a decision support tool correctly addresses the needs of the business user.

Also presented are the performance measures that are used in response to the business need. Performance measures are a sampling of common ratios used in sales and marketing. As they relate to R/3™, performance measures will be considered in greater detail when we get to the analysis stage (Chapter 5). Table 4–1 shows what needs to be measured and how they relate to the other two columns.

Table 4–1 Assessing Sales and Marketing Business Drivers

Business Need	Typical Questions	Performance Measure
Monitor customer spending/ordering habits	Which customers spend the most/least? How much does a customer typically spend?	Net sales per customer Average order size Deflated change in average order size
Increase revenue	What is the net/gross sales revenue trend over time? How do the regions/channels compare with one another? (contribution) How many new customers are needed to achieve our revenue goals for the next period/year?	Sales growth Sales per customer
Increase customer satisfaction	In which region/district are customers returning goods? Which product lines have the most returns?	Customer satisfaction ratio
Execute effective marketing	Are our price discount programs effective? What is the effect of our product promotions on net sales value? Am I spending too much on marketing? What is the break-even value?	Average order response Average sales value response Average return on marketing Marketing growth

Table 4–1   Assessing Sales and Marketing Business Drivers (Continued)

Business Need	Typical Questions	Performance Measure
Increase customer loyalty	Are we successfully selling into current customer base? Are we marketing to existing customers effectively?	Customer growth Customer solicitation ratio
Increase market share	What is our market share and that of our competition?	Market share trend Order growth
Maximize profitability	What are my costs per order/transaction?	Return on sales Profit growth

Once you have a good idea of what the business drivers are for the company report and have supplied the answers to the most pressing questions, you should document these in a report or spreadsheet. This document will help you determine exactly what the report is supposed to accomplish. An example is provided in Chapter 8.

4.2   *ASSESSING R/3™ SALES INFORMATION*

Table 4–2 indicates the main R/3™ sales information available for customer and material (sales orders) data. This information will be useful in assessing what standard reports are currently available in the R/3™ system.

Table 4–2   Assessing Sales Information by Customer and Material

Report Type	Description
Customer incoming orders	Net and gross values of incoming orders by customer. Provides data on orders quantity, order items, and open orders quantities and values.
Customer returns	Net and gross values of incoming returns, listed by customer. Includes net and gross orders in currency, quantity of returns, and item number.
Customer invoiced sales	Net and gross value of all invoiced sales, listed by customer. Also provides data on invoiced quantities and cost of invoiced sale.
Customer credit memos	Net and gross value of credit memo (a posting that reduces payables or receivables). Includes data on cost and quantity of credit memo.

Table 4–2   Assessing Sales Information by Customer and Material (Continued)

Report Type	Description
Customer master record	Provides master data information, including general data (address, marketing, contact person, etc.), company code data (accounting info, withholdings, correspondences, etc.), and sales area data (sales, shipping, billing, etc.).
Credit master sheet	Includes data on checks, credit limit, liabilities, payment history, balance, days in arrears, etc.
Material incoming orders	Net and gross values of incoming orders by material. Provides data on orders quantity, order items, and open orders quantities and values.
Material returns	Net and gross values of incoming returns, listed by material. Includes net and gross orders in currency, quantity of returns, and item number.
Material invoiced sales	Net and gross value of all invoiced sales, listed by material. Also provides data on invoiced quantities and cost of invoiced sale.
Material credit memos	Net and gross value of credit memo. Includes data on cost and quantity of credit memo.
Material master	Provides master data information, including general data (address, marketing, contact person, etc.), company code data (accounting info, withholdings, correspondences, etc.), and sales area data (sales, shipping, billing, etc.)

4.3   UNDERSTANDING SALES BUSINESS PROCESSES

We will now consider the business process scenarios that cover all the business areas that were identified in our business drivers document. Reviewing the business processes will help us determine what sales data can be derived from R/3™. The business process scenarios identify what areas will be measured in the report, how the report will be used, and where (that is, what organizations, people, etc. will be affected by the report).

To understand R/3™ Sales and Distribution business processes, we take you through the main processes and then single out one, the direct mail campaign, as an illustrative example.

Business-to-business Sales in SAP™ R/3™

The R/3™ sales logistics business process scenario allows users to manage sales and distribution activities in an effective manner. The business processes include scenarios for sales, shipping, billing, sales support, and sales information. With real-time, on-line access to sales information, such tasks as order entry, delivery, and billing are all streamlined. In addition, sales and distribution can be integrated with procurement and production planning, improving turnaround time up and down the value chain.

The core processes of R/3™ sales and distribution scenarios include:

- Providing sales support for acquiring prospective customers through various marketing channels
- Handling of customer inquiries and ultimately processing sales orders
- Conducting credit limit checks, guarantees for open receivables, and generally overseeing risk management
- Controlling shipment deliveries and issuing goods
- Managing warehouse and overseeing stock placement and removal
- Providing quality management checks for quality assurance, including inspections and checks of deliveries and returns
- Coordinating transportation, including planning and shipping deadlines
- Means of transport and assigning routes
- Providing shipment for international customer, including Foreign Trade tax, export control, and declarations to authorities
- Tracking billing procedures via an invoice, credit/debit memo, and rebate processing

These core processes provide the basis for the following business process scenarios for R/3™ Sales and Distribution:

- Direct sale to industrial consumer
- Direct sale to internal consumer
- Direct sale to retail company
- Customer order processing
- Component supplier processing
- Third-party order processing

Direct Sale to Business Customer Value Chain

When assessing business processes it is useful to identify the value chain in R/3™ that includes the business processes for which you require data. To illustrate a typical flow of the sales and distribution business process scenarios, we focus on a single value chain, the direct sale to an industrial consumer. Figure 4–1 summarizes this flow:

▶ **Figure 4–1**   Direct Sale to Business Customer: Value Chain

The following activities are represented within this value chain:

- Mailing promotion processing
- Sales activity processing
- Customer contract processing
- Delivery processing
- Sales order processing
- Credit control
- Picking
- Goods issue
- Rebate processing

As these are common processes to all R/3™ Sales and Distribution scenarios, the remainder of this chapter summarizes the main activities in each process.

Mailing Promotions

The mail promotions business process is used by sales support to acquire a prospective customer through some marketing channel. This process begins by recording sales activities with customers, such as phone calls, meetings, and product presentations. Direct mail campaigns can be planned and monitored. As these activities result in customer inquiries, they are recorded in the system. A quotation, valid for a specified time period, is created on the basis of this inquiry.

Direct mail campaigns can be created, using all of the sales information already stored in the system, such as the addresses of customers and prospective customers. Mailing campaign processing involves three events:

1. Determination of business partners: that is, deciding which customers or prospective customers to target and making an address list
2. Initiation of correspondence: writing sales letter, special offer, trade show invitation, etc.
3. Preparation of enclosures for the mailing campaign: creating product sample, brochure or documentation

Once these tasks are accomplished, the mailing campaign may begin.

Sales Activities

Any kind of customer contact—a sales call, a telephone call, a sales letter—is considered a sales activity. When stored as data, different kinds of sales activities can be valuable sources of information for employees in the sales department. Information about one sales activity (e.g., a direct mailing campaign) forms the basis for other sales activities (e.g., telemarketing calls).

Sales activity processing begins by determining what type of activity will take place. Three options are possible:

- Personal—an in-person sales call
- Telephone—a phone sales call
- Written—a sales letter

One of these three kinds of sales activities will lead to the next task: determine business partners and/or a contact person. When we determine this information and enter it into the system, we can then record a description of the sales activity. For example, we may record a short comment about the activity, date and time of the activity, reason, outcome, analysis or status of the activity, and follow-up action. When the outcome of the sales activity is known, it can also be entered as data.

The outcome of sales activity leads to nine possible outcomes, some of which trigger other tasks:

- Unsuccessful sales activity
- Agreed-upon follow-up sales activity
- Request for a quotation (RFQ) from the contact—triggers the task customer RFQ processing
- Quotation from the contact—triggers the task customer quotation processing
- Order from the contact—triggers the task standard order processing
- Credit or debit memo from the sales activity—triggers the task credit/debit memo request processing
- Return order from the sales activity—triggers the task returns processing
- Free-of-charge delivery from the sales activity—triggers the task free delivery processing
- Consignment sales order from the sales activity—triggers the task consignment
- Fill-up order processing

All of the possible tasks that follow sales activity processing are included in the sales and distribution business process scenario.

Customer Inquiries

As a result of the mailing campaign sales activity, a customer may inquire by mail or phone about such things as prices, terms of delivery, a description of the products, etc. The customer may also enter a request for a quotation (RFQ) from the company.

A quotation is an offer from a company to sell or deliver goods or services to a customer within a certain period of time and under certain conditions (prices, delivery times, terms of delivery, and material specifications). A quotation can be created with or without reference to a customer inquiry. For example, the company may want to let its customers know about a special offer or a new product. In this case, the quotation is created without reference to a customer inquiry. Alternatively, a quotation is created as a result of a customer inquiry. Inquiries and quotations provide important presales information that can be used to gauge market trends and help plan business strategies.

The task customer inquiry processing leads to two tasks: 1) determine customer inquiry business partner and 2) enter customer inquiry processing items.

These events lead to the next task: check inquiry item. Checking the inquiry item includes four possible events:

- Item is a make-to-order product.
- Item is kept in stock.
- Item is not kept in stock.
- Item is a material that can be configured.

If the last event is triggered—that is, if the item is a material that can be configured—the different parts of the material must be determined.

The next step is to edit the customer RFQ data by incorporating information from checking the inquiry item. Then, the final request for the quotation can be created. After the final request's creation, the next two steps in the chain are 1) monitor the request—since all quotations have a validity date, monitoring the request ensures that the inquiry or quotation is responded to quickly and within the relevant time period, and 2) check acceptance of the request.

The task check acceptance of the request is linked to two possible events: reject request and create quotation from the request. If the request is rejected for some reason, the request for quotation is canceled and the customer inquiry items are rejected. If a quotation is created from the request, the next task in the chain, customer quotation processing, can begin.

Customer Contracts

Both sales activity processing and customer RFQ processing are linked to the task customer quotation processing. Under sales activity, a quotation is created from a contact. Under customer inquiry, a quotation is created because of a request. In both cases, we enter the quotation into the system, triggering the following events: 1) determination of the business partners of the quotation, and 2) determination of quotation items.

Deliveries

Several different tasks in both sales and procurement logistics can set off delivery processing. These include: standard order processing, customer contract call processing, free delivery processing, subsequent delivery processing free-of-charge, consignment fill-up order processing, consignment issue processing, returnable packaging issue processing, customer schedule agreement processing, and purchase order processing for stock transfer. It's also possible that the process begins without any reference to an order.

Standard order processing prompts delivery processing once an order is released. The first task is to monitor the delivery date. Two events may follow: 1) delivery date takes place, or 2) delivery date doesn't take place.

When the delivery date does take place, the next task is to choose the kind of delivery. This choice involves four possibilities:

- Create without reference to an order
- Create from an individual sales order
- Create from delivery due list (a work list made up of all sales orders and scheduling agreements that are due within a specified period of time)
- Create from stock transport order

The first choice leads to the task determine delivery items. The second choice prompts: open delivery from sales order. The third choice leads to edit delivery due list. And the fourth choice is followed by open delivery from stock transport order.

All four tasks lead to the next step: open delivery. Once opened, the following task is carry out credit control. This task connects to finance. One of two things may now happen: credit requirements are fulfilled or delivery can't be created.

Sales Orders

In R/3™, a standard order is a document representing a one-time customer demand for products within standard delivery and accounting parameters. This scenario manages the following activities:

- Helping a customer decide what to buy
- Processing customer orders
- Coordinating delivery and related logistics
- Producing customer invoices

R/3™ Standard Order Handling integrates order handling activities with the workflow of downstream delivery and logistics operations. Logistics operations include transportation planning, as well as picking, packing, and shipping of products. The credit and material availability checks made during order entry are similarly available in this workflow. As goods leave the plant or warehouse, stock and value adjustments are made in the materials management system. To complete this scenario, invoices are processed and sent to customers. The appropriate cash management, accounts receivable, and profitability systems are updated.

A typical scenario begins by recording sales activities with customers, such as phone calls, meetings, and product presentations. Direct mail campaigns can be planned and monitored. As these activities result in customer inquiries, they are recorded in the system. A quotation, valid for a specified time period, is created on the basis of this inquiry.

Upon customer acceptance of the quotation, a standard sales order is processed. A standard sales order can also be processed directly from a customer without a quotation. The sales order documents the customer's demand, prices the order, and checks both customer credit and material availability. The sales order function in R/3™ utilizes a configurator to select configured products as well as a "conditions" program to manage complex pricing scenarios. The sales order process sends requirements to manufacturing.

Credit Control

If credit control is successful, a series of tasks follow: determine or transfer delivery route; determine serial numbers of delivery item; and, finally, check delivery items. Checking the delivery items triggers one of two events: 1) item is not in stock, or 2) item is in stock.

If the item is in stock, the next task is to determine the picking location. This leads to checking to see if the item is handled in batches or not. Three possible events follow: Item is handled in batches, the item is not handled in batches, or warehouse management determines delivery batch.

When the item is not batch-handled, the next steps are to choose a batch and to check if batch splits are allowable. Batch splitting designates transferring a certain amount of one batch to another. These tasks lead to: determine delivery batch. Now another task in the chain can begin: check availability of delivery item. Here, two possible outcomes exist: 1) delivery items are available, or 2) delivery items are partially available. If the items are only partially available, the next task is to see if partial delivery is allowed. This leads to: 1) correct delivery quantity, or 2) reject delivery item.

If the items are available or partial delivery is allowed, the following task occurs: check out use of warehouse management during picking. This task involves either picking with warehouse management or picking without warehouse management.

Picking

Picking with warehouse management involves no other tasks. Picking without warehouse management involves creating a picking list and then carrying out the picking without the help of warehouse management. Picking leads to two events: 1) delivery items are completely picked, or 2) delivery items are partially picked.

After complete picking of items, packing can take place. However, if not all of the items are picked, the results must be edited in the system. This is followed by two activities: 1) create partial delivery, or 2) create full delivery by picking again.

Pack delivery items follows. Once done, delivery information is edited and then a delivery is created. This task triggers seven possible outcomes in sales and distribution (SD) or materials management (MM):

- Check to see if billing is relevant (SD)
- Create or transmit shipping papers (SD)
- Goods issue processing for stock material (MM)
- Batch goods issue processing (MM)
- Consignment goods issue processing (MM)
- Create stock transport order (SD)
- Release scheduling agreement (SD)

It's also possible to monitor only the delivery without performing any of these tasks. The second, third, fourth, and fifth events all lead to the task of billing in sales and distribution. In the case of the sixth event, create stock transport order, the next step is to update the order. In the seventh event, release scheduling agreement, the subsequent task is to adapt the agreement quantity.

Goods Issue

Goods issue processing for stock material comes after delivery processing in sales and distribution. Delivery processing includes credit control, which offers two possibilities: either the credit limit is sufficient or it is not. If there is enough credit, the process continues. Two options follow: post goods issue or select valuation type. If the goods issue is posted, links to project system and sales and distribution occur in the form of project update, delivery processing, local shipping, or printing of goods receipt slip.

It's also possible that warehouse management will remove the goods from storage. This leads to goods issue/removal from storage processing. Another possibility is that the warehouse isn't maintained by warehouse management. In this case, the material is simply issued.

Rebate Processing

Billing can be the result of several different sales and distribution functions, from delivery and returns to rebate settlement and third-party order. The first task is to choose the type of invoice. This activity can include creating the invoice from a single document or from a billing due list. Once either is accomplished, a billing document is created.

The next task is to determine or transfer the billing prices and taxes. Two events may follow: a pro forma invoice and a billing document relevant to accounting. Here, it's possible the billing document is transmitted and then transferred, which leads to the function of project update in project system. Other tasks in other areas may also take place.

The invoice may just be monitored. It may also be checked to see if it has any connection to a volume-based rebate. Finally, controlling may take over the document for its profitability analysis, or finance may use the document for customer invoice processing.

5

Analyzing R/3™ Sales Information

MAP▶ **I**n the analyzing phase of reporting, the most important activity is to identify all the relevant information available for the report. Here, you need to match up the business needs defined in Chapter 4 with what is available in the R/3™ system. This analysis will entail examination of the business information contained in the system, including knowledge of ratios used to measure performance, organizational dimensions used, and the source data. An analysis of the following areas will help us access this information in R/3™:

- Business objects
- Performance measures
- Decision support applications
- Information sources (characteristics, key figures, and ratios)

5.1 UNDERSTANDING SALES BUSINESS OBJECTS

Business objects help us identify the characteristics that are important for reporting purposes and determine which characteristics are available in R/3™. A business object encapsulates the business logic of a certain information object type, for example, a sales order. The object contains various levels of information, such as the possible header types, available organizations, item data, objects types, and other information useful for reporting purposes.

The primary business objects for R/3™ Sales and Distribution are represented in the following:

- Sales Order
- Customer Delivery
- Product
- Customer

Sales Order Business Object

This business object contains all the information in the SAP™ system relating to a sales order. The data represents the contractual arrangement between a sales organization and a sold-to party (customer) concerning goods to be delivered or services to be rendered. A sales order contains information about prices, quantities, and dates. The request is received by a sales area, which is then responsible for filling the order.

The sales order is, of course, the most important source of information for your sales reporting. It records the basic information on all transactions with your customer.

The following tables list important fields in the sales order. We divide these into characteristics (Table 5–1), which represent the criteria you will use to select values, and key figures (Table 5–2), which represent the values. Key figures are used to create performance measures, normally expressed as ratios, which are used to evaluate a business process or activity. We have included the technical names of the fields, since they are often useful when communicating requirements to your SAP™ Technical Staff.

Table 5–1   Characteristics of the Sales Order Business Object

Characteristic	Technical Name	Description
Sales document number	VBAK-VBELN	Number that uniquely identifies a sales document. You require this field in your report if you require information specific to a sales order or contract.
Sales document item number	VBAP-POSNR	Number that identifies the item in the sales order. You require this field in your report if you require information specific to a sales order or contract.
Material number	VBAP-MATNR	Number that identifies the product ordered.
Sales Item description	VBAP-ARKTX	Text describing the order.
Document date	VBAK-AUDAT	Date the sales document was sent to the customer.

Table 5–1   Characteristics of the Sales Order Business Object (Continued)

Characteristic	Technical Name	Description
Document currency	VBAK-WAERK	Indicates the currency of the document, expressed as the standard codes set forth by the International Standards Organization.
Sales organization	VBAK-VKORG	Topmost organizational unit responsible for the entire sales process.
Distribution channel	VBAK-VTWEG	How the product or service is sold to the customer, (e.g., wholesale or retail).
Division	VBAK-SPART	Groups together the goods sold through a distribution channel (e.g., food and non-food divisions).
District	VBKD-BZIRK	Organizational unit responsible for selling in a geographical region.
Sales employee	VBAP- PVRTNR	Identifies the person responsible for the order.

Table 5–2   Key Figures for the Sales Order Business Object

Key figure	Technical Name	Description
Sales order net value	VBAK-NETWR	The net value of the order, after discounts have been applied, in the currency of the document.
Target quantity	VBAP-ZMENG	Target quantity to deliver, expressed in the sales unit of measure.
Sales taxes	VBAP-MWSBP	Tax amount in document currency.
Cumulative confirmed quantity	VBAP-KBMNG	Quantity confirmed to deliver after the system has performed an availability check.
Net value of order item	VBAP-NETWR	Net value of orders that have not yet been shipped.
Net value of returns for a sales order item	VBAP-NETWR	Net value of returns that have yet to be processed.
Gross value of a sales order item	VBAP-KZWI1	Gross value of incoming orders.
Gross value of returns for a sales order item	VBAP-KZWI1	Net value of returns that have yet to be processed.

Table 5–2   Key Figures for the Sales Order Business Object (Continued)

Key figure	Technical Name	Description
Quantity of order	VBAP-KWMENG	Total quantity ordered.
Quantity of returns	VBAP-KWMENG	Total quantity of returns.
Invoice quantity	VBRP-FKIMG	Total invoiced quantity.
Cost of order	VBAP-WAVWR	Total cost of order, determined from the price of the material from its material master record. This price is used to value a particular material stock in inventory.
Credit memo value	VBRP-KZWI6	Total value of credits issued to customer in a credit memo.

Customer Delivery Business Object

The customer delivery business object is a document that is used to manage and process delivery of goods to a customer. It is used as the basis for:

- Picking operations for order fulfillment
- Creating shipping documents to accompany the delivery
- Determining the transportation routes for the delivery
- Determining the amount to bill the customer

You require information related to the delivery business object when you need to create reports that describe deliveries made to customers.

Table 5–3 identifies the characteristics and key figures relevant to deliveries.

Product Business Object

All product information in the SAP™ R/3™ system is contain in the material master. Each product is defined in the single material master record, which identifies:

- What customers can order
- The value of the products ordered
- The total quantity in stock and quantity available to order
- The relevant units of measure for identifying the amount to order
- Quality control information
- Information on how the product is delivered
- Information for accounting and billing purposes

Table 5–3   Characteristics and Key Figures for Deliveries

Characteristic	Technical Name	Description
Delivery	LIKP-VBELN	Number that uniquely describes the delivery. You require the delivery number if the user of the report needs to identify deliveries.
Delivery date	LIKP-ERDAT	Date the delivery was entered.
Shipping point	LIKP-VSTEL	Physical location, such as a warehouse, from which the delivery was shipped.
Delivery type	LIKP-LFART	Defines the purpose of the delivery (e.g., cash sale or returns).
Shipping conditions	LIKP-VSBED	Code defining how the goods will be shipped to the customer.
Ship-to party	LIKP-KUNNR	Number that identifies the party to ship the goods to, if different from the sold-to party.
Sold-to party	LIKP-KUNAG	Number that identifies the receiver of the goods.
Order number	LIKP-AUFNR	Number of the order that the delivery references.
Bill of lading	LIKP-BOLNR	The bill of lading number for the delivery.
Route	LIKP-ROUTE	Route taken to reach the customer or ship-to party.
Forwarding agent	LIKP-SPDNR	Number that identifies the freight forwarder.
Destination country	LIKP-LLAND	Key identifying the country to which the items are being delivered.
Total weight	LIKP-BTGEW	Total weight of the delivery.
Total volume	LIKP-VOLUM	Volume of the delivery.
Time for deliveries on hand	MCVKENNZ1-ARBLA	Total time for deliveries.
Returns weight	LIKP-BRGEW	Total weight of returns.
Returns volume	LIKP-VOLUM	Total volume of returns.

Materials that are composed of different parts or assemblies can be described in a bill of material. The bill of material aggregates all of the components that make up an assembly in a structured list.

Materials can also be further broken down into batches, which is relevant if the product needs to be managed by different production lots.

The material master is the single source for describing the products and goods that your company sells to its customers. Therefore, it is an important component in planning your sales reporting requirements.

R/3™ stock levels can be determined at a variety of organizational levels. You can view the total stock held for a plant or storage location, for example. This gives you flexibility in determining from where to order stocks.

Table 5–4 lists the characteristics and key figures relevant for products.

Table 5–4   Characteristics and Key Figures for Products

Characteristic	Technical Name	Description
Material number	MARA-MATNR	Number that uniquely describes a product, part, or item that your company carries in inventory.
Material description	MAKT-MAKTX	Description of the product.
Plant	MARC-WERKS	The organizational unit responsible for producing and/or providing the product.
Storage location	MARC-LGORT	The stock location of the material.
Material group	MARA-MATKL	Logical grouping of similar materials (e.g., men's wear).
Manufacturer number	MARA-MFRNR	Control number used by the manufacturer to identify the part.
Batch number		Control number that identifies the batch.
Base unit of measure	MARA-MEINS	Unit of measure in which the product is managed in inventory. (Note: this may differ from the unit used to ship the item.)
Unrestricted use stock	RMMG3-LABST	Total quantity of stock that can be ordered and issued for delivery.
Restricted use stock	RMMG3-EINME	Total quantity of stock that has restrictions, used for materials handled in batches.
Returns stock	RMMG3-RETME	Total quantity of stock returned by customer.

Table 5–4 Characteristics and Key Figures for Products (Continued)

Characteristic	Technical Name	Description
Gross weight	MARA-BRGEW	Gross weight of product expressed in the unit of weight field.
Net weight	MARA-NTGEW	Net weight of product expressed in the unit of weight field.
Standard price	MBEW-STPRS	The standard price of the material, used for valuation purposes.
Moving average price	MBEW-VERPR	The valuation price of the material, if the moving average price method is used. In this method, the price continually fluctuates when the procurement price changes.
Total value of products in stock	MBEW-SALK3	Total value of stock—value that is actually posted to the balance sheet in financial accounting.

Customer Business Object

The customer business object is the key to all information regarding your company's business partners. In R/3™, customer information is contained in the customer master record. The customer master record contains information relevant for:

- Ordering
- Marketing
- Shipping
- Billing
- Contact management

In addition, the customer master record contains certain control fields that are used to manage the ordering and delivering process automatically. Thus, for example, price discounts for preferred customers can be defined in the customer master record and then automatically applied to all orders by the customer.

In the SAP™ R/3™ system, customer data is stored in customer master records. Each ship-to and sold-to party identified in a sales order is identified in a customer master record.

In a similar fashion, customer data is maintained for various organizational units or entities, such as the sales organization, distribution channel, and division. This allows for optimum flexibility in specifying customer needs across sales regions and channels.

Your company can use the customer master record as well as the customer material info record to record vital information about customers. You can use the customer master to record important contacts, delivery information, and market research data.

Table 5–5 lists some important characteristics and key figures for reporting on customer master records.

Many of the key figures in Table 5–6 also apply to the sales order key figures.

Table 5–5   Characteristics for Customer Master Records

Characteristic	Technical Name	Description
Customer number	KNA1-KUNNR	Number that uniquely identifies a customer.
Customer contact	KNA1-NAME1-NAME4	Names of key contacts at the customer site.
Sales organization	KNAP-VKORG	Sales organization
Distribution channel	KNAP-VTWEG	Distribution channel
Division	KNAP-SPART	Division
Industry	KNA1-BRSCH	Key that identifies the industry to which the customer belongs (e.g., high tech or agriculture).
Customer class	KNA1-KUKLA	Field that defines important attributes of the customer, such as the total yearly revenue expected.
Nielson indicator	KNA1-NIELS	The regional division according to the A.C. Nielson market categories.
Region	KNA1-REGIO	The state or province of the customer.
Zip code	KNA1-PSTLZ	The zip code to which the customer belongs.
Tax ID	KNA1-STCD1	The tax identification number of the customer.
URL	KNA1-URL	Web site address for your customer.
Country	KNA1-LAND1	The country code for the customer.
Partner function	KNVP-PARVW	Code that identifies the purpose of the customer (e.g., sold-to party or ship-to party).
Personnel number of the person responsible	KNVP-PERNR	Personnel number of the contact person.

Table 5–6   Key Figures for Customer Master Records

Key Figure	Technical Name	Description
Annual sales	KNA1-UMSA1	The total annual sales of the customer.
Net value of order item	VBAP-NETWR	Net value of orders that have not yet been shipped.
Net value of returns for a sales order item	VBAP-NETWR	Net value of returns that have yet to be processed.
Gross value of a sales order item	VBAP-KZWI1	Gross value of incoming orders.
Gross value of returns for a sales order item	VBAP-KZWI1	Net value of returns that have yet to be processed.
Invoiced sales	VBRP-NETWR	Net value of invoiced orders.
Open orders	VBAP-OAUWE	Order value for which sales orders are recorded but delivery has not been made.
Quantity of order	VBAP-KWMENG	Total quantity ordered.
Quantity of returns	VBAP-KWMENG	Total quantity of returns.
Invoice quantity	VBRP-FKIMG	Total invoiced quantity.
Cost of order	VBAP-WAVWR	Total cost of order, determined from the price of the material in its material master record. (This price is used to value a particular material stock in inventory.)
Credit memo value	VBRP-KZWI6	Total value of credits issued to customer in a credit memo.

5.2   UNDERSTANDING ORGANIZATIONAL STRUCTURES IN SALES

As a reporting analyst, you will need to understand how a typical sales organization is defined in R/3™ sales. The reason for this is that your reports will necessarily have an organization dimension. For example, if your report is relevant to a particular region and distribution channel, you will need to understand the relationship between these organizational entities in R/3™ and how they have been configured in your R/3™ system.

Product and Channel Organization in Sales

Figure 5–1 illustrates how the sales organization, distribution channel, and division are used to describe the R/3™ sales channels your company uses to sell and market its products.

Sales Organization

The sales organization, the highest organization level within sales, is ultimately responsible for all customer interactions and transactions. All selling transactions, for example, require a sales organization. The sales organization is responsible for product liability and claims made by customers.

Sales reports nearly always will include the sales organization as the primary selection criteria.

Distribution Channel

The distribution channel designates the mode through which your company services and supplies its customers. Retail distribution, direct to consumer, and wholesale distribution are all examples of distribution channels.

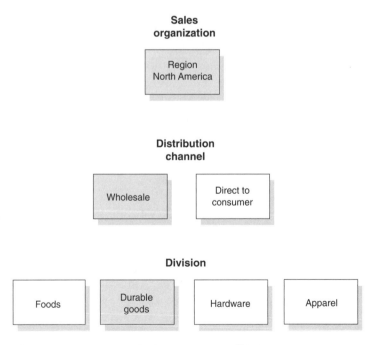

▶ **Figure 5–1**   Product and Channel Organization in R/3™ Sales
Note: The shaded boxes represent one sales area.

Division

A division is used to designate a product line in the SAP™ R/3™ System. The R/3™ System allows your company to make customer-specific arrangements for pricing, for example. You can use the division to analyze data for separate product lines within a division.

Sales Area

A sales area represents any given combination of sales organization, distribution channel, and division. You can carry out separate analyses by sales area.

Personnel Organization in R/3™ Sales

Figure 5–2 illustrates how your company's internal sales organization is defined in the R/3™ system.

Sales Office

The sales office is the geographical location responsible for a district or region.

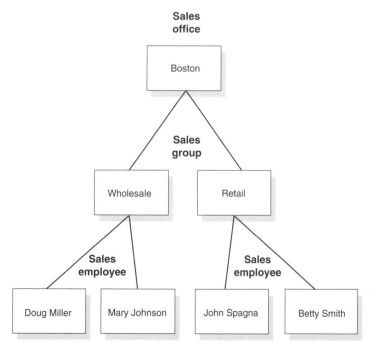

▶ **Figure 5–2** Personnel Organization in R/3™ Sales

Sales offices are assigned to sales areas, described previously. This links the sales office to a specific product division and distribution channel.

Sales Group

The sales employees of a sales office can be further subdivided into one or more sales groups, according to the distribution channels or product lines for which they are responsible. For example, sales groups can be defined for individual divisions.

If you create reports that measure the performance of various sales departments, then you will need to use the sales group as one of your selection criteria.

Sales Employee

Individual sales personnel are described as sales employees in the R/3™ system.

Organization in Shipping

Figure 5–3 illustrates the organizational units relevant for shipping. You will need to understand these relationships if your sales reports need to include information about deliveries to customers.

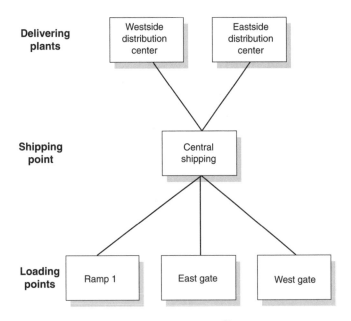

▶ **Figure 5–3** Organizational Units for Shipping in R/3™

As shown in Figure 5–3, shipping points can be subdivided into several loading points (i.e., where trucks and other transportation means are loaded for shipment).

In R/3™, all deliveries must be made through a designated shipping point. The shipping points and loading points available to the shipping department in your company are defined in R/3™ in this fashion.

The shipping point can serve one or more delivering plants, that is, the location providing the goods to be shipped. One thing to remember is that R/3™ can automatically determine the shipping point to use for deliveries, depending on how your system is configured. This automatic determination may depend on such factors as the geographic location of the shipping point relative to the distribution center or plant, or the mode of transportation used (train or truck, for example).

5.3   *UNDERSTANDING SALES PERFORMANCE MEASURES*

Performance measures are the main source of content for the report and contain the most important information for analysis purposes. They provide the key figures and ratios that are used to measure performance. R/3™ has a number of information sources built into the system that provide you with standard ratios that measure performance in an R/3™ sales system.

For your convenience, we have included a list of some standard ratios used to measure performance in a sales and marketing environment. The following is a list of commonly used sales performance measures.

Marketing Ratios

The key performance measures for marketing are:

Average Order Size
Ratio of net sales to total number of transactions over a given period of time.

Management uses AOS to select new products and to indicate customers' propensity to spend.

Deflated Change in Average Order Size
This year's deflated average order size reduced by last year's average order size.

$$\text{Deflated Change in AOS} = \frac{\text{AOS} \times \text{Price Index Last Year}}{\text{Price Index}} - \text{Average Order Size}$$

Order Growth

Difference between the number of transactions this year and last year (or any number of previous years) divided by last year's number of transactions, expressed as percentage.

$$\text{Order Growth} = 100 \times \frac{\text{Trans This Year} - \text{Trans Last Year}}{\text{Trans Last Year}}$$

Customer Growth

Difference between this year's number of customers and last year's number of customers.

$$\text{Customer Growth} = 100 \times \frac{\text{No. Custs. This Year} - \text{No. Custs. Last Year}}{\text{No. Custs. Last Year}}$$

Sales per Customer

Net sales value divided by average number of customers.

This ratio reveals how many new customers are needed to implement sales growth plans.

$$\text{Sales per Customer} = \frac{\text{Net Sales}}{\text{Customers}}$$

Customer Solicitation Ratio

Number of promotions to existing customers divided by total number of solicitations.

This ratio measures the extent to which the company directs sales efforts to the existing customer base.

$$\text{Customer Solicitation Ratio} = 100 \times \frac{\text{No. Solicitations to Existing Customers}}{\text{Total Solicitations}}$$

Average Return on Marketing

Compares the average marketing expense with the net sales value.

$$\text{Avg. ROM} = \frac{\text{Net Sales This Year} + \text{Net Sales Last Year}}{\text{Marketing Expense This Year} + \text{Marketing Expense Last Year}}$$

Average Order Response

Average number of transactions divided by average number of solicitations, expressed as percentage.

$$\text{AOR} = 100 \times \frac{\text{No. Trans. This Year} + \text{No. Trans. Last Year}}{\text{Solicitations This Year} + \text{Solicitations Last Year}}$$

Average Sales Response
Differs from average order response in that it looks at the dollar value instead of the number of transactions.

$$ASR = \frac{\text{Average Net Sales}}{\text{Average No. of Solicitations}}$$

Customer Satisfaction Ratio
Ratio of value of return goods as percentage of gross order value.

Sales Ratios

The key performance measures for sales are:

Sales Growth
Percentage growth of gross and net sales over previous year, expressed as percentage.

$$SG = 100 \times \frac{\text{Net Sales} - \text{Net Sales Last Year}}{\text{Net Sales Last Year}}$$

Sales Growth Trend
Number of consecutive years that sales revenues have exceeded those of the previous year.

Deflated Sales Growth
Difference between this year's deflated net sales and last year's net sales, divided by last year's net sales, expressed as percentage.

Deflated Sales Growth =

$$100 \times \frac{(\text{Net Sales} \times \text{Price Index Last Year} \div \text{Price Index}) - \text{Net Sales Last Year}}{\text{Net Sales Last Year}}$$

Break-Even Sales Factor
Gross profit divided by total expenses, expressed as percentage.

$$\text{Break-even Sales Factor} = 100 \times \frac{\text{Gross Profit}}{\text{Total Expenses}}$$

Sales per Employee
Net sales divided by average number of employees.

Revenue to Space
This ratio shows the amount of real estate needed to create revenue.

$$RTS = \frac{\text{Net Sales}}{\text{No. Square Feet of Plant Space}}$$

Profitability

The key performance measures for profitability are:

Profit Growth
Difference between this year's net profit after taxes and last year's net profit after taxes, divided by last year's net profit, expressed as percentage.

$$PG = 100 \times \frac{\text{Net Profit After Taxes} - \text{Net Profit After Taxes Last Year}}{\text{Net Profit After Taxes Last Year}}$$

Return on Sales
Net profit after taxes divided by net sales, expressed as percentage.

Measures the difference between what a company takes in and what it spends in conducting its business.

$$ROS = 100 \times \frac{\text{Net Profit After Taxes}}{\text{Net Sales}}$$

Operating Margin
Net profit before taxes plus interest expense and depreciation, divided by net sales, expressed as percentage.

Profit per Sales Employee
Net profit after taxes divided by average number of employees.

$$\text{Profit per Sales Employee} = \frac{\text{Net Profit After Taxes}}{\text{No. Sales Employees}}$$

6

Understanding the R/3™ Sales Information System

In this chapter, we examine some options that are available for presenting R/3™ data to end users. As you recall, the presentation phase of building reports focuses on transferring knowledge to other users. Practically speaking, this process will decide the most effective form for the report to clearly transmit information to end users. The goal for the presentation phase is to design a finished report, a template, or a proto-report that will organize essential information into a structured report. For this phase of our scenario, we can carry over much of the information that we identified earlier in the managing and analysis phase. For example, we can draw upon knowledge of the business drivers, performance measures, and business objects not only to select the subjects and headings for the report, but to decide upon the best presentation software as well.

For this chapter, we use the Sales Information System (SIS), SAP™'s primary sales reporting tool, as the presentation software. We examine the standard analyses available in the SIS, and then delve into main characteristics, key figures, and ratios available for sales reports. Finally, we take a look at a specific report that can be created using the SIS as the primary presentation application.

6.1   SALES INFORMATION SYSTEM

The Sales Information System is a component of the Logistics Information System (described in Chapter 3), an R/3™ reporting tool that can be used to create reports as well as to present the data that is collected. The SIS accesses business information called infostructures. An infostructure is a kind of three-dimensional data cube that contains data that has been collected from R/3™ transactions. For example, a customer infostructure (S001 in the Sales Information System) contains data that has been collected for customers. It will contain information on invoices, sales orders, deliveries, and so forth.

The data is collected as characteristics, key figures, and time period. As we noted earlier, characteristics are the objects you report on, such as customer or material. Key figures are the statistical values used to forecast or measure performance, such as "invoiced sales." Key figures are usually expressed as a value or quantity. The last part of the data cube is an aggregate of the data by time period, for example, by daily, weekly, monthly, or fiscal periods.

The SIS contains standard reports that can be accessed with the standard analysis tool. Standard reports are available for such key sales areas as:

- Customer
- Material
- Sales Organization
- Shipping Point
- Sales Employee
- Sales Office

6.2   STANDARD ANALYSES IN THE R/3™ SALES INFORMATION SYSTEM

Table 6–1 lists the types of analyses provided in the R/3™ Sales Information System. You can use this list to identify the reporting analyses that you may require for your organization.

Each decision support tool provides:

- ABC analysis (Pareto)
- Top N listing (list of values based on a key figure)
- Trend analysis
- Exception analysis (based on trend or threshold)
- Ability to dynamically switch currencies
- Time-series breakdown (from year to month to week to day)
- Planned vs. actual (where appropriate)
- Display access to master data records, in the case of customer and product, respectively

Table 6–1   Standard Analyses in the R/3™ Sales Information System

Decision Support Tool	Information Delivery
Customer analysis	Summarizes the order quantities and values resulting from business transactions with customers. Lists breakdown statistics of customer, including period, sales organization, and distribution.
Product analysis	Summarizes the order quantities and values for articles or products (material) resulting from transactions with business partners.
Sales office	Contains the ordering activities and customer transactions by sales office and sales group.
Sales documents	Retrieves detailed information about specific sales orders.
Deliveries	Analyzes total deliveries and returns for one or more shipping points.
Sales organization	Summarizes the ordering activities and customer transactions by sales organization.

Customer Analysis

The customer analysis provides access to sales information based on the customer and independent of the organizational unit (e.g., sales organization or sales area). The customer analysis reports on statistical figures that are based on:

- Incoming orders
- Returns
- Invoiced sales orders
- Credit memos
- Sales activities
- Customer hierarchy

Product

The product analysis provides access to sales information based on a particular product, part article, or material. The product analysis provides statistical data based on:

- Incoming orders
- Returns
- Invoiced sales orders
- Credit memos

- Configurable materials
- Product hierarchy

Sales Office

The sales office analysis provides access to sales figures for a branch office or district. The sales office analysis provides total values based on:

- Incoming orders
- Returns
- Invoiced sales orders
- Credit memos

Sales Documents

The sales documents analysis provides access to sales figures based on a particular type of sales document for a customer, material, or sales organizational unit. The sales documents analysis provides totals for a customer/product combination based on:

- Inquiries
- Quotations
- Deliveries
- Invoices

6.3   *CHARACTERISTICS, KEY FIGURES, AND RATIOS*

Each of the data elements displayed in a decision-support tool can be a characteristic or key figure. As we noted earlier, characteristics are the objects you report on, such as customer or material. Key figures are the statistical values, such as "invoiced sales," used to forecast or measure performance. Key figures are usually expressed as a value or quantity.

Ratios combine a characteristic and associated key figure that can be used as a performance measure. For example, "Sales per employee" is a performance measure composed of a key figure (sales or sales value) and a characteristic (employee).

| TIP | Characteristics and key figures are described via the business object, while ratios are tools to measure performance. |

Table 6–2 is a list of the characteristics and key figures required for each of the decision support tools described previously.

Table 6–2 Decision Support Tool Characteristics and Key Figures

Decision Support Tool	Characteristic	Key Figure	Performance Measure
Customer	Sales organization Distribution channel Division Customer Product	Credit memo value Credit memo quantity Billing document value Billing document quantity Gross credit memos Gross order value Gross order quantity Gross order freight quantity Incoming order value Incoming order quantity Invoiced sales Invoiced quantity Invoiced sales cost Open order quantity Open order value Returns value Returns quantity	Customer growth Sales per customer Customer satisfaction ratio
Sales Employee	Sales organization Distribution channel Division Sales employee Sold-to party Material	Credit memo value Credit memo quantity Billing document value Billing document quantity Gross credit memos Gross order value Gross order quantity Gross order freight quantity Incoming order value Incoming order quantity Invoiced sales Invoiced quantity Invoiced sales cost Returns value Returns quantity	Sales growth per employee Profit per employee

Table 6–2   Decision Support Tool Characteristics and Key Figures (Continued)

Decision Support Tool	Characteristic	Key Figure	Performance Measure
Product	Sales organization Distribution channel Material	Credit memo value Credit memo quantity Billing document value Billing document quantity Gross credit memos Gross order value Gross order quantity Gross order freight quantity Incoming order value Incoming order quantity Invoiced sales Invoiced quantity Invoiced sales cost Open order quantity Open order value Returns value Returns quantity	
Sales Organization	Sales organization Distribution channel Division Customer Product	Credit memo value Credit memo quantity Billing document value Billing document quantity Gross credit memos Gross order value Gross order quantity Gross order freight quantity Incoming order value Incoming order quantity Invoiced sales Invoiced quantity Invoiced sales cost Returns value Returns quantity	Sales growth Sales growth trend Deflated sales growth Operating margin

Table 6–2   Decision Support Tool Characteristics and Key Figures (Continued)

Decision Support Tool	Characteristic	Key Figure	Performance Measure
Deliveries	Shipping point Route Carrier Destination	Delivery volume Delivery work load Gross weight delivery Gross weight returns Net weight Net weight returns Unit of weight	Customer satisfaction ratio
Sales Documents	Sales organization Distribution channel Division Sales office Sales group Sold-to party Material Sales document type	Gross order value Net order value Order quantity	Average order size Deflated change in average order size Customer solicitation ratio Average sales response

6.4   SIS SAMPLE REPORT

To perform a sales standard analysis by customer (IDES values):

1. Log on to your IDES system.
2. Choose the following path from the SAP™ main menu:
   Logistics > Logistics controlling > Sales information system.
   The sales information screen displays.
3. From the Standard Analysis menu, select Customer.
   The customer analysis selection criteria screen displays.
4. In the Sold-to party text boxes enter the range 1000, then 2000.
5. In the Period to analyze text boxes enter the range: 01.1997 and 01.1998.
6. Click on the Execute icon.
   The Customer Analysis Initial List report displays (Figure 6–1).

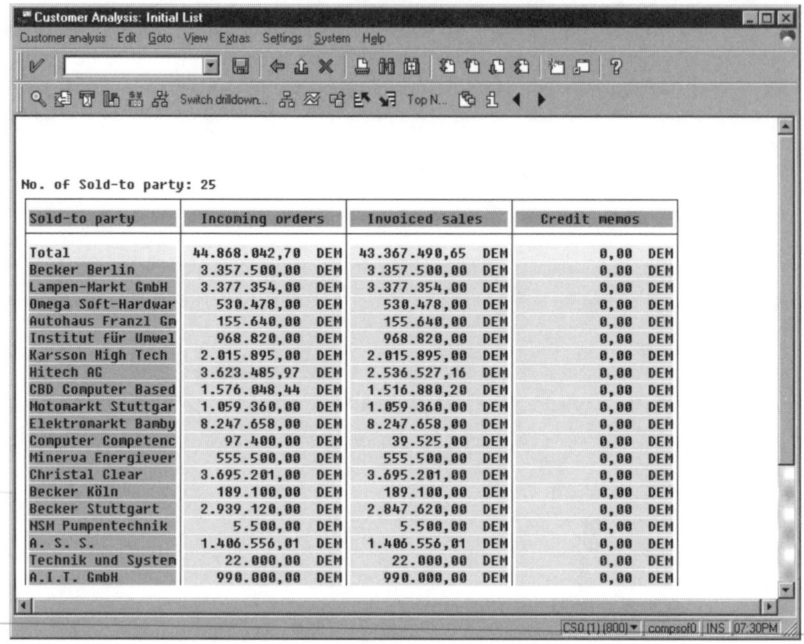

Sold-to party	Incoming orders	Invoiced sales	Credit memos
Total	44.868.042,70 DEM	43.367.490,65 DEM	0,00 DEM
Becker Berlin	3.357.500,00 DEM	3.357.500,00 DEM	0,00 DEM
Lampen-Markt GmbH	3.377.354,00 DEM	3.377.354,00 DEM	0,00 DEM
Omega Soft-Hardwar	530.478,00 DEM	530.478,00 DEM	0,00 DEM
Autohaus Franzl Gm	155.640,00 DEM	155.640,00 DEM	0,00 DEM
Institut für Umwel	968.820,00 DEM	968.820,00 DEM	0,00 DEM
Karsson High Tech	2.015.895,00 DEM	2.015.895,00 DEM	0,00 DEM
Hitech AG	3.623.485,97 DEM	2.536.527,16 DEM	0,00 DEM
CBD Computer Based	1.576.048,44 DEM	1.516.880,20 DEM	0,00 DEM
Motomarkt Stuttgar	1.059.360,00 DEM	1.059.360,00 DEM	0,00 DEM
Elektromarkt Bamby	8.247.658,00 DEM	8.247.658,00 DEM	0,00 DEM
Computer Competenc	97.400,00 DEM	39.525,00 DEM	0,00 DEM
Minerva Energiever	555.500,00 DEM	555.500,00 DEM	0,00 DEM
Christal Clear	3.695.201,00 DEM	3.695.201,00 DEM	0,00 DEM
Becker Köln	189.100,00 DEM	189.100,00 DEM	0,00 DEM
Becker Stuttgart	2.939.120,00 DEM	2.847.620,00 DEM	0,00 DEM
NSM Pumpentechnik	5.500,00 DEM	5.500,00 DEM	0,00 DEM
A. S. S.	1.406.556,01 DEM	1.406.556,01 DEM	0,00 DEM
Technik und System	22.000,00 DEM	22.000,00 DEM	0,00 DEM
A.I.T. GmbH	990.000,00 DEM	990.000,00 DEM	0,00 DEM

Figure 6–1 Customer Analysis Report

As Figure 6–1 illustrates, the SIS report that we have created is a standard analysis for a customer. The report lists the customer, the net value of all incoming orders from that customer, the net value of invoiced sales, and the net value of credit memos.

7

Sales Information Delivery

MAPP **M**any reporting analysts believe that the reporting process ends with the Presentation stage. Having put together a very well organized, useful report, they conclude that their work on it is finished. This is a typical mistake, especially in companies that haven't yet established good reporting processes. As any IS staff can corroborate, the number one reporting request is for new reports that have already been implemented! Most reports, often some of the best that a company designs, are never used because no one knows about them.

In the MAPP process, Publishing is designed to create a system that improves the circulation, knowledge, and awareness of reports within the company. The main objective of the publishing strategy is to get a report into the hands of the end users who can make the best use of the report data. In other words, we need to make sure that the right people in your organization have the right information at the right time.

Chapter 7 draws on our experience with sales professionals in a wide range of industries and provides information on creating a publishing system especially suited for sales reporting.

Areas covered in this chapter include:

- Web-based R/3™ sales publishing
- Enterprise Information Portal
- Scenarios for sales publishing
- Sales report circulation plan
- Rollout issues for sales reports
- Improving knowledge transfer
- Publicizing sales reports

7.1   WEB-BASED R/3™ SALES PUBLISHING

The choice of medium for publishing sales reports must take into account two sales realities: sales professionals are often on the road and sales organizations tend to be dispersed across the country and beyond. In the past, this wide distribution of sales professionals hindered the ability for effective communication in general and collaborative efforts in particular. Enterprise information systems such as SAP™ R/3™ did not make matters any easier. R/3™'s complexity hindered remote use of reports and required too much training and support. Moreover, the difficulty in printing and publishing reports with real-time information made collaboration using R/3™ data increasingly less likely.

Today, however, with the emerging sophistication of web-based solutions, publishing R/3™ sales information can be one of the strengths of a sales reporting system. Throughout this chapter we recommend the corporate information portal, a leading technology in web-based content management, as an effective medium for publishing R/3™ sales information. With corporate information portal technology, companies can create an effective sales publishing system by more effectively distributing information, encouraging collaboration, and making ERP-based sales reports easier to create and share.

Internet Information Portals

Information portals are not content sites, but rather launch pads to other content. First introduced to the consumer market with Internet information gateways such as Yahoo™, MSN.com™, and the Go™ network, information portals organize and simplify information. Yahoo, for example, presents the user with a search engine and a descriptive catalog of web content. This technology has allowed Internet users to customize and filter information, making it more relevant to their individual needs. The unwieldy Internet, with its tendency to induce information overload, has been effectively tamed through these personalized portals.

Corporate information portals are an extension of gateway technology, but instead of bringing the user sports scores and stock tips, they bring a personalized view of corporate content and applications over a company *intranet*. Whereas "classical" reporting was mostly concerned with basic figures and ratios, corporate portals allow reports to mix data and other kinds of business content. Corporate portals allow end users to view and access such company information as:

- Shared documents
- Email
- Calendars

- Workflow
- Reports
- Project management
- Applications

With corporate portals, users can create their own personalized profiles for data, information, and applications. For example, a portal could be customized so that a user can make travel reservations, check sales performance, or submit expense reports—all from a desktop.

The latest entries into the corporate portal market have taken on enterprise applications, creating portals that allow users to access and use business information data. Corporate portals make it possible to create an easy-to-use corporate web system for distributing and publishing enterprise reports and report-related information.

Enterprise Information Portal

The Enterprise Information Portal (EIP) is a web product that provides a Yahoo-like functionality to enterprise users. The product acts as a clearinghouse for information from enterprise applications and lets users determine how they want their reports and information presented. In particular, it provides a unique interface to R/3™ data and real-time data access. Designed to work with a variety of devices such as Windows CE™ and wireless, the product can reach large numbers of corporate end users.

Unlike other web systems such as Outlook/Exchange™ (see Chapter 12), the EIP is not "client heavy"; instead, it uses a Yahoo-like web browser to call up information on a server rather than downloading and installing information on the client. To deliver views of data, the EIP uses Microsoft's Internet Information Server™ (IIS), which also retrieves live data from the R/3™ system. Figure 7–1 illustrates this arrangement.

The client receives the information on a report from the IIS in one simple step. When the data needs to be updated, the user hits the Refresh button and live data is queried and received from R/3™. Figure 7–2 shows an ActiveSheets "e-report" in the EIP web browser.

Publishing with the EIP

For publishing purposes, the EIP allows you to use the web to distribute information to your sales force. It is dynamically configured to deliver the right information to the right users. Moreover, the EIP creates a web-based environment in which sales people can collaborate, use, and distribute sales content. Adminis-

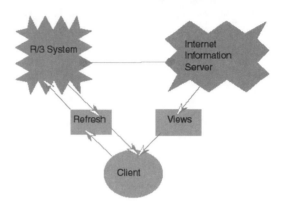

▶ **Figure 7–1**   Web-Based Reporting Architecture

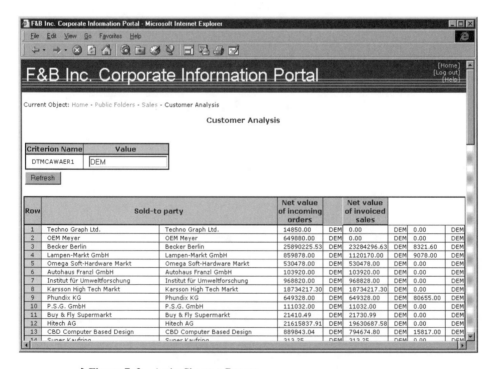

▶ **Figure 7–2**   ActiveSheets e-Report

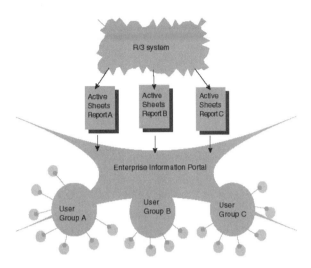

▶ **Figure 7–3**   Information Delivery via the Enterprise Information Portal

trators can monitor and approve content, as well as provide common areas for sharing information.

The basic model for our publishing strategy is illustrated in Figure 7–3. Here, we imagine R/3™ sales reports have been created in Excel with ActiveSheets. The report administrator designates the reports for use according to certain roles or user types. Users who fit that role will receive the report in their individually configured enterprise information portal. Any user who needs the report can access the file simply and easily by downloading it. They can also upload the file and post it to a public area if desired.

Scenario for Sales Report Publishing with the EIP

The head office has put together a projected sales scenario and would like to get input from its district sales managers. They want to examine revenue based on current period and current year with a projected 10% increase by product and 20% increase by district. They would like the districts to run these reports and provide comments on them. Although the sales managers are spread across the country, they need to be able to collaborate on putting the plan together.

Since they cannot work this way in R/3™, the company has decided to use the Enterprise Integration Portal solution. They will do the reports in Excel with a live data link to R/3™. They will set up folders or views in the EIP for a more effective collaboration platform.

The folders or views are created so that they can post their reports to a place where others can see and use them. Permissions are set up so that all can access

▶ **Figure 7–4**   Collaboration in the Enterprise Information Portal

the information through the portal. Also, different views are set up for different users according to their reporting roles.

The reports themselves are done in Excel with a live connection to R/3™. By using Excel everyone will not only be working with real data in the R/3™ system, but they will also be able to comment on the numbers using Excel's annotation feature (Figure 7–4). Within the district itself, the district managers can have their sales people contribute to the reports, put in their own comments, and perhaps try out new plan scenarios. When the deadline approaches, the reports make their way back up the line through the district sales managers and back to the head office. In this way, many people are able to provide valuable input on putting together realistic numbers for the plan.

7.2   CIRCULATION

Once a medium such as a web solution is decided upon, information delivery is the next step to consider in the Publishing phase. A good circulation plan takes into account such issues as:

- What permissions are necessary for which users?
- What media will be used to circulate the report?
- Is there a routing procedure?
- When and how often does the report get used?
- Who gets the report and when?
- What are the roles or views that need to be set up?

The first priority of a circulation plan is, of course, that the report gets to the target user groups. A secondary goal, however, is that you make sure you take into account the best delivery capability for users—even if that capability should be as antiquated a system as paper. If people in the organization want to distribute reports by paper, then you need to take that into account.

Yet another goal is to make sure that there is an effective communication strategy for the report. Ongoing updates and pertinent information should be circulated to the many constituencies involved in the creation and delivery of the report. A system needs to be in place to channel this information to the appropriate members of the organization. Information may include:

- Updates to business sponsors of the report
- Summaries to users
- General updates to the organization
- Correspondence to IS management
- Communications among implementation team members
- Administrative updates and reports

Role-based Reporting

An ideal method for circulating enterprise reports is role-based information delivery systems. In role-based information delivery, the business information is organized and structured according to "views." The views represent user types or profiles set up so that the user gets only information that fits with his or her roles in the company or in the reporting process. Once each user has been assigned a role associated with his/her position and responsibility, he/she can access the data in various self-created directories. Figure 7–5 shows a typical user profile with "public" and "private" views of business information.

A simple scenario for common reporting roles could be a sales rep, a sales executive, and an administrator. The sales user would have a view of reports and reporting information typical of a report consumer. Likely, the reports in this view would have fixed content; that is, the user cannot change the report's contents, but rather can only update the data. The sales executive would have an expanded role. He or she would not only have different kinds of reports avail-

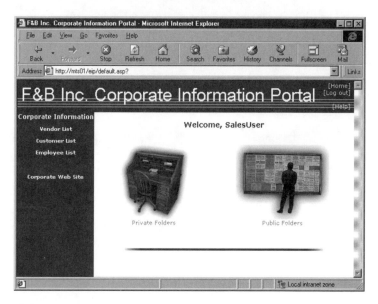

▶ **Figure 7–5** Public and Private Views in the EIP

able in the portal, but would also have expanded permissions to view reports of employees. The administrator's role would allow access to all reports in both public and private areas. The administrator, for example, would be responsible for monitoring the reporting process and making sure that all posted reports go through the proper approval channels. For example, Figures 7–6 and 7–7 compare the administrator's and the sales rep's views.

In the EIP, these views are controlled through a log on process. Different users can log on with different roles to get different views of business information. Views can also be exchanged. For example, using a sales executive logon, a procurement executive could see the kinds of reports that are available in the sales areas of the company and perhaps implement them in his or her organiza-

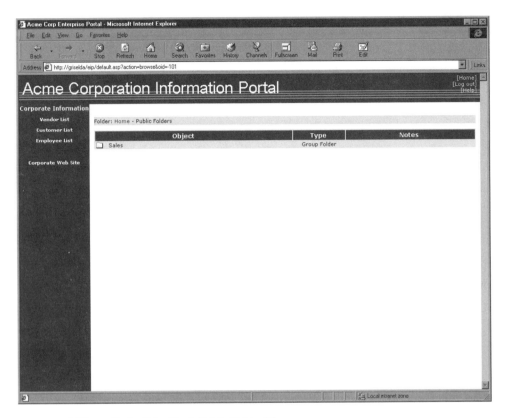

▶ **Figure 7–6**   Sales Rep's Public Folder View

tion. Exchanging views in this manner can facilitate collaboration among users and departments.

The EIP also comes with a User Manager Console that is fully integrated with Microsoft's Management Console. The User Manager allows the administrator to define roles for users and groups of users, thereby ensuring that individuals access reports or documents that fit their previously defined roles.

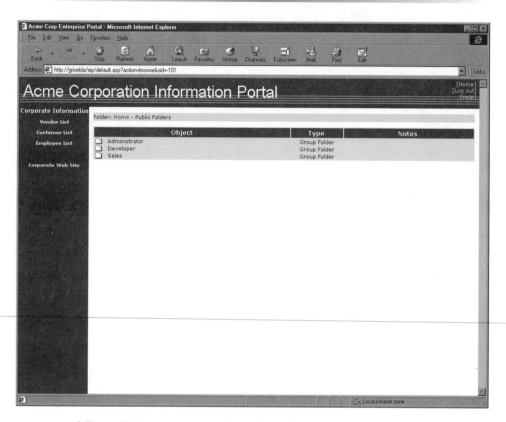

▶ **Figure 7–7**   Administrator's Public Folder View

7.3   KNOWLEDGE TRANSFER

The next stage of the Publishing phase is to devise a strategy for how rollout, training, and feedback will be conducted for the report. These are largely responsibilities of the report administrator, who will coordinate all activities and create a plan for the effective communication of all report information within the organization.

The rollout plan should focus on creating and maintaining the rollout schedule, from initial training to the implementation of the report. To facilitate training, all materials should be located in a central area or folder where they can be easily accessed by the report's consumers. In addition, all training activities need to be publicized and coordinated with training personnel. Finally, there should be a feedback system created for the continuous improvement of the report's content and use.

Rollout Administration

The rollout schedule should consist of three components: time, audience, and materials. Time establishes the logistics of the rollout schedule—for example, finding out when and where the training will take place and publishing this information. Another important time factor is the duration of the approval cycle—for example, how long before a manager should be reminded that she or he needs to approve or reject a report proposal?

When examining the audience for a rollout, the administrator should consider once again the roles for the report. Understanding the roles entails listing all of the report's consumers and grouping them by user types. Many times during a rollout, the administrator doesn't know exactly who the users are; instead, they have a profile that tells them what the user roles are. These roles need to be defined by asking such questions as: If a variety of users needs the report, how will differing needs be addressed? Will some users require updates? Will others need full training? Do users outside the company need the report? What will they require?

The final component, materials, describes all information that exists outside the report itself that will need to be handed out during rollout. Examples of materials include: documentation, announcements, training materials, video, email, and posters.

The following is a list of typical questions that the rollout plan should consider:

- What's the process for the rollout?
- What is the training schedule?
- Where will training be conducted?
- Who needs to be involved in the rollout?
- What materials need to be written?
- How will materials be transmitted?
- How will documentation be handled?
- Who is responsible for documentation/materials?
- When will the report be made public?
- Who is responsible for final sign-offs?

Report Administration with Information Portals

Organization in a publishing system is crucial for enterprise reporting simply because a reporting system has to be more structured and regulated than every-day business activities. When people create or use a report, they are making a decision important to the business. Thus, you must have a publishing process that can control the amount and quality of information that is available. This should be the role of an administrator, web master, or anyone who manages report information flow.

In the reporting process, the administrator provides oversight, functioning as an official who ensures that rules are adhered to when reports are distributed. As a report is posted to the general public or implemented by a certain group, the administrator should ask such questions as:

- Does the report meet certain criteria?
- Have the right people signed off on it?
- Are there reports already like it?
- Is the report the right size and in line with report protocol?

The administrator must walk a fine line between encouraging end users to share information and ensuring that standards remain in place. You wouldn't, for example, want someone to flash out to the general public a report that hasn't been approved.

The EIP role-based information delivery has a monitoring function that allows users to create and submit reports, but controls the process by which they are posted for general use. Users are encouraged to create and post reports to their personal portal, but they can only make them generally available via the appropriate approval channels. In this way, an organization has structured information that goes through an approval process and ultimately is shared for the greater good.

For example, a sales rep has created a report in a private folder and wants to make it available to other people. A note is attached to it that says: "This is a great file—wouldn't it be great if other business units were using it?" In Figure 7–8 the sales rep "publishes" the report by selecting "Approve" so it can be sent for approval to the manager or the administrator.

The EIP allows individuals to publish reports and documents to the portal, but administrative features ensure that only approved material finds its way into the portal's public folders. The administrator can go in, have a look at it, get it approved, and then publish it in the public folder.

Training Coordination

In the Publishing phase, all training activities among the various levels of consumers for the report should be coordinated and publicized. Typically, training is a weak area in the reporting process, in part because it requires collaboration between and among different parts of the organization. But training is the key to the effective communication of ideas in the report. When devising a training plan for the report, the following types of questions should be addressed:

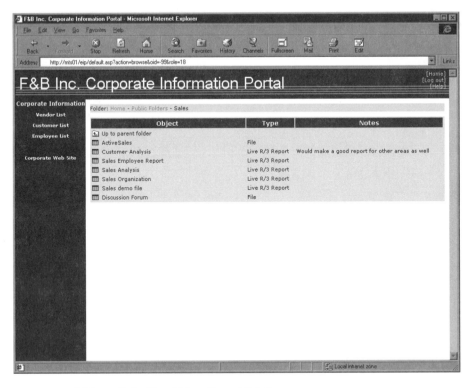

▶ **Figure 7–8** User-Driven Report Solution

- What training materials must be created?
- Who will require training?
- Where will training take place?
- What training materials will be available and where?
- After the rollout, what is the plan for training new end users?
- How will changes to the report be transferred?

The training system should be integrated so that producers, training personnel, and consumers are all in sync. Again, effective communication is key among all the groups involved. Department heads, report producers, or even HR personnel will need to make report administrators aware of new users of the report.

Remote Training

For sales personnel especially, remote training should be given high priority, because the sales force tends to be dispersed beyond company headquarters. In order to facilitate training and collaboration among sales personnel who might not be able to attend on-site events, web-based training files can be posted to EIP public folders.

One significant advantage of the EIP is that any Office-compliant document can be passed along among the users. Files can consist of a wide range of training media, from Word documents to videos. Figure 7–9 illustrates a live screen cam in the Windows Media Player that shows the sales user a detailed technical process.

Feedback Solicitation

All business processes, including the reporting process, need to adapt to continuous change. Feedback is one of the primary tools for improving the reporting process. A good feedback system is important not only for troubleshooting, but for making sure that the report stays useful and relevant.

In all stages of the MAPP process, there is a feedback "loop," in which appropriate personnel are periodically consulted for approval. When Managing, for example, we submit a "scoping" document to get necessary input from man-

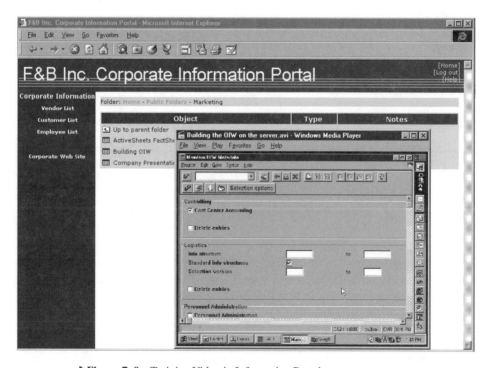

▶ **Figure 7–9**   Training Video in Information Portal

agers and business sponsors of the report. In the Publishing stage, feedback from all consumers and producers of the report should be solicited. In order for all parties involved in the process of the report to voice their concerns, report managers need to consider carefully the medium through which feedback will be solicited and delivered. Other feedback issues to consider are:

- Should a formal feedback document be created?
- Is a feedback forum appropriate?
- Who will be responsible for logging and responding to feedback?
- What is the routing procedure for types of feedback?
- How will common feedback concerns be converted into change?

Lastly, we also recommend that a formal post-implementation assessment be conducted among business users. This assessment should actively solicit feedback from users on issues such as deployment, training, and support. Our goal is to achieve immediate improvements in the initial stages of the report deployment.

Feedback Forum in the EIP

As business-to-employee communication moves from the server to the Internet, web-based forums for feedback will become increasingly important. Remote discussion forums are especially effective for sales people. As in Figure 7–10, web-based discussion groups allow both users and consumers to monitor and participate in a range of issues such as content, technology, and process.

7.4   *BUILDING AWARENESS*

After all the logistics of the delivery of the new report are in order, the last step in the Publishing phase is to devise a marketing plan to increase awareness about it. Increasing awareness is really nothing more than finding effective ways to publicize the activities surrounding the rollout, training, and continuous use of the report.

Certain facts of the report will need to be on hand to design an effective publicity campaign. A list of the users will need to be created, as well as a grouping by user types (for future users of the report). All matters relating to the reporting schedule must be clear. For example: When should the report be delivered? When is the rollout? When will training begin? Other useful facts to gather are:

- Who are the sponsors of the report?
- What purpose will the report serve?
- Where can people go to find out more?

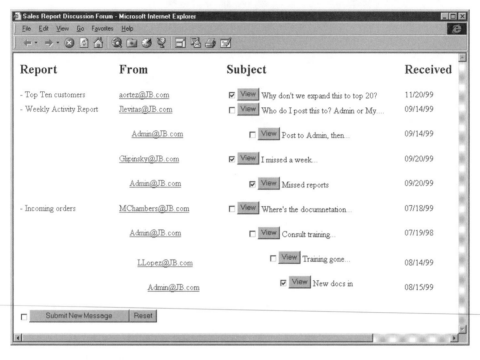

▶ **Figure 7–10**   Web-Based Discussion Forum

- What are the important dates to remember?
- When should I run the report?

After all the facts are collected, they must be documented and approved by the report producers and all others involved in the transmission of the report (IS, for example). Then public relations documents will need to be written and distributed via appropriate channels. Media possibilities for distribution may include:

- Emails
- Web link
- Posters
- Presentations
- Meetings

Publicizing Events

There is perhaps no better medium in terms of cost and distribution than the corporate web. There are many possibilities for publicizing report information over

▶ **Figure 7–11**   Publicity Newsletter

the web. You could build links in public folders to documents that promote publishing activities.

Another possibility is to create a separate web devoted to report publishing activities. If kept current, such a web site can function as a kind of reporting newsletter. In this way, you can reduce your publicity efforts to the constant promotion of the web site. Using the public folders forum, you can direct different user groups to the web site when appropriate or provide employees with brief updates to the new content on the site. This is not only a cost-effective strategy, it is less time-consuming and less labor-intensive. Figure 7–11 illustrates a newsletter style site for publicizing reporting information.

8

Putting It All Together: Creating an R/3™-based Sales Reporting System Using the MAPP Method

$\mathbf{A}$ systematic approach to building reports in R/3™ can help a business evaluate and analyze information crucial to an organization's health. In this chapter we show you how to use the MAPP method to build sales reports so that your company can more clearly assess, and ultimately improve, sales performance.

In the following example we study the efforts of the reporting team at our case company, General Consolidated Products, Inc. (GCP). The senior Sales Reporting Analyst at GCP, Diane Wilson, is responsible for building the sales reports that are distributed to its US-based sales organization.

Sales Organization for GCP

For Diane to respond effectively to her department's reporting requirements, she must have a clear understanding of the organization's business needs and drivers. Our reporting examples reflect the organizational structure of the sales division at GCP, which we have outlined in Figure 8–1.

8.1 MAPPING PHASE I: MANAGE THE SALES REPORTING ENVIRONMENT

As a producer of sales reports, Diane is responsible for the entire sales reporting cycle, from research to delivery. Using the MAPP method, Diane begins by gathering information that will help her manage the entire reporting process. By accessing and using information in R/3™ more efficiently, Diane is able to determine:

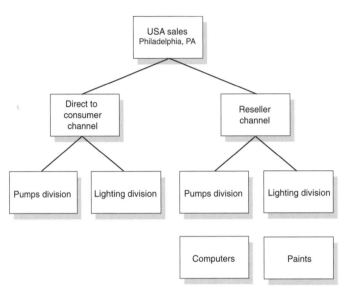

- The business problem that the reporting solution needs to solve
- The business process(es) on which the reporting solution will focus
- The existing reporting tools that the solution can leverage (for instance, analyses already in R/3™)
- The reporting tools that will have to be built or customized

Business Needs Analysis

MAPPing reporting solutions to the business needs and drivers in your organization is absolutely key to producing meaningful reports. While this connection might seem self-evident in many of the reporting solutions you develop for your organization, clearly identifying the problem that a report addresses will help you focus on the information that the target audience really needs. By clarifying the problem to be addressed, you will avoid producing reports with extraneous information. Instead, you will be able to get the right information to the right users at the right time.

Understanding the key business goals of your audience is crucial if you want to produce reports that matter. For example, if the stated goal of a sales organization is to shorten the order-to-cash cycle, you can create a report that compares, period by period, the length of time it takes to process the order, deliver it, invoice it, and receive payment. Your report could also provide breakdowns of sales period, customer, or sales organization.

Getting Started

First, you need to get the big picture of what your organization, its departments, and its people are trying to achieve. Too often the overwhelming details of building a reporting solution prevent us from seeing the larger goals of the organization. Before planning your reports, talk to the managers who will use them. They will be able to articulate their department's needs and goals, and you will better understand how your reports can help them achieve results.

Second, establish a dialog with key report users to discuss where their current problems lie in order to identify any "hot buttons." Understand, however, that many of these problems might not be visible to your users. Many users abhor change, and are quite happy with legacy report solutions because: "We've always done it *this* way." By initiating a conversation with your target audience early on you can determine whether these users understand the goals of their department as set forth by management, and at the same time, you can help the business user understand how your reporting solution will help them meet management's goals.

If senior management is the primary user of your reports, try to ascertain what information is crucial to their needs and what information is less vitally important.

If you are new to the organization or to the role of "report analyst," evaluating business needs is a great way to open up a genuine dialog with your user community so that you can better understand how to serve them and your business.

The Business Needs Analysis at GCP

Back at GCP, Diane began to recognize that users were dissatisfied with their current reporting solution. However, she was finding it difficult to pin down the main cause of their frustration and to prioritize their problems.

Diane knew that an overarching goal of the North American sales organization was to improve customer responsiveness. Management wanted sales and service efforts to be proactive at every customer interaction: in sales, delivery, and service. The goal of this "customer-focused" approach was to increase customer retention, the rate of which had been falling steadily for several years. The effort was dubbed the "Customer One" initiative. Diane knew that to achieve this goal, management would need timely information about customer orders and returns. Regional and district managers, for instance, would need to monitor their organization's responsiveness to customers at every customer engagement.

Diane decided to ask her report users whether they had the appropriate tools to help North American sales achieve this goal. She prepared a survey, which she sent to the regional VPs and district managers. The survey included the following questions:

- How do you plan to monitor your organization's compliance with Customer One?
- Are you satisfied with the customer reports you now receive?
- Do you receive the reports in a timely fashion?
- Do you have sufficient raw data to monitor compliance?
- What are some of the ratios/measurements you would like to see included in the reports?
- How are reports distributed to people in your organization?
- Does everyone in your department have access to the North American SAP™ system?
- Do you feel that you receive timely access to information?

After emailing the questionnaire to the appropriate members of the sales division, she followed up with each manager by telephone. She then analyzed and documented the results.

Diane also interviewed John Meyers, the VP of the Northeast Region. She knew John had a good handle on the reporting issue, and his buy-in would be essential for the project. John became the executive sponsor of the project, and he confirmed the conclusions she had derived from the survey:

- Many of the managers did not have sufficient reporting tools to adequately monitor Customer One.
- Very few of the sales managers and their direct reports had access to the SAP™ system. Instead, they would request the reports from the sales support center or from customer service.
- The sales managers had a good idea of the kind of information they needed, but were unsure of where and how to get it. Diane got some great tips on the type of values and ratios they were looking for.
- Many managers were not always sharing information with their direct reports because it had not been done in the past.
- Almost no one trusted the numbers they were seeing because they felt that they were never up-to-date.
- Some managers requested reports that already existed in the R/3™ system.
- The sales managers and national and global account reps complained that they did not know what happened after an order was placed.

As a regional VP, John felt frustrated that he was not able to measure his organization's compliance with Customer One. He wanted to tie the incentive compensation for account reps to the average. He also noticed that management was not evaluating the same information. The regional reports had different information than the district reports and so on. John felt that if Diane could find a system where the VPs, district managers, and account mangers were evaluating the same information, they could respond to customer problems effectively and efficiently.

Identify Business Processes

Diane quickly realized that she would need to supply critical information to a variety of users across several departments in the organization. Because these users needed to communicate with each other to achieve management's goals, Diane knew that she had to take a cross-functional approach to the reporting solutions she developed for the Customer One initiative. Since the source for much of the raw data that Diane used in her reports was from the North American SAP™ system, she began by consulting with the SAP™ implementation team at corporate headquarters. She learned that she would need to focus on the following business processes:

- Sales order processing
- Delivery processing
- Billing processing[1]

The bulk of North American Sales and Service employees had some degree of interaction with these business processes. By analyzing these business processes, Diane was able to develop an overview of the key activities and organizational entities involved in the Customer One initiative. Understanding these business processes helped Diane achieve a cross-departmental perspective on the problem of customer retention, showing her how customers interacted not only with the sales division, but also with the shipping services and accounts receivable departments.

Identifying Roles

Roles define the tasks and responsibilities that your users perform. Defining the roles that your reporting solutions support will help you focus on the needs of your audience. For example, the needs of a district manager are different from those of a shipping expediter or demand planner.

---

1. For a description of these processes, please see Chapter 4.

You may find it necessary to go through a few iterations before settling on the exact roles you need to support. When defining roles, you should always start from a general understanding of responsibilities and move to a more detailed understanding of the tasks involved. Do not equate roles with job titles at your company. One reporting role might include the duties of several employees within the organization. Conversely, one user may be responsible for many roles. When you define a role, you should consider the kinds of tasks that would typically be performed. It is also important to understand the interactions between roles. For example, the customer service managers and distribution managers may have similar reporting needs, even though they have different responsibilities and expertise.

Finally, remember that you may also have primary and secondary user groups in your audience. For example, a report you provide to a budgeting analyst may also be sent to certain cost center managers.

Roles at GCP

By analyzing the business processes and the business needs survey, Diane Wilson identified the following roles for the Customer One reporting solution at GCP's North American sales operations:

Regional VPs

The regional VPs are ultimately responsible for Customer One compliance. They need access to the latest summary figures for customers and for the sales districts in their region. Their focus is on retaining key customers in their region and acquiring new ones.

District Managers

The district managers need access to tactical information about their district's response to customer needs. Ultimately, they are responsible for customer satisfaction in their districts. The district managers require up-to-the-minute statistics for monitoring customers by year-to-date revenues.

Account Managers (Direct Resellers)

The account managers need information related to inquiries, orders, delivery, and billing for their specific accounts. They also need information about their customers' businesses in order to respond quickly to their needs.

Many account managers are independent resellers with no direct link to the company's computing system. Currently, their reports are mailed or faxed to them on a weekly basis. This information delay almost always led to faulty customer shipments or over-deliveries. Trying to resolve these matters often involved lengthy games of "phone tag" with the customer support center.

Customer Service Manager

The customer service manager needs access to all reporting and transactional information about customer orders, deliveries, and billing.

Distribution Manager

The distribution manager needs information relating to customer deliveries and the shipping points that serve them.

As-Is Analysis

The as-is analysis takes stock of the current reporting environment, the information sources, and the reporting solutions. The goal of this phase is to ask:

- What reports do we use today?
- What reports are available out of the box with SAP™?

Often, you may find that a report exists, but for one reason or another, the user groups are not aware that the report exists. This situation is not uncommon in many organizations, and may be due to the lack of communication between those responsible for creating the reports and those using them.

Another problem may be that the existing reports are missing some important information or are organized incorrectly. Sometimes it is much easier to fix what is broken instead of reinventing the wheel, and the as-is analysis will help you do this.

As-Is Analysis at GCP

Armed with a keener understanding of the problems her reporting solution has to solve, as well as a familiarity with the reports' users, Diane moved to the next activity: assessing the current reporting environment and determining ways to improve it.

Table 8–1 lists the reports that Diane felt would be useful to support the reporting requirements for the Customer One initiative in North American sales.

TIP You can identify the reports available in sales by selecting "General Report selection" from the "Information systems" menu in SAP™ R/3™. This will display the report tree. Select Sales and Distribution to display the sales report.

Table 8–1   As-Is Analysis

Report	Source	Business Process	Primary User
Sales orders by customer	SAP™	Sales order processing	Customer service manager
Sales order revenue by region	SAP™	Sales order processing	VP sales
Deliveries by shipping point	SAP™	Delivery processing	Distribution manager
District comparison	SAP™	Sales order processing	Regional VPs
Market share analysis	Corporate market database (Lotus notes)	N/A	Regional VPs, district managers
Customer revenue by sales employee	SAP™	Sales order processing	District manager
Returns by region	SAP™	Sales order processing	VP
Credit memos by district	SAP™	Billing processing	District manager
Credit memos by customer	SAP™	Billing processing	Account manager, customer service manager

Reporting Needs Analysis

The reporting needs analysis defines the delta between the reporting solutions today and where your reporting needs lie. The reporting needs analysis identifies the deficiencies in your current reporting solution. In this step, you simply map the report with the business needs it must fill.

We strongly advise that you validate the findings of your analysis with representatives from your user community. This will give you insightful feedback and help you define improvement areas. In addition, a sign-off from users and management on what reporting requirements need to be addressed will help you accurately determine the scope of the solution and provide you with goals that can be tangibly measured.

It is important to note that the reporting needs may change as you navigate through the mapping process. While building the solution or rolling it out to users, you might identify additional reports that would be of service to your user.

Reporting Needs Analysis at GCP

Diane Wilson recognized that one important need at GCP was to get more information into the hands of the account managers in the field. The customer service and the distribution managers had instant access to online information in their SAP™ system, but the account managers and representatives in the reseller distribution channel had virtually no direct access to the same information. They relied on printed reports, emails, and calls to the sales support staff, overloading sales personnel with unnecessary work. In short, GCP had the right reporting tools available, but they weren't getting the information to the right people.

Table 8–2 lists the most important information that Diane found the North American sales organization needed to support GCP's Customer One initiative.

Table 8–2   Solution Tool

Need	Solution
Timely information on customer revenue for account reps	Order value report (my customers)
Up-to-the-minute information for account managers on what customers are ordering	Incoming order report
Help sales support staff with reporting chores	Enable field sales force to access reports themselves, especially resellers
Make sure that the regional VPs and district managers are comparing "apples with apples"	Make current regional reports available to sales offices

At this point in the process, Diane has all the information she needs to determine the organization's reporting needs and goals. Before she can do that, however, she needs to take stock of what she has learned thus far.

The Scoping Document

Diane summarized all the information she gathered in the Manage phase into a Scoping Document. The Scoping Document describes:

- The exact problems the reporting solution needs to solve
- Who the reporting solution is for
- What the current reporting solution offers
- What the new reporting solutions need to achieve

From this exercise, she determined that the people in the organization with the most pressing reporting needs were the sales personnel and their account managers and account representatives. Each sales office needed instant information about orders for the companies.

One problem she encountered is that only the district managers had live access to the SAP™ reporting data. Only sales transaction users, in customer service or shipping, for instance, along with the regional and district management, had access to the SAP™ system. It was too costly to train the direct sales personnel in SAP™, and the re-sellers would be too difficult to support. For this reason, Diane would have to find a way to provide the field staff with the same live reports in Excel format or via a Web browser.

8.2   *MAPPing Phase II: Analyze the Sales Reporting Solution*

Good reports need good data. In phase two of MAPPing, we analyze the data required to build meaningful reports. By analyzing business information available within the SAP™ system or accessible elsewhere in other systems, you can produce a detailed description of the reporting solution(s) you need to provide. In this phase, we define the:

- Business objects used in the report
- Time (periods) to cover in the report
- Organization entities, or units, for which the report is valid
- Characteristics, key figures, and ratios that we use in the report

Business Objects

A business object can be a valuable source of information for organizing information in your report because it identifies the report's main data point. The business object gives a high-level, aggregate view of the data required in the report, an important advantage in building reporting solutions.

Time Periods

In Enterprise reporting, performance is usually measured in relation to a particular time period, whether by month, quarter, or fiscal year. Identifying an appropriate time period can answer important questions about performance, such as: "Are we performing better than last year/last month?"

It is important to identify the time periods for which the report is valid. While a typical report contains month-to-month comparisons, your users may need access to data that is more current, down to the week, day, or minute.

For the most part, SAP™ provides you with access to up-to-the-minute data. However, for performance reasons, your site may decide to update the records at less frequent intervals.

You also will need to determine how many previous years data you require. Many SAP™ installations store one prior year of data, with summary records for previous years. While this is sufficient for most business needs, you may need to reach back further into the past if, for example, you are asked to develop a trend analysis.

Organizational Units

You must identify the exact SAP™ organizational entities for the report. The organizational units are used to slice the information along departmental lines in your company. Management may use this to compare one region or district with another, for example.

In sales business processes, the following organizational entities are relevant:

- Sales organization
- Distribution channel
- Division
- Shipping point
- Delivering Plant
- Profit center

Characteristics

Characteristics tell us what needs to be analyzed in the report. A characteristic is used to summarize different types of information, such as "Material."

Business objects and organizational units are actually two examples of the characteristics you can use in your reports. In sales reporting, for example, the sales order and the sales organization are both examples of characteristics.

Key Figures and Ratios

Key figures and ratios are the statistical values used to forecast or measure performances, such as "total value of invoiced sales per district." They normally take the form of a quantity or value and are expressed in a currency or unit of measure or as a percentage.

The Sales Report Analysis at GCP

Diane Wilson, the Senior Reporting Analyst at General Consolidated Products, used the information from the Manage phase to determine the requirements for building the sales district report solution. After analyzing the available data, she summarized the information in the report as shown in Table 8–3.

Table 8–3   Data for Sales Office Report

Business Object	Organizational Unit	Ratio/Key Figure	Time
Sales order	Sales organization	Incoming order value	Quarterly
Material	Sales group	Invoiced sales value	Monthly
Customer	District	Returns value	Weekly
		Credit memo value	Daily
		Gross order value	Current YTD
		Net order value	Previous YTD
		Ratio gross order value to returns	

The next step was to make sure that the data was appropriately organized into an information structure in SAP™. The info structure assembles the raw data used in the report, and provides the report with the data summarized by characteristic (business object and organizational unit), ratio, and time.

Creating the Sales Info Structure

To create the sales info structure, do the following:

1. In the SAP™ command box, enter transaction MC21 (i.e., /omc21). The Create Info Structure Screen displays (Figure 8–2).

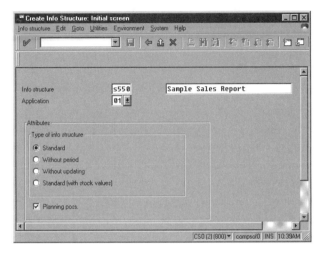

▶ **Figure 8–2** Create Info Structure

2. Enter the name of the info structure.

   The name is four characters long: the first character must be "S" and the remaining three characters can be any value between 501 and 999.

3. Enter a description for your report.

4. Enter the application number ("01" for Sales).

   If a similar info structure exists, enter the name of the info structure in the Copy from Info Structure field.

5. Press Enter to display the Enter Characteristics screen.

6. Press the Select Characteristics button. The characteristic selection screen appears.

7. Select the field catalog that contains the source data of the sales report.

   When you double click on a field catalog entry, a list of the fields contained within the catalog appears on the left as shown in Figure 8–3.

8. Press Copy and Close to enter the characteristics in the info structure.

9. Press the Select Key Figures button.

   A list of the available key figures appears. Select the key figures that you want to have summarized based on the characteristics in your report.

10. When you have finished, the info structure should appear as in Figure 8–4, with the characteristics on the left, and the key figures on the right.

11. Select Info Structure ──▷ Check to have the system check the validity of the info structure.

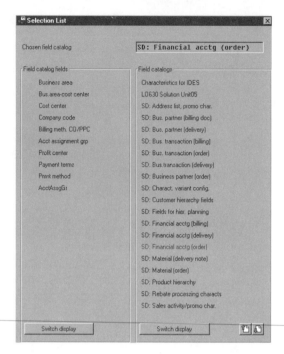

▶ **Figure 8–3**   Selection List Screen

12. Select Info Structure ⎯▷ Generate to save and activate the info structure in your system.
If the Correction and Transport system is active, you will need to enter the development class in your system (see your system/project administrator for the development class and correction number to enter).

13. When the info structure is active, review the log for any errors.

8.3   MAPPING PHASE III: PRESENTING THE RESULTS

In this phase, you will use the raw data and report definitions developed in the Analyze phase to create the report. In the Presentation phase, you are finally able to transform data into a valuable document for the end users who have been waiting for the information you've assembled. Not only do these users need timely and accurate data, they also need to be able to use that information efficiently. To help you present your reporting solutions advantageously, we have divided the Presentation phase into two processes: 1) creating templates in order to validate your report design with selected users and 2) creating appropriate formats for your final presentation.

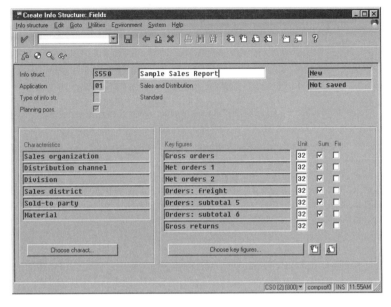

▶ **Figure 8–4**   Info Structure Fields

Creating the Report Template

Think of the report template as the prototype of your report. While the actual report may be created in a variety of media—an SAP™ report, an Excel spreadsheet, a web page in HTML, or a presentation in hard copy, we recommend that you design a template in electronic form, since you will constantly return to the template as you make changes and improvements to the report.

A good reporting tool for this purpose is Microsoft Excel. Because Excel is a familiar business format, you can use it to show your audience exactly what's in the report and how the information will be displayed. And with an electronic format, you can email the report to users for feedback.

Sample Report Template: GCP

Diane Wilson created the following report template in Excel to use as validation with end users. To document the fields used in the report, she used the Excel "insert comment" feature. This helped those users validating the report to locate the exact fields of the report and understand its characteristics and key figures. Figure 8–5 shows the report template for the Sales District reporting solution at GCP.

Month	Month	Sold-to party ID	Sold-to party Text	Material ID	Material Text	Incoming orders
06.1998..08.1998						
	071998	1171	Hitech AG	PC_SERVICE_A	PC Service Plus	43,560.00
Sold-to party ID	061998	1171	Hitech AG	PC_SERVICE_CONF	PC Service (Configurable)	-
1171..1172	071998	1171	Hitech AG	PC_SERVICE_CONF	PC Service (Configurable)	23,466.67
	081998	1171	Hitech AG	PC_SERVICE_CONF	PC Service (Configurable)	-
	061998	1171	Hitech AG	REPAIR_SERVICE	Desktop Repair Service(non configurable)	-
	071998	1171	Hitech AG	REPAIR_SERVICE	Desktop Repair Service(non configurable)	14,850.00
	061998	1171	Hitech AG	S-1000	Maintenance Computercenter complete	-
	071998	1172	CBD Computer Based Design	DPC1002	Harddisk 1080 MB / SCSI-2-Fast	79,920.00
	071998	1172	CBD Computer Based Design	DPC1009	Standard Keyboard - EURO Model	12,239.50
	071998	1172	CBD Computer Based Design	DPC1013	Professional keyboard - NATURAL Model	15,324.42
	071998	1172	CBD Computer Based Design	DPC1017	SIM-Module 4M x 36, 70 ns	6,589.80
	061998	1172	CBD Computer Based Design	PC_SERVICE_A	PC Service Plus	-
	071998	1172	CBD Computer Based Design	PC_SERVICE_A	PC Service Plus	16,335.00
	061998	1172	CBD Computer Based Design	PC_SERVICE_CONF	PC Service (Configurable)	-
	071998	1172	CBD Computer Based Design	PC_SERVICE_CONF	PC Service (Configurable)	35,100.00
	061998	1172	CBD Computer Based Design	REPAIR_SERVICE	Desktop Repair Service(non configurable)	-
	071998	1172	CBD Computer Based Design	REPAIR_SERVICE	Desktop Repair Service(non configurable)	37,125.00
	081998	1172	CBD Computer Based Design	REPAIR_SERVICE	Desktop Repair Service(non configurable)	-

▶ **Figure 8–5**   Sales District Report

The Dos and Don'ts of Report Design

- Make sure the report heading clearly states the purpose of the report, the time frame in which it was created, and the person who generated the report.
- Make sure that your report does not contain more than 9 characteristics or more than 9 key figures on any one page. Avoid unnecessary clutter.
- Don't crowd the report with unnecessary graphics.
- For online reports, use drilldowns when appropriate to reduce the amount of information.
- Use business graphics to help users interpret values, trends, etc.
- Avoid cryptic abbreviations.
- Make sure all online reports are easy to print.

Reporting Query

A query describes a view of the actual data a user will see. Typically, a query selects the:

- Organizational units
- Characteristics
- Time period

For example, consider the query "Present the sales report for all sales offices in the Northeast region." Figures from regions other than the Northeast would obviously be excluded from the report.

When designing the report, you should carefully consider the queries users will need to enter, and try to make the queries as easy as possible. Most users have difficulty formulating queries. Make sure that the query entry is as automatic as possible for ad hoc reports.

Formats

The format of the report identifies the actual output of the report. You may have an established format in your organization for printed and online reports.

When choosing a format, you should take into account the media you will use. In the example that follows, we show how to create a report in three online formats: SAP™, Excel, and HTML. Using the template approach, we can keep the core design of the report separate from its output format.

Creating the Sales Report in SAP™

At GCP, Diane has decided to create the Sales District Report in the SAP™ Info System. This report can be used by the Customer Service Manager, who has SAP™GUI access to the SAP™ system.

In SAP™, sales reports are created as so-called "Evaluations" for specific information structures.

1. Start transaction MC11 by entering /omc11 in the command line.
   The Create Evaluation screen appears.
2. Enter the application "01" (for sales) in the application field.
   You will need to enter the info structure created earlier in the Evaluation Structure field.
3. Enter a four-character code and description for the evaluation in the Evaluation fields, as in Figure 8–6.
4. Press Enter to display the Create Evaluation: Definition Screen (Figure 8–7).
5. Select the Characteristics button to choose which characteristics to include. These are proposed from the info structure.
6. Select the key figures required. These are proposed from the info structure.

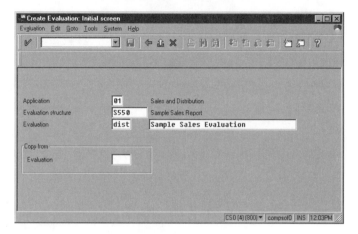

▶ **Figure 8–6**   Create Evaluation Screen

7. To create a formula, select Insert formula. Then, select the key figures for which you want to enter a mathematical expression.
   In Figure 8–8, we have created the key figure "Adjusted sales" by subtracting the value of customer returns from the gross order value.
8. Select Evaluation –> Generate to activate the evaluation.
9. Select Evaluation –> Execute to test the evaluation.
10. Enter the selection criteria, then press F8 to execute the report.

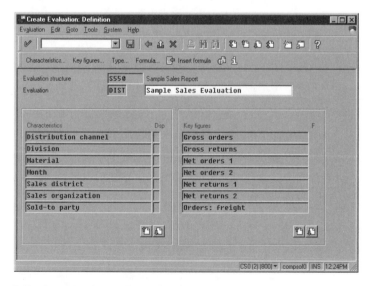

▶ **Figure 8–7**   Create Evaluation Definition Screen

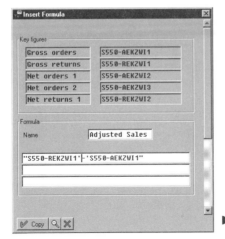

▶ **Figure 8–8**   Create Adjusted Sales Screen

Incoming Sales Report in Excel

We now examine a similar report, using Excel as the primary presentation application. In this example, we will create an incoming sales report for analysis purposes within Excel.

In an enterprise, not every manager requires the same level of information on incoming sales orders. For example, a monthly summary of incoming orders may be adequate for a senior executive but a line manager may need a different summary of the same data. In this example, we show you how an ActiveSheets report can meet the unique information needs of both users through its Excel interface to live R/3™ data.

Our sales order report examines incoming sales orders. This report will help you answer such questions as:

- What materials have been sold?
- To whom have the materials been sold?
- When was it sold?
- What is the net value of the incoming order?

In this example, we create a report that displays a list of all incoming sales orders by customer and material.

To build our sales order report, we will use the ActiveSheets interface in Excel to browse the Sales and Distribution folder, find the Sales Organization subject, and select the sales organization data source (Figure 8–9).

▶ **Figure 8–9**   Sales Organization

ActiveSheets now provides a list of possible columns for our report (Figure 8–10). We will transfer the available R/3™ data fields on the left to the listbox on the right. For our report, we want to analyze the incoming orders from customers within a certain time period. Our first column will contain the month. Our second will contain the customer ID and a short textual description of the customer. Our next column is the material ID and its description. Finally, we provide a listing of the net values of all incoming sales orders.

On the next page, ActiveSheets will limit the report to a selection criteria that we define (Figure 8–11). Since we are building a report based on a certain time range, we must specify that time. We'll also specify the customer.

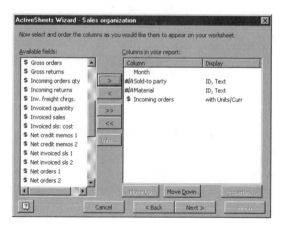

▶ **Figure 8–10**   Fields and Columns of the Sales Report

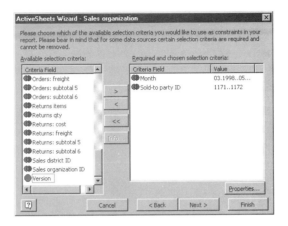

▶ **Figure 8–11** Selection Criteria

We've now come to the last page of the wizard. Here, we format the report using Excel's predefined style sheets. ActiveSheets now returns the results, places the report, and then formats it. In Figure 8–12, we now have a report that analyzes all incoming orders for the months of June through August, 1998.

Let us suppose that we've received this report as an email from our district manager, but we want to look at different months than the ones originally designated. ActiveSheets allows you to edit the live data in the report without leaving

Month	Sold-to party ID	Sold-to party Text	Material ID	Material Text	Incoming orders
071998	1171	Hitech AG	PC_SERVICE_A	PC Service Plus	43,560.00
061998	1171	Hitech AG	PC_SERVICE_CONF	PC Service (Configurable)	-
071998	1171	Hitech AG	PC_SERVICE_CONF	PC Service (Configurable)	23,466.67
081998	1171	Hitech AG	PC_SERVICE_CONF	PC Service (Configurable)	-
061998	1171	Hitech AG	REPAIR_SERVICE	Desktop Repair Service(non configurable)	-
071998	1171	Hitech AG	REPAIR_SERVICE	Desktop Repair Service(non configurable)	14,850.00
061998	1171	Hitech AG	S-1000	Maintenance Computercenter complete	-
071998	1172	CBD Computer Based Design	DPC1002	Harddisk 1080 MB / SCSI-2-Fast	79,920.00
071998	1172	CBD Computer Based Design	DPC1009	Standard Keyboard - EURO Model	12,239.50
071998	1172	CBD Computer Based Design	DPC1013	Professional keyboard - NATURAL Model	15,324.42
071998	1172	CBD Computer Based Design	DPC1017	SIM-Module 4M x 36, 70 ns	6,589.80
061998	1172	CBD Computer Based Design	PC_SERVICE_A	PC Service Plus	-
071998	1172	CBD Computer Based Design	PC_SERVICE_A	PC Service Plus	16,335.00
061998	1172	CBD Computer Based Design	PC_SERVICE_CONF	PC Service (Configurable)	-
071998	1172	CBD Computer Based Design	PC_SERVICE_CONF	PC Service (Configurable)	35,100.00
061998	1172	CBD Computer Based Design	REPAIR_SERVICE	Desktop Repair Service(non configurable)	-
071998	1172	CBD Computer Based Design	REPAIR_SERVICE	Desktop Repair Service(non configurable)	37,125.00
081998	1172	CBD Computer Based Design	REPAIR_SERVICE	Desktop Repair Service(non configurable)	-

▶ **Figure 8–12** Incoming Sales Report in Excel

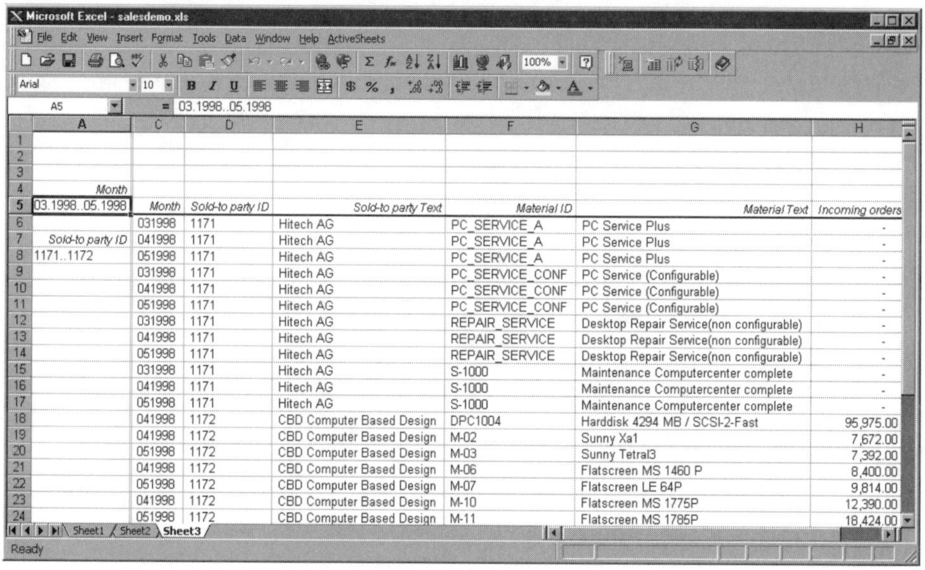

▶ **Figure 8–13**   Incoming Sales Report (March–May, 1998)

Excel. Simply change the date on the spreadsheet, and ActiveSheets returns the values (Figure 8–13).

Now suppose we only want to examine our own set of customers. We simply change the presentation of the information by revising the customer ID to the range we want. ActiveSheets then returns the desired range (Figure 8–14).

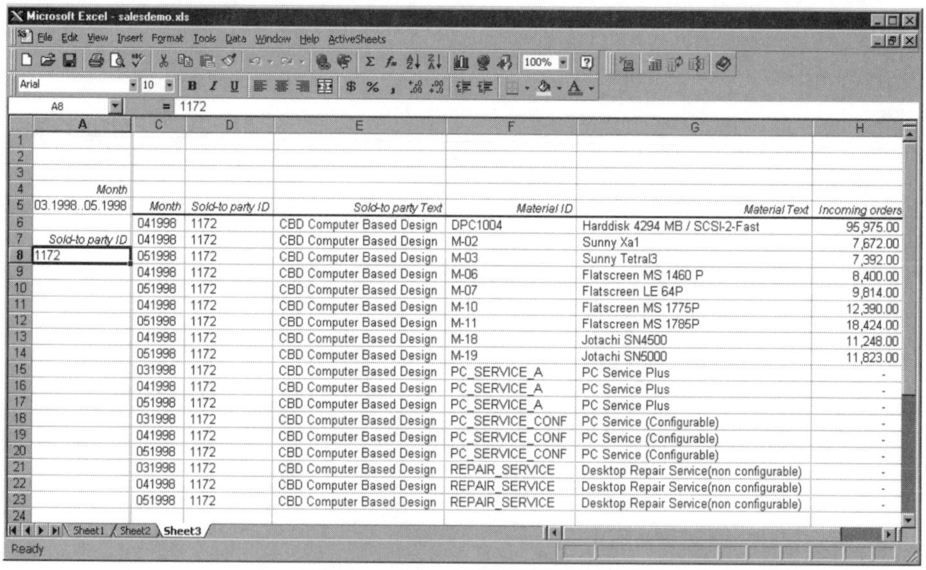

▶ **Figure 8–14**   Incoming Sales Report: Customer Drilldown

8.4   *MAPPing Phase IV: Publishing the Report*

In this phase, we focus on getting the report into the hands of the end users and making sure they know how to use it when it gets there. The goal of this phase is to put together a detailed description of the publishing plan for the report solution. In this section, we concentrate on facilitating knowledge transfer, designing a circulation plan, and increasing awareness of the report within the organization.

Facilitating Knowledge Transfer

One of the main reasons reports never become solutions is that too often a report is a company's best-kept secret. Companies may extend some efforts in the rollout phase, but after this phase the report is left to fend for itself in the organization. What follows then is all too typical: the report is either performed perfunctorily for years on end without change or it disappears with the changeover of personnel.

Knowledge transfer is achieved through efficient training and feedback. A good feedback system will make sure the report improves and remains applicable to the business problems it is meant to solve. A good training system will make sure the report is effectively employed by knowledgeable users. Both systems can be effectively planned in the rollout phase. That is, if the rollout plan incorporates effective training procedures, documents them, and creates a knowledge base that can be accessed throughout the life cycle of the report, then training data will always be readily available for the report—even if trainers are not. Moreover, if the rollout creates a good feedback system for the report, then it should be easy to maintain over time.

In the rollout phase, carefully plan out the training and feedback systems that will remain "attached" to the report long after its initial use. Encourage the producers of the report to write down the important aspects of the report. If this is not possible (and it is often difficult to get managers to write), have someone interview them and transcribe their thoughts. This is the beginning of a knowledge base that you can distribute with the report. Also, those documents that we have prepared in the first three phases will prove very effective in explaining the uses and intents of the report. Post these to a common area as well. If there is formal training that goes with the report by a training department, make sure that you have the electronic files as well as the hard copy documents themselves. That way you can post these to a knowledge base area, perhaps in a public folder in Exchange (see Chapter 7). The next step, then, is to plan out an advanced education and refresher education strategy for the report. This will ensure that the report not only stays relevant, but improves with time and use as well. Don't forget that there should be a strategy for training new hires.

The rollout plan should solicit feedback from all the key consumers and producers of the report to gauge performance against the predetermined success criteria. It should also create a general sense of satisfaction among the reporting community. Feedback should be solicited also from the business users, asking them to grade such areas as training, deployment, and support. When you get the results of this feedback, publish it. Put it in a public feedback area. The goal here is to create a history of feedback, and to get the members of the reporting community actively involved in suggesting further improvements. Getting this input is crucial for all successive stages of the report's development and use.

Knowledge Transfer at GCP

As we noted earlier, one of the key obstacles to Diane's reporting solution is that there was little money in the budget for training. Hence, knowledge of SAP™ systems among reps was very low. Moreover, the sales force was widely scattered all over North America, making onsite training difficult, time-consuming, and costly. For these reasons, Diane ruled out onsite training for all except those reps in the main office. For the others, she chose an online solution.

Diane's online solution was to arrange a series of training sessions using Microsoft Windows NetMeeting (Figure 8–15). She sent around a signup sheet and held training sessions at convenient times during the week. All the users had to do was dial in using the NetMeeting GUI, and the users were able to watch a video and then have a question and answer chat session with the online trainer. After the rollout, the video was made available for new employees, and new online training classes for the report were offered three times a year.

▶ **Figure 8–15**   NetMeeting Training

Designing a Circulation Plan

The circulation plan considers the best way to get both the report and information concerning the report to those who need it. This goal necessarily involves choosing the appropriate media for the report. This assessment must be realistically based on the capabilities of the organization. If paper is the best medium at the time of the report's delivery, then paper should the medium of choice.

TIP   Sometimes the best way to cut short the paper trail is to make the online file look as much like the paper file as possible. In this way, in time you can wean hard copy users off their paper dependency.

The circulation plan should also be concerned with delivering updates to the reporting community. This is important for changes in dates, content, process, etc. Moreover, constant communication is generally a good idea to maintain a dialogue with the reporting community. If appropriate, an email newsletter can be distributed at regular intervals.

It is also a good idea to make sure that pertinent information goes to the appropriate personnel. If you constantly send out data that is not relevant to many people, your efforts will begin to be ignored. Most important, routing plans need to consider if the report itself has to travel through different groups during its cycle of information delivery. Figure 8–16 illustrates a sales routing plan that begins with the financial analyst, who hands the report over to the district managers, and so forth.

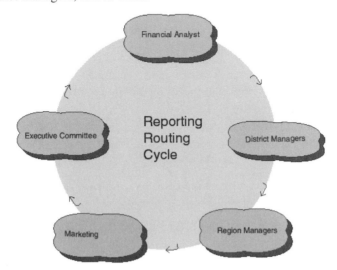

▶ **Figure 8–16**   Routing Plan

The Circulation Plan at GCP

Earlier, Diane defined a number of roles in the Scoping document she created at the end of the Managing phase. These roles will help her define the circulation plan, as well as the routing schedule. The main users of the report are: Regional VPs, District Managers, Account Managers, Customer Service Managers, and Distribution Managers.

To make sure the report follows this routing plan, Diane has chosen the Enterprise Information Portal (see Chapter 7) as the main publishing medium. Using this medium will allow her to set up the three main roles for the report and to circulate pertinent information to the five types of users.

Diane has set up a routing procedure in which Regional VPs deliver the report with the "blessed" numbers to the administrator who publishes it in the other managers' various public folders. The managers then return the report with their input back to the VPs. They are ultimately responsible for Customer One compliance, and this routing procedure will ensure that the Regional VPs have the latest summary figures for customers and for the sales districts in their region.

After the document travels through the various managers, it ultimately ends up in the public folders of the Regional VPs. After this process, the VPs transfer the report to the Marketing public folder. Figure 8–17 illustrates this arrangement.

Diane has also set up the folders to filter different kinds of information to the groups of report users. Table 8–4 represents what information will go to which group.

Table 8–4   Information Organization Plan

Report Group	Information
Regional VPs	Information on key customers in their region and data related to acquiring new customers.
District Managers	Tactical information about their district's response to customer needs.
Account Managers	Inquiries, orders, delivery, and billing for their specific accounts.
Customer Service Managers	All information about customer orders, deliveries, and billing.
Distribution Managers	Customer deliveries and the shipping points that serve them.

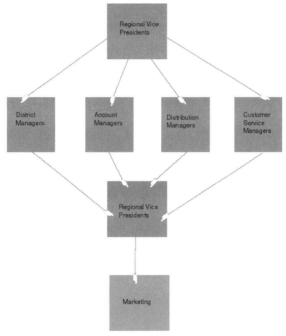

▶ **Figure 8–17**   Routing Plan at GCP

Building Awareness

The last step in the publishing phase is to make sure everyone knows about the report. The main objective is to extend the community of the report beyond the initial reporting team. The method of increasing awareness should be included in the circulation plan. In the publicity plan, the focus should be less on how the report gets publicized, and more on the content of the overall publicity plan.

The publicity plan should take a long-term approach to the report. In the initial rollout, publicity should target all new users, communicate the training plan and the schedule, and extol the virtues of the new report. After the rollout, periodic updates should be planned. For example, the plan should consider communicating the schedule for the training of new hires. A quarterly newsletter might be planned for publishing feedback or success stories.

The publicity documents themselves are up to the tastes of the publisher. As a rule, the reporting method works well for individual communications. Make sure that in every form of communication you answer the reporter's basic questions of Who? What? Where? and When? For example, for training, the publicity document should answer:

- Who will require training?
- What will be the subject of the training?
- Where will the training take place?
- When will training be available?

Increasing Awareness at GCP

For publicizing the report's issues and activities, Diane has decided to leverage GCP's internal marketing for the Customer One initiative. Part of this marketing plan has been to create a Customer One website, which Diane will use to update the company and users about all information pertaining to the report.

Keeping the needs of the different user groups in mind, Diane will also post web links to the various groups' public folders. These links will bring pertinent information and updates to the report users. In this way she can keep all involved abreast of new developments, as well as keep them informed about Customer One initiatives that may directly affect their areas of concern.

The Publishing Plan Document

Having isolated the basic needs and an overall plan of information delivery for the report, Diane puts together a publishing plan that will eventually be submitted for final approval. The publishing plan is outlined in Table 8–5.

Table 8–5   Publishing Document

Roles	Training	Rollout	Feedback	Routing	Updates
VPs	On-site 09/15	TBA	Updates	To: Managers From: Managers To: Marketing	Email
District	NetMeeting 09/15–22	09/23	Feedback Forum	From: VP To: VP	Links in public folders
Account	NetMeeting 09/15–22	10/01	Feedback Forum	From: VP To: VP	Links in public folders
Customer Service	On-site 09/18	TBA	Feedback Forum	From: VP To: VP	Links in public folders
Distribution	NetMeeting 09/15–22	TBA	Feedback Forum	From: VP To: VP	Links in public folders

Diane's publishing plan reflects the business needs of those who will be using the report and establishes an approved plan for delivery, training, and feedback. As we have been emphasizing throughout this chapter, to ensure that corporate information reaches those who need it most, a good reporting solution needs a good publishing strategy. By providing you with a MAPPing solution for sales reporting, we've demonstrated how you can more effectively distribute critical information and collaborate on key projects. Whether you choose a web-based R/3™ solution, a corporate portal, Excel, or even a bound paper report, the MAPP process can facilitate knowledge transfer between and among your sales constituency.

SECTION 3

Business-to-Business Procurement

This section describes elements in procurement in the R/3™ transaction system such as requirements planning, sourcing, invoicing, and so forth. It also provides the business background of external procurement with the high-level business rules governing procurement in R/3™.

We focus on the following areas:

- Procurement business drivers
- R/3™ procurement reports
- Procurement value chains and business processes
- Purchasing tasks and activities
- Purchasing business objects
- R/3™ procurement organizational units
- Procurement performance measures
- R/3™ purchasing information system
- Decision support tools
- Procurement characteristics, key figures, and ratios

9

Understanding R/3™ Procurement Information

MAPM   The management stage of the MAPP-ing method entails identifying what needs to be measured in the process of the successful deployment of a report. That includes providing the following types of management assessments:

- Business drivers
- "As Is" assessment
- Business processes
- Audience (company specific)[1]
- Priority (company specific)

In this chapter, we examine these business background and decision support requirements from a purchasing perspective. We take a look at the data that is available for procurement reporting in the R/3™ system and map out the key areas for managing activities. These areas include:

- Business drivers analysis
- Business needs assessment
- "As Is" assessment
- Value chain analysis
- Business process analysis
- Tasks and activities analysis

---

1. Both the audience and priority will be specific to your company's needs, usages, and requirements. Thus, they cannot be dealt with adequately here.

9.1   TYPICAL BUSINESS DRIVERS IN PROCUREMENT

A large portion of the managing phase has to do with assessing reporting needs. To identify those needs, we examine the common business drivers for procurement. Understanding the business drivers behind the report will ultimately help you define the necessary content of the report.

Table 9–1 categorizes the key business requirements that drive purchasing activities in the SAP™ R/3™ system. It also includes cross-references for these business drivers and some of the typical questions that a user of a procurement report might ask.

Table 9–1   Key Business Drivers for Purchasing

Key Business Driver	Determining Factors	Questions Addressed
Lower ordering costs	Every purchasing transaction a company executes has costs associated with it (this can be 300 USD per order line item). A single PO item can generate subactivities and thus costs in goods receipt, inventory, shipping, manufacturing, and accounts payable. One way to lower costs is to lower the number of orders for a particular material by evaluating the ratio of quantity ordered to number of orders for a material for a given time period.	What is the ratio between quantity ordered and number of orders? Do we have too many vendors for the same material? Which vendors do not have long-term agreements for total orders over a certain dollar value?
Improve buyer efficiency	Buyers are evaluated via the purchasing group. Buyers are judged by: • Ordering efficiency • How well inventory levels are managed • Number of completed orders handled (delivered, invoiced) • Fewest vendors for each class of material ordered • Number of long-term agreements • Number of RFQs • Optimum cycle time between requisitions and delivery • Lowest prices	What is the ratio between the quantity ordered and the number of orders per buyer? Which buyers have too many vendors for the same material? Which buyers have too few long-term contracts? Are buyers not getting enough bids? Which buyer has the best on-time performance for requisitioned material? Which buyers have the best price?

Table 9–1   Key Business Drivers for Purchasing (Continued)

Key Business Driver	Determining Factors	Questions Addressed
Evaluate vendor price development	Prices by: • Vendor • Material	How has pricing changed for a material? How have vendors for a particular material/class of materials changed their pricing over time? How does this compare to the market price?
Evaluate rebate arrangements	Rebates/bonuses agreements in place and rebates/bonuses paid	Do we have rebate agreements with vendors? Which vendors give us the best rebates based on business volume?
Improve vendor on-time delivery	Analyze vendor quality	Which vendors deliver on time? Which do not? Which vendors under/over deliver?
Improve relationships with key suppliers	Analyze ordering activities for vendors/suppliers by: • Material • Purchasing organization	Who are my top ten vendors by order volume/order value? What is the ordering trend for the top vendors?
Concentrate procurement activities on materials most often procured	Analyze ordering activities for material by: • Vendor/supplier • Purchasing organization • Plant	Which ordered materials represent the greatest portion of the total order value? What is the ordering trend for the materials?
Analyze orders for purchasing organizations	In given timeframe: • Total orders by vendor • Total orders by material • Total volume by vendor • Total paid to each vendor • Total ontime/late deliveries by vendor • Total ontime/late deliveries by purchasing organization	Which vendors have the most order volume? What is the ordering trend for each purchasing organization?

Table 9–1   Key Business Drivers for Purchasing (Continued)

Key Business Driver	Determining Factors	Questions Addressed
Approve supplier list	Only approved suppliers out of key sources above	Which parts or materials have an approved vendor? Which vendors are explicitly approved? Can materials be procured internally / externally?

The business drivers considered here are:

- Lower costs per order
- Buyer efficiency
- Vendor price development
- Rebate/bonus level settlement
- Vendor quality control
- Key sources of supply and vendors
- Vendor management
- Approved supplier list

Once you have a good idea of what the business drivers are for the company report, you should document these in a report or spreadsheet. The goal of this document should be to help you determine exactly what the report is supposed to accomplish.

9.2   ASSESSING R/3™ PURCHASING INFORMATION

Table 9–2 indicates the main purchasing information available in R/3™. This information will be useful in assessing what standard reports are currently available in the R/3™ system.

9.3   UNDERSTANDING EXTERNAL PROCUREMENT BUSINESS PROCESSES

We should now consider the business process scenarios that cover all the business areas that were identified in the business drivers document. Reviewing the

Table 9–2   R/3™ Standard Reports

Report Type	Description
Material purchasing values	Summary of values for purchasing material items. Provides data on the value of the purchase order including discounts, discharges, etc.; value of goods received in local currency; the invoiced amount as set by vendor; the purchase order price; and the average invoice price.
Material purchasing quantities	List of quantity data relating to purchasing materials. Includes data on the amount of ordered materials from purchase orders and scheduling agreements; the quantity of material at goods receipt; amount entered in invoice upon receipt of invoice; and the target delivery amount in base unit of measure.
Material delivery reliability	Number of material deliveries that fall within predefined range limits. Range limits are based upon actual and projected delivery dates.
Material delivery quantity	Number of purchase order or scheduling agreement items that fall within an assigned variance range. Variance is based on quantity ordered and quantity delivered.
Material Master	Master record of material item, including data on general information, material classification, sales organizations, imports, exports, MRP, forecasting, quality management, accounting, costing, and storage.
Vendor purchasing values	Summary of purchasing values by vendor. Provides data on the value of the purchase order including discounts, discharges, etc.; value of goods received in local currency; and the invoiced amount as set by vendor.
Vendor delivery reliability	Number of vendor deliveries that fall within predefined range limits. Range limits are based upon actual and projected delivery dates.
Vendor quantity reliability	Number of purchase order or scheduling agreement items that fall within an assigned variance range. Variance is based on quantity ordered and quantity delivered.
Vendor frequencies	Number of all items of the created request for quotation (RFQ), position of all acquired quotations, recorded purchase orders, created contracts, scheduling agreements, and deliveries.
Vendor evaluation scores	Provides scores for vendors based on quantity reliability criteria for a given period of time.
Ranking lists	Ranking of vendors according to purchasing organization. Measures quality of deliveries, price, and average variance.

Table 9–2   R/3™ Standard Reports (Continued)

Report Type	Description
Evaluation comparison	Evaluation of vendors based on material. Ranks pricing, quality, shopfloor complaints, delivery, service, etc.
Vendor master record	Vendor master data, including vendor number, purchasing organization, address, control, payment transactions, purchasing data, and partner functions

business processes will provide us with a better understanding of how the purchasing data can be derived from R/3™. The business process scenarios will also help us identify what areas will be measured in the report, how the report will be used, and where (that is, what organizations, people, etc. will be affected by the report).

To understand R/3™ procurement business processes, we take you through the main processes and then single out one, the procurement of stock material business process scenario, as an illustrative example.

Business-to-Business Procurement in SAP™ R/3™

The process of purchasing, delivering, and paying for materials or services from a third party is known as external procurement, the business process scenario we analyze here. Internal procurement, on the other hand, deals with the process of fulfilling the demand for a material or services from within the company—a manufacturing plant or distribution center, for example.

External procurement describes the operational tasks and responsibilities for:

- Determining the requirements for a material or service (that is, what the organization needs, in what quantity, and by what time) across the enterprise
- Assessing which suppliers are qualified to provide goods or service
- Monitoring and expediting deliveries from suppliers
- Acceptance of goods or services from suppliers on behalf of the company
- Monitoring the quality of goods or services
- Handling and approving invoices for payment

Procurement has the main organizational responsibility for maintaining relationships with suppliers. This includes contract negotiation, quality management, and periodic evaluation for vendors. While the exact organizational structure varies from industry to industry, the purchasing agent owns the contract negotiation process, including pricing and the terms and conditions set with a vendor for payment.

> **NOTE** The terms "vendor" and "supplier," while used interchangeably here, do have slight nuances in meaning. "Vendor" reflects the financial relationship between the parties in the accounts payable sense. Supplier reflects the demand fulfillment aspect of the relationship.

In R/3™, the responsibilities of procurement are within the scope of the Materials Management module. Materials management provides core functionality for the R/3™ Logistics system, including Purchasing, Inventory Management, and Invoice Verification (for accounts payable).

Procurement Value Chain

Figure 9–1 represents a procurement value chain in the R/3™ System. Each link in the chain represents the interaction of key R/3™ purchasing components from a high-level view.

Represented in Figure 9–1 is a general outline of how a typical procurement process flows. The value chain depicts the subsequent workflow of converting the proposed supply plan for purchased material into commercial arrangements with suppliers, monitoring the status of these purchases, and receiving the items into inventory. Workflow events are configured to each company's requirements by taking into consideration the degree to which automated or manual controls are required. These steps include:

- Approving the planned requirements and generating a requisition
- Associating the requirement with a preplanned "source of supply" (contract or delivery schedule)
- Creating Requests for Quotations and obtaining bids from suppliers
- Issuing a purchase order

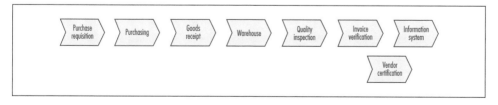

▶ **Figure 9–1** Value Chain: Procurement (Procurement of Stock Material)

- Sending the purchase order to a supplier
- Generating an EDI purchase order
- Receiving a shipping notification from the supplier
- Receiving the items into inventory
- Issuing items to production or to maintenance orders
- Receiving items from production

Procurement of Stock Material Business Process Scenario

R/3™ realizes procurement in the following business processes:

- Procurement of stock material
- Procurement of consumable material
- Procurement of services

The main difference between stock material and consumable material is how the material is used after it is received by the company (otherwise known as "goods receipt"). Stock material consists of finished goods, parts, assemblies, or raw materials that are carried in inventory. For example, raw material used in a production process is carried in inventory until it is released for production in the "goods issue" process.

Consumable material, on the other hand, is *not* carried in inventory but used (or consumed) by the ordering department directly after the goods receipt has occurred. Maintenance, repair, and operating (MRO) supplies are examples of types of materials that are often procured as consumable material.

This scenario does *not* cover procurement of external services. The reason for this is that the processes and their underlying data vary significantly. This is due to the fact that purchasing services as opposed to purchasing parts, assemblies, or raw materials is very different operationally.

The following areas detail the main activities in procurement of stock material.

Material Requirement Planning

The primary entry point for this scenario is the forecasting and material requirements planning (MRP) processes. The MRP uses a variety of deterministic or statistical methods to anticipate future demand for each stock item. The supply plan for these items is balanced with current demand and is consistent with the company's inventory investment and strategy. Hence, the materials planning incorporates "demand" information into the procurement activities. For example, information about current demand can consist of reservations for material required by a given functional area (e.g., when a production process requires a given quantity on a given day). The material reservations are collectively used to identify demand for a material at a given time.

Requisition Processing to Stock Material

When a new requirement for material is identified, the result is a purchase requisition. A purchase requisition is a formal request that instructs purchasing to produce a material (or service) in a given quantity by a certain date. An item can be requisitioned in two ways: with a source of supply or without.

- With: There are existing contracts or buying history with a supplier, or the material can be sourced internally (i.e., from an existing plant).
- Without: The purchasing department must find a supplier on the open market by using a bidding process.

If the purchase requisition has a source of supply, the next step is purchase order processing. If not, a few more activities are necessary to begin purchase order processing. First, vendor inquiry processing takes place. (A vendor is an external source of materials and services.) Under this task, the inquiry is sent to vendor and the quotation arrives. Once the quotation arrives, vendor quotation processing begins. After that, the next task, purchase order processing, begins.

Processing of RFQ Issued to Vendor

Companies receive quotations from different vendors by sending out a Request for Quotation (RFQ). A quotation contains a vendor's pricing and conditions for certain goods or services. A request for quotation can be created with reference to a purchase requisition or can be entered manually.

A RFQ is used to communicate requirements for a material or service to potential suppliers. In this process, requirements specified in authorized purchase requisitions for which no source of supply has been identified are copied into the RFQ. (The RFQ can also be entered manually.) The buyer specifies the deadline for the supplier's quote or bid. When the RFQ contains all items required, including desired quality and the delivery date, the buyer then enters the address information (either from the vendor master record or manually) for each potential supplier. An RFQ is created for each vendor, but the items within each RFQ are identical. The buyer can specify a code to monitor all RFQs belonging to a single bidding process. Finally, the RFQs are sent to the respective vendors. When the deadline for the submission of quotations passes (or when all vendor quotations have been received), the process "vendor quotation processing" is triggered.

Vendor Quotation Processing

Vendor quotation processing occurs after the vendors have responded to the previous request for quotation and sent their quotation back. Once their information has been entered into the system it is possible to compare bids. Price comparison is the most important step of vendor quotation processing.

This task leads to three possible events: 1) select quotation, 2) information record processing, and 3) subcontractor information record processing (see Figure 7–2b).

If the quotation isn't selected, a rejection notice is transferred. If the quotation is selected, three tasks may take place: 1) purchase order processing for stock material, 2) purchase order processing for subcontracting, and 3) purchaser order processing for consumable material.

Purchase Order Processing for Stock Material

Purchase order processing of stock material begins as a result of a number of different tasks in the areas of procurement (materials management) and production (production planning) logistics. It falls under the responsibility of warehouse management. In this case, we'll examine how the previous two tasks— vendor quotation processing and vendor RFQ processing—trigger this step.

In vendor quotation processing, a quotation and data about the order item are first selected and then transferred for vendor data processing.

In the case of vendor RFQ processing, three possible events can occur:

- Creation of a purchase requisition with a source of supply
- Creation of a purchase requisition with a vendor
- Creation of a purchase requisition without a source of supply
  (following this, a source of supply and a vendor must be determined)

All three lead to selection of data about the item, transfer of the order item, and processing of vendor data.

It is possible that a demand for the item exists but no source of supply is yet available. If this is the case, we determine a supply source and vendor and then select a category for the order item (for example, normal). Now, vendor data processing can begin.

Vendor data processing includes processing all vendor-related information and then checking or entering the material. Once completed, we determine stock material with a master record. Stock material is something that's always kept in stock (for example, a raw material) and has a material master record, allowing companies to manage and keep track of the amount of material they possess. Determining stock material leads to five possible actions:

- Enter order as detail data
- Maintain goods released control
- Process purchase order conditions
- Specify key acknowledgments
- Enter additional item data

All five are linked to the next task, enter supplier schedules. After this, we create the purchase order. A purchase order includes such data as terms of delivery and payment and detailed description of the item (What kind of material is it? How much has been ordered? When is it to be delivered? How much does it cost?). In this phase, the goal is to process purchase orders as quickly as possible, using reference information from previous tasks, such as purchase requisition processing.

Now, one of three things can happen: 1) monitor order, 2) transfer order, or 3) process information record. If the order is transferred, it triggers the next task: send a delivery letter.

Goods Receipt Processing

Goods receipt processing follows the sending of a letter to a vendor asking for the delivery of an ordered item. Goods receipt processing begins when the ordered material arrives or a material arrives with a shipping notification. At this point, two events occur: checking material slip and determining storage and removal.

By checking the material and shipping slip, we can see whether the shipment is correct or needs to be returned. Once we determine the purchase order and material storage arrangements, we adjust purchase order dates and select valuation type.

First, it's possible that the goods receipt can't be posted, and the process stops. However, other events can also take place:

- Material posted to warehouse stock—opens two possibilities:
  - Warehouse management moves material into storage—triggers next task, storage processing of goods receipt

- Warehouse management doesn't maintain warehouse (i.e., warehouse is independently managed)—material is simply placed in stock
• Material posted to quality inspection stock
• Material posted to blocked stock

In all three cases, two tasks follow: inform purchasing and print goods receipt-and-issue slip.

10

Analyzing R/3™ Procurement Information

MAP In the analysis phase of reporting, the most important activity is to identify all the relevant information available for the report. Here, you need to match up the business needs defined in the last stage of the game with what is available in the R/3™ system. This analysis will entail examination of the business information contained in the system, including knowledge of ratios used to measure performance, organizational dimensions used, and the source data. An analysis of the following areas will help us access this information in R/3™:

- Business objects
- Performance measures
- Decision support applications
- Information sources (characteristics, key figures, and ratios)

10.1 UNDERSTANDING PURCHASING BUSINESS OBJECTS

Business objects help us identify the characteristics that are important for reporting purposes and locate what characteristics are available in R/3™. A business object encapsulates the business logic of a certain data source, for example, a sales order. The data source contains various levels of information, such as the possible header types, available organizations, item data, objects types, and other information useful for reporting purposes.

The primary business objects for R/3™ Materials Management are represented in the following:

- Purchase order
- Vendor
- Material
- Purchase requisition
- Vendor–material info record
- Vendor invoice

Purchase Order Business Object

The purchase order is a key source of information for your procurement reporting. It records the basic information on all transactions with your vendors. By definition, the purchase order business object is a request or instruction from a purchasing organization to a vendor (external supplier) or a plant to deliver a certain quantity of material or to perform certain services at a certain point in time. The business object defines a request to a supplier (external vendor or internal plant) to deliver a material or service in a specific quantity at an agreed-upon price and date. A purchase order (PO) consists of a number of items, for each of which a procurement type is defined, as for subcontracting, consignment, stock transfer, or service.

Tables 10–1 and 10–2 list important fields in the purchase order. We divide these into characteristics, which represent the criteria you will use to select values, and key figures, which represent the values. Key figures are used to create performance measures, normally expressed as ratios, which are used to evaluate a business process or activity. For your convenience, we have listed the important purchase order characteristics and key figures, along with a brief description, in the tables that follow. We have included the technical names of the fields, since they are often useful when communicating requirements to your SAP™ Technical Staff.

Vendor Business Object

The vendor is a business partner that supplies your company with goods and services. In R/3™, vendors can be *internal* or *external*. This means that an organization within your company can also be your supplier. (Note: the terms "vendor" and "supplier" are used interchangeably in R/3™).

The vendor information is maintained by both the purchasing and accounts payable departments. Purchasing is responsible for the vendor pricing and business communication information. Accounts payable is responsible for recording the financial transactions with the vendor and therefore needs to maintain such information as the bank account information for direct wire transfers.

Table 10–1   Purchase Order Business Objects

Characteristic	SAP™ Technical Name	Description
Purchasing document number	EKKO-EBELN	Number that uniquely identifies a purchasing document, such as a quotation, purchase order, or contract. You must have this field in your report if you require information specific to a purchase order or contract.
Purchasing document type	EKKO-BSART	Code that defines the characteristics of a purchasing document, for example, what type of order or contract it is. Purchasing documents can have many different properties, depending on how they are used in your company's implementation of SAP™ R/3™.
Purchasing document item number	EKPO-EBELP	Number that identifies the item in the purchase order. You need this field in your report if you require information specific to a sales order or contract.
Material number	EKPO-MATNR	Number that identifies the product ordered.
Item description	EKPO-TXZ01	Text describing the order.
Document date	EKKO-AEDAT	Date on which any item in the purchasing document was changed or created.
Document currency	EKKO-WAERS	Indicates the currency of the document, expressed as the standard codes set forth by the International Standards Organization.
Purchasing organization	EKKO-EKORG	Topmost organizational unit responsible for managing the relationship between your company and its suppliers. In the purchase order or contract, this field indicates the purchasing organization responsible for the order.
Bid or quotation number	EKKO-ANGNR	Number of the bid or quotation submitted for the order.
Company code	EKPO-BUKRS	The code of the company responsible for paying the order. The company is derived from the purchasing organization, since a purchasing organization can manage the relationship with vendors that supply more than one company.
Plant	EKPO-WERKS	The code identifying the plant or site that will receive the ordered goods when they are delivered.

Table 10–1   Purchase Order Business Objects (Continued)

Characteristic	SAP™ Technical Name	Description
Storage location	EKPO-LGORT	The code identifying the physical location where the products will be stored after delivery.
Purchasing group	EKPO-EKGRP	The person or department responsible for a buy.
Requirements tracking number	EKPO-BEDNR	The code identifying a particular buy or sourcing activities. The requirements tracking number groups all sourcing activities, such as bid processing and ordering.
Material group	EKPO-MATKL	Indicates a product group or service with common characteristics—dairy products, for example.
Cost center	EKPO-KOSTL	The number of the cost center to charge the purchase to.
Profit center	EKPO-KO_PRCTR	The number of the profit center to charge the purchase to.
Fund	EKPO-GEBER	The number of the funds reservation to charge the order to.
Business area	EKPO-GSBER	The code of the business area to charge the order.

Table 10–2   Key Figures for Purchase Orders

Key Figure	Technical Name	Description
Order quantity	EKPO-MENGE	Quantity ordered.
Order price	EKPO-NETPR	Net order price as expressed in the order price unit (for example, per box or per piece) after quantity discounts have been applied.
Gross order value	EKPO-BRTWR	Value of the order before application of price discounts.
Net order value	EKPO-NETWR	Net value after price adjustments.

The vendor account number is required for most activities in purchasing. For example, all purchase orders require a vendor account number in R/3™. However, requisitioning activities do not include vendors.

The vendor business object holds the data you need for reporting on business partners in purchasing and accounts payable. The characteristics and key figures within the vendor business object are listed in Tables 10–3 and 10–4.

Table 10–3   Vendor Business Objects

Characteristic	SAP™ Technical Name	Description
Vendor number	LFA1-LIFNR	Number that uniquely identifies a supplier in the R/3™ system.
Vendor communication	(Multiple fields in R/3™ table LFA1)	The address field includes such information as the state, province, country, and postal code of the vendor, as well as the Internet address (Uniform Resource Locator or URL) of the vendor.
Purchasing organization	LFM1-EKORG	Vendor information may be maintained for more than one purchasing organization.
Purchasing group	LFM2-EKGRP	The purchasing group (person or department) responsible for the vendor.
Currency	LFM1-WAERS	The currency that the vendor requires payment in.
Language	LFA1-SPRAS	The language of the vendor. If configured in your system, your vendor can receive purchasing documents in its own language, even if it differs from the language your company uses in its business.
Industry key	LFA1-BRSCH	The code of the industry to which the vendor belongs (e.g., retail, service, etc.).
Tax jurisdiction	LFA1-TXJCD	The code indicating the tax jurisdiction (e.g., state and county). This information is used to calculate applicable tax.

Table 10–4   Key Figures for Vendor

Key Figure	SAP™ Technical Name	Description
Minimum order value	LFM2-MINBW	Minimum dollar value for purchase orders sent to the vendor.
Planned delivery time in days	LFM2-PLIFZ	Number of days the supplier requires for deliveries, on average. This value is one of the variables used to estimate the delivery time in purchasing and material requirements planning.
ABC indicator	LFM2-LFABC	Key used to rank vendors, by dollar value, for example. Use this field to report on vendors that are responsible for the largest portion of your annual purchasing budget.

Table 10–4   Key Figures for Vendor (Continued)

Key Figure	SAP™ Technical Name	Description
Effective order value	MCEKKZ-EFFWR	Effective value of the purchase order, including discounts and delivery charges.
Invoiced amount	MCEKKZ-REWRT	Total amount invoiced for the vendor.
Number of purchase orders	MCEKKZ-ABEST	Number of purchase orders created.
Number of deliveries	MCEKPO-ALIEF	Number of goods receipts from vendor.
Value of deliveries	MCEKET-WEWRT	Dollar value of the goods received.
Value of returned goods	MCEKKZ-EFFWR_R	Effective value of goods returned to supplier.
Number of late deliveries	MCEKKZ-TABW1	The number of late deliveries from the supplier.
Total delivery time	MCEKPO-LFZTA	Number of days between order date and delivery for a purchase order.

Purchasing Material Business Object

In R/3™, goods purchased externally are described in the material business object. A material here refers to the goods, parts, or articles that your company requires to carry out its business. The material business object contains data specific to purchasing and inventory management. The material business object identifies:

- The products that can be procured by your organization
- The plant or site that holds the material in inventory
- Inventory management information, such as the minimum level of material to hold in inventory at all times (safety stock) or the stock level at which an order should be placed for the material (reorder point)
- Shipping instructions, which are automatically sent to the vendor when the material is ordered
- The price used to valuate the quantity of material to hold in inventory
- Foreign trade data, such as export licenses or certifications

The material business object also determines how the material is accounted for on your company's books when it is delivered, consumed, or used in production.

Please note that purchased materials need not be defined in the R/3™ system; that is, they do not require a material master record. Users can enter a textual description of what to order when they place an order. However, if the material is carried in inventory, as opposed to being directly consumed by a cost center, for example, a material record with its material number is required.

Tables 10–5 and 10–6 list the important characteristics and key figures for the material business object.

Table 10–5   Purchasing Material Business Object

Characteristic	SAP™ Technical Name	Description
Material number	MCEKPO-MATNR	Number that uniquely identifies a material.
Plant	MCEKPO-WERKS	Key that identifies the site or manufacturing facility that will hold the material in inventory or accept delivery of the material.
Storage location	MCEKPO-LGORT	Code for the physical location to store the material
Material group	MCEKPO-MATKL	Code for the class or product line of the material.
Manufacturer part number	MCEKPO-MFRPN	The part number of the material assigned by the manufacturer.
Batch number	MCEKPO-CHARG_D	The batch number identifying the material in batch status management.

Table 10–6   Key Figures for Purchasing Material

Key Figure	SAP™ Technical Name	Description
Quantity of requirements	MCBKENN-MNG08	Quantity allocated to a cost center for consumption or to sales orders.
Total stock	MCBKENN-GSBEST	Total stock in inventory.
Total stock coverage	MCBKENN-RWGSBEST	The range of coverage for the stock as calculated by total stock divided by the average daily usage of the material.

Table 10–6   Key Figures for Purchasing Material (Continued)

Key Figure	SAP™ Technical Name	Description
Total stock turnover	MCBKENN-UHGESBEST	Measures the number of turns for the material and is calculated by dividing the total usage by the average usage.
Safety stock	MCBEST-EISBE	Quantity that should always be in stock.
Valuated stock value	MCBEST-WBWBEST	The total value of the stock held in inventory.
Book inventory value	MCISEG-IBUGVO	The value of the stock after physical inventory.
Restricted use stock	MCBEST-KUEIN	Stock that is on hand that is not available for production or consumption within the company.

Units of Measure for Material

When creating reports with quantities levels, you need to understand the units of measures available in the R/3™ system. The R/3™ system provides for a variety of units of measure:

Base unit of measure
Unit of measure in which the material is managed in inventory. This is the unit of measure which R/3™ actually converts any alternative units of measure.

Order unit of measure
Unit of measure in which a material is ordered. Often in purchasing, goods are ordered in different units of measure than that in which that are managed in inventory. For example, you may order a material by the box but manage it by the piece. The significance of this is that the R/3™ system will need to calculate the number of pieces in the box before posting orders for the material in inventory.

Purchase Requisition Business Object

The business object purchase identifies the material, goods, or services required by your company to produce products or operate its business. The purchase requisition is a key input business object to purchasing. It summarizes the key data for requirements for goods or services: the material or service (what), the delivery date (when), the person or department requiring the goods or service (for whom).

In R/3™, purchase requisitions can be entered manually or generated automatically by the MRP facilities of the system. That is, the system can create requisitions based on forecasted requirements.

Requisitions may also require approvals from management. The requisition cannot be fulfilled unless it has been approved by the appropriate persons to whom the system has submitted the requisition for approval.

Tables 10–7 and 10–8 list the characteristics and key figures for the business object purchase requisition.

Table 10–7 Purchase Requisition Business Object

Characteristic	SAP™ Technical Name	Description
Purchase requisition number	EBAN-BANFN	The number identifying a purchase requisition.
Purchasing group	EBAN-EKGRP	The code of the person or department responsible for sourcing the requisition.
Material	EBAN-MATNR	The number identifying the material to the R/3™ system.
Plant	EBAN-WERKS	The code identifying the plant that requisitioned the material.
Requisitioner	EBAN-AFNAM	The name of the person who ordered the material.
Requirements tracking number	EBAN-BEDNR	The code identifying a particular buy or sourcing activities. The requirements tracking number groups all sourcing activities, such as bid processing and ordering.
MRP controller	EBAN-DISPO	The key of the person or group responsible for planning orders of the material for production.
Desired vendor	EBAN-LIFNR	The vendor that the requisitioner prefers.
Number of reservation	EBAN-RSNUM	The number or the material reservation to which the requisition is assigned.

Purchasing Info Record

The purchasing info record contains vendor information specific to a material, such as the vendor's pricing for a material. The purchasing info record therefore holds a wealth of information for buyers sourcing a material.

Information from purchasing activities is automatically updated in the info record. For example, when you create a quote from a vendor, a purchasing info

Table 10–8 Key Figures for Purchase Requisition

Key Figure	SAP™ Technical Name	Description
Delivery date	EBAN-LFDAT	The date that the requisitioned materials are to be delivered or the service is to be provided.
Quantity	EBAN-MENGE	The quantity to order.
Release date	EBAN-FRGDT	The date that the requisition has been released for ordering.

record is created if it did not exist. The info record also contains the purchase order price from the last purchase order cut for the vendor.

The characteristics and key figures for the purchasing info record are identical to the purchase order. We only mention the info record here so that you understand its significance in R/3™ Procurement.

Vendor Invoice Business Object

The vendor invoice business object contains information regarding the amount to pay a supplier for goods or services rendered. It is used to verify that the invoice submitted by the vendor actually matches the quantity delivered and price set forth in the purchase order.

The vendor invoice entered in the R/3™ system is used as input to the Accounts Payable business process. When the invoice is recorded, the automatic payment facility in R/3™ will initiate payment to the vendor.

Tables 10–9 and 10–10 list the characteristics and key figures in the vendor invoice.

Table 10–9 Vendor Invoice Business Objects

Characteristic	SAP™ Technical Name	Description
Document date	RBKP-BLDAT	The date the invoice was entered in your system.
Posting date	RBKP-BUDAT	The date the invoice was entered and released for payment.
Fiscal year	RBKP-GJAHR	The fiscal year in which the invoice is posted for payment.

Table 10–9   Vendor Invoice Business Objects (Continued)

Characteristic	SAP™ Technical Name	Description
Vendor	MCEKKO-LIFNR	The account number of the supplier in financial accounting.
Purchase order number	MCEKKO-EBELN	The number of the purchase order referenced by the invoice.
Company code	MCEKKO-BUKRS	The legal entity responsible for paying the invoice.
Vendor billing document number	RBKP-BELNR	Records the financial transaction between the paying company and the invoicing party or vendor. The vendor billing document specifies the company code and the amount of the payable owed the invoicing party.
Goods receipt document number	MCMSEG-MBLNR	Identifies when the goods were actually received.

Table 10–10   Key Figures for Vendor Invoice

Key Figure	SAP™ Technical Name	Description
Gross order value	MCEKKO-MC_BRTWR	Value of the order before discounts have been applied.
Order value	MCEKKO-EFFWR	Value of the order including discounts and delivery costs.
Invoiced value	MCEKKO-REWRT	Amount specified by the vendors in the invoice.
Order quantity	MCEKKZ-MENGE	Order quantity from the purchase order.
Quantity invoiced	MCEKKZ-REMNG	Total quantity that the vendor has invoiced.
Goods receipt quantity	MCEKKZ-WEMGM	Total quantity received of the purchase order quantity.
Target quantity	MCEKPO-KTMNG	Total quantity that the vendor may deliver under a specific contract, blanket order, or scheduling agreement.

10.2   *UNDERSTANDING ORGANIZATIONAL STRUCTURES IN PROCUREMENT*

As a reporting analyst, you will need to understand how a typical purchasing organization is defined in R/3™ materials management. The reason for this is that your reports will necessarily have an organization dimension. For example, if your report is relevant to a particular region and distribution channel, you will need to understand the relationship between these organizational entities in R/3™ and how they have been configured in your R/3™ system.

Organizational Entities in Procurement

Organizational units describe the entity designated to perform a certain set of functions within a company. The purchasing business processes in R/3™ involve the following organizational units:

Company Code

Used in all financial transactions. The company code contains the chart of accounts and thus is the organizational unit referenced for all statutory reports, such as the balance sheet and profit and loss statements. In R/3™ purchasing, the purchasing organization is assigned to a company code.

Purchasing Organization

Organizational unit responsible for the buying process. The purchasing organization identifies and approves suppliers and negotiates terms with vendors.

Plant

Production facility or branch office. The plant is the destination area for ordered goods. A plant can also function as a source of supply.

Purchasing Group

A buyer or group of buyers that monitors and expedites the buying process. The purchasing group is the main contact with a vendor and is internally responsible for the procurement of a class of materials or services.

10.3 *UNDERSTANDING PROCUREMENT PERFORMANCE MEASURES*

Performance measures are the main source of content for the report and contain the most important information for analysis purposes. They provide the key figures and ratios that are used to measure performance. R/3™ has a number of information sources built into the system that provide you with standard ratios that measure performance in an R/3™ Procurement system.

Performance measures reflect the goals of a purchasing department. These goals are:

- To ensure the firm has the quantity and quality of goods required for efficient production
- To buy at prices as competitive as possible
- To get delivery as fast as possible to ensure stocks are available as required
- To build a good relationship with suppliers
- To ensure suppliers are prompt and reliable

There is always a trade-off in all purchasing transactions. The buyer will often be able to negotiate better prices if the quantity ordered is larger. However, there may be an opportunity loss when money is tied up as a result of the large quantity stocks. Therefore, there are various costs from stocks that must be considered.

For your convenience, we have included a list of some standard ratios used to measure performance in a purchasing environment. A list of commonly used sales performance measures follows.

Inventory Ratios

The key performance measures for inventory are:

Inventory to cost of sales
Comparison between the inventory value and cost of sales, expressed as a percentage

$$\text{Inventory to cost of sales} = 100 \times \frac{\text{Inventory value}}{\text{Cost of sales}}$$

Inventory turnover ratio
Ratio of cost of sales to average inventory, expressed as a percentage

$$\text{Inventory turnover ratio} = 100 \times \frac{\text{Cost of sales}}{\text{Average inventory}}$$

Average days of inventory
Indicator of effectiveness of inventory management

$$\text{Average days of inventories} = \text{\# of days in period} \times \frac{\text{Period end inventory balances}}{\text{Total cost of sales}}$$

Estimated inventory balance
Validated average age of inventory, given projected cost of sales

$$\text{Estimated inventory balance} = \text{Projected cost of sales} \times \frac{\text{Average age of inventory}}{\text{Days in period}}$$

Sales to inventory ratio
Measure of inventory to support the given level of sales

$$\text{Sales to inventory ratio} = \frac{\text{Sales}}{\text{Average inventory balance}}$$

Annual sales to inventory
Annualized sales to inventory

$$\text{Annual sales to inventory} = \frac{\text{Quarterly sales} \times 4}{\text{Average inventory balance}}$$

Inventory to working capital
Average inventory value to average working capital (net current assets)

$$\text{Inventory to working capital} = \frac{\text{Inventory}}{\text{Working capital (current assets} - \text{current liabilities)}}$$

Purchasing

Economic order quantity (also, economic lot size)
Order quantity that represents the best quantity to order from the cost perspective. The economic order quantity or EOQ balances the cost of holding inventory (inventory space, capital costs) with the cost of ordering.

$$\text{EOQ} = \sqrt{2 \times \frac{\text{Annual demand} \times \text{Order cost}}{\text{Carrying cost}}}$$

Stockouts
Component parts stocked out for the current year, expressed as a percentage

$$\text{Stockout} = 100 \times \frac{\text{Stockouts}}{\text{Total number of components}}$$

Market price vs. Vendor price
Ratio of the market or spot price for a commodity and the vendor price

$$\text{Market/Vendor price} = \frac{\text{Market price}}{\text{Vendor price}}$$

Range of coverage
Calculates the safety stock "dynamically." The safety stock is the amount that needs to be kept in inventory to satisfy possible requirements within a given time period.

$$\text{Safety stock} = \text{Average daily requirements} \times \text{Range of coverage}$$

Here, the range of coverage is the number of days in the future the requirement needs to be met.

Ontime deliveries
Percentage of deliveries (for a vendor or a material) in which the delivery is made on or before the delivery date specified in the purchase order or scheduling agreement.

$$\text{Ontime delivery} = 100 \times \frac{\text{Late deliveries}}{\text{Total deliveries}}$$

Buyer performance versus budget
Ratio of dollars spent versus budget for a specific purchasing group or product line

$$\text{Budget performance rating} = \frac{\text{Total invoice value}}{\text{Total order value} - \text{total returns}} \div \text{Budget}$$

Average value per purchase order
Measures how effective the purchasing organization or purchasing group is in managing the order process.

$$\text{Average value per purchase order} = \frac{\text{Total order value}}{\text{Total number of purchase order items}}$$

Accounts Payable

Purchases in payables
Amounts payable to an organization's total purchases for a given period

$$\text{Days purchases in payables} = \frac{\text{Accounts payable, ending balance}}{\text{Period purchases/days in period}}$$

Purchases and Disbursements

How much a company purchases versus how much it disburses in a given period

$$\text{Days purchases in disbursements} = \frac{\text{Cash disbursements}}{\text{Period purchases/days in period}}$$

Accounts payable turnover

Number of times accounts payable paid out in a period

$$\text{Accounts payable turnover} = \frac{\text{Period purchases}}{\text{Accounts payable/ending balance}}$$

Disbursement to accounts payable

Determines whether accounts payable were under or over paid in a given period.

$$\text{Disbursements to accounts payable} = \frac{\text{Disbursements}}{\text{Accounts payable}}$$

Days purchasing outstanding

Ability to meet trade payable commitments on schedule

$$\text{Days purchasing outstanding} = \frac{\text{Trades payable}}{\text{Period purchases/days in period}}$$

11

Understanding the R/3™ Purchasing Information System

MAPR ▶ **I**n this chapter, we examine some options that are available for presenting R/3™ data to end users. The first we examine is the Purchasing Information System, SAP™'s primary procurement reporting tool. Next, we take a look at a specific report that can be created using the PIS as the primary presentation application.

11.1 PURCHASING INFORMATION SYSTEM

The Purchasing Information System is a component of the Logistics Information System (described in Chapter 3), an R/3™ reporting tool that can be used to create reports as well as to present the data that is collected. The Purchasing Information System accesses business information based on the underlying infostructures, which describe the data purchasing applications can access. These infostructures are a kind of multi-dimensional data cube that contain the data that has been collected from R/3™ purchasing transactions. For example, the infostructure S012 contains data from purchase order activities, such as the total value ordered by a purchasing group or purchase organization.

The data is collected as characteristics, key figures, and time period. As we noted earlier, characteristics are the objects you report on, such as customer or material. Key figures are the statistical values used to forecast or measure performance, such as "invoiced sales." Key figures are usually expressed as a value

193

or quantity. The last part of the data cube is an aggregate of the data by time period, for example, by daily, weekly, monthly, or fiscal periods.

11.2   STANDARD ANALYSES IN THE R/3™ PURCHASING INFORMATION SYSTEM

The Purchasing Information System contains standard reports that can be accessed with the standard analyses shipped with R/3™. Standard reports are available for such key procurement areas as:

- Vendor
- Material
- Purchasing group
- Purchasing documents, including
    - Vendor quotations
    - Contracts
    - Scheduling agreements
    - Purchase orders

The following is a list of the types of analyses provided in the R/3™ Purchasing Information System. You can use this list to identify the reporting analyses that you may require for your organization.

Each decision support tool provides:

- ABC analysis (Pareto)
- Top N listing (list of values based on a key figure)
- Trend analysis
- Exception analysis (based on trend or threshold)
- Ability to dynamically switch currencies
- Time-series breakdown (from year to month to week to day)
- Planned vs. Actual (where appropriate)
- Display access to master data records, in the case of customer and product, respectively

Material

For each purchasing organization, material, and plant within a given period, the Material report provides information regarding the value and quantity of articles purchased, on-time deliveries, and the frequency of orders.

Vendor

The vendor analysis provides information on total dollar value of purchase orders with a vendor, the vendor's on-time delivery history, and current and projected value of any rebate arrangements with the vendor.

Purchasing Group

The purchasing group analysis provides you with the order activities for one or more purchasing groups within a purchasing organization. The order activity is also broken down by vendor.

Purchasing Documents

The Purchasing Information System provides analysis for the purchasing document type (PO, contract, vendor quotation, etc.).

Order Value Analysis

The order value analysis provides you with an ABC analysis, a comparison period analysis, and a value frequency analysis on your purchasing data. It lets you define the sort sequence of the characteristics (purchasing organization, group vendor, plan, and material), as well as the output sequence of the key figures in the report.

11.3   *CHARACTERISTICS, KEY FIGURES, AND RATIOS*

Each of the data elements displayed in a decision-support tool can be a characteristic or key figure. Characteristics are the objects you report on, such as customer or material.

Key figures are the statistical values used to forecast or measure performance, such as "invoiced sales." Key figures are usually expressed as a value or quantity.

Ratios combine a characteristic and associated key figure that can be used as a performance measure, as described previously, for example.

Table 11–1 is a list of the characteristics and key figures required for each of the decision-support tools described previously.

Table 11–1   Decision Support Information

Decision Support Tool	Characteristic	Key Figure
Purchasing Information	Material Material group Plant Purchasing organization Vendor	Invoice price Invoiced amount Order quantity Order value Quantity of goods received P.O. price Target delivery quantity
Outline agreements	Purchasing organization Purchasing group Vendor	Contracts Deliveries Quotation items RFQ items Schedule agreements
Subsequent settlement	Granter of condition Material group Plant Procurement vendor Purchase organization Purchasing group	Agreement Arrangement end date Condition record income Income (final settlement) Provision of income Volume Total income
Vendor	Material Material group Plant Purchasing organization	Invoice price Invoice amount Invoice quantity Mean delivery time Order quantity Order value Schedule agreement items Target delivery quantity Value of goods received Deliveries
RFQ	Material Material group Plant Purchasing organization Vendor	Analysis currency Contract items Deliveries Invoice price Invoice amount Invoice quantity Mean delivery time Order quantity Order value Schedule agreement items Target delivery quantity

11.4   *EXAMPLE PURCHASING INFORMATION SYSTEM REPORT: THE ORDER VALUE ANALYSIS*

The following example describes how to perform an order value analysis using Purchasing Information System.

The order value analysis provides the following reports:

- Totals analysis
- ABC analysis
- Analysis using comparison periods
- Frequency analysis

Totals Analysis

Totals analysis affords you an overview of the value and number of POs.

You will obtain a list of all materials ordered for a plant, the net order value, and the average value per PO. Below this, the following data is displayed for each plant and purchasing organization:

- the total net order value
- the total average value per PO

ABC Analysis

The ABC analysis is used for classifying vendors or materials by order value. The ABC indicator has the following characteristics:

A   percentage with a high order value.
B   percentage with an average order value.
C   percentage with a low order value.

The ABC analysis allows you, for example, to determine the relative importance of the individual vendors in your vendor base. It provides you with an overview of any changes that may occur in your relationships with vendors.

Analysis Using Comparison Periods

This analysis allows you to easily detect changes in purchasing activities. For example, you can determine how much was ordered from which vendor by which purchasing organization or purchasing group, and by how much the total order value of one period differs from that of a comparison period.

In this analysis, you can display all the data that you have previously displayed in the totals analysis.

Frequency Analysis

Use this analysis to determine which net order values most frequently occur for which purchasing organizations.

The frequency analysis can be used as a basis for negotiations with vendors. For example, you may find that you have issued many individual purchase orders with a value larger than $2000 to vendor X, and an individual percentage quantity discount would be more favorable than the existing period-end rebate based on total business volume over a period.

You can choose one of the four options, combine several of the analyses, or use all the options in one analysis.

Running an Analysis of Order Values

You invoke all four of the above analyses as follows:

1. Choose *Purchase documents* —▷ *Reporting* —▷ *Order value analysis* from the Purchasing Information System main menu
2. On the document selection screen, specify the scope of data for the analyses. For example, enter the currency for the analysis, and the purchasing organization and other criteria as shown in Figure 11–1.

> **TIP** For best performance, you should make the selections as narrow in scope as possible. You should always leave the "interactive analysis" field checked. This field determines whether only the totals of the purchasing documents are selected for the analyses (that is, total value and total quantity key figures). The detail records are selected when requested by the user from the resulting report. This results in a much faster response time when you start the report.

3. On the order value analysis control screen, specify the parameters for the analysis you wish to run.

  The screen is subdivided into four parts as shown in Figure 11–2. The first is the totals analysis part. However, it also contains the fields for the sort and output sequence to which the other three analyses refer.

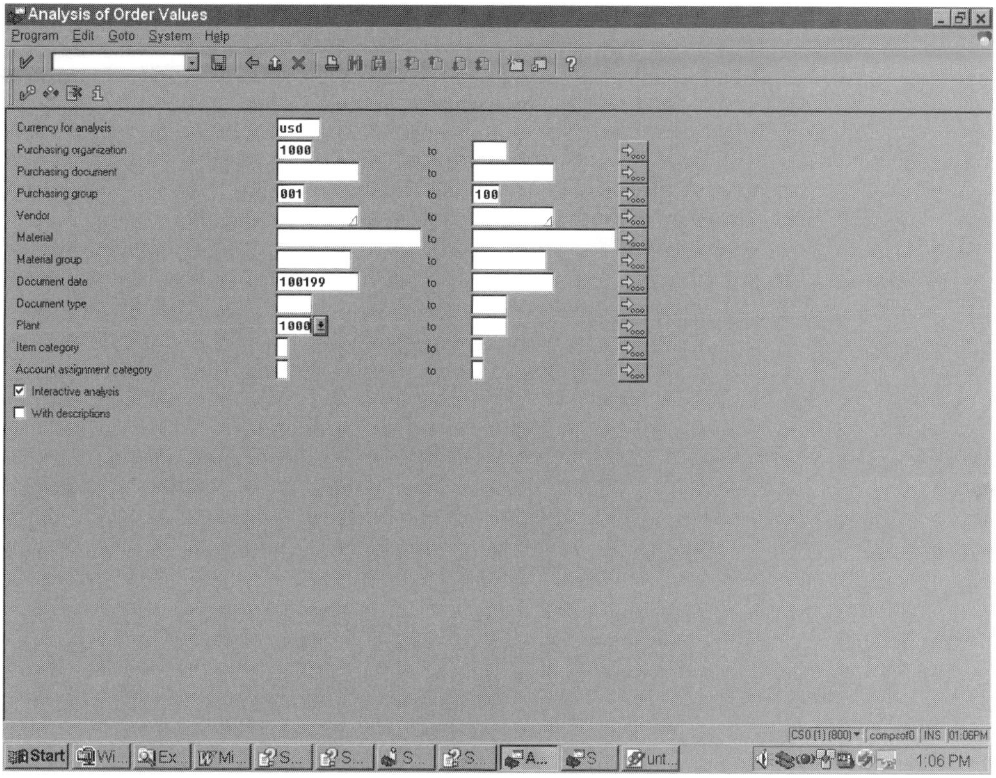

▶ **Figure 11–1** Analysis of Order Values

TIP	To run voluminous analyses in the background, you must create a variant. In this variant, you must delete the indicator *Interactive analysis*. All results of the analysis are then printed successively in a list.

In the left part of the screen you can specify the totaling (summary) levels:

- Purchasing organization
- Purchasing group
- Vendor
- Plant
- Material group
- Material

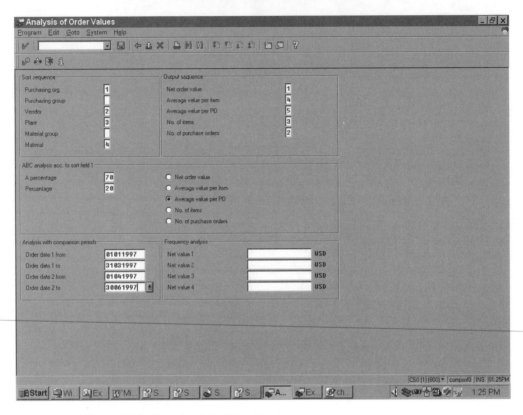

▶ **Figure 11–2**   Data for Order Values Analysis

In the part of the screen to the right, you specify which values (e.g., net order value) you wish to have, and the sequence in which they are to be displayed in the list.

4. Run the analysis. The base report displays as shown in Figure 11.3.

PO Value Analysis in Currency USD: Totals

List   Edit   Goto   System   Help

ABC analysis   Period comparison

Material		Net order value	No.POs	No.itm	Average val./item	Average value/PO
1400-750		395.906,64	7	7	56.558,09	56.558,09
AM2-320		2.248,40	1	1	2.248,40	2.248,40
Plant	1000	398.155,04	8	8	49.769,38	49.769,38
Vendor	200	398.155,04	8	8	49.769,38	49.769,38
		14.666,74	1	1	14.666,74	14.666,74
100-700		2.860,78	15	15	190,72	190,72
1300-241		121,89	1	1	121,89	121,89
1300-251		121,89	1	1	121,89	121,89
AM2-540		133,34	2	2	66,67	66,67
AM2-550		133,34	2	2	66,67	66,67
AM2-900		0,00	1	1	0,00	0,00
Plant	1000	18.037,98	23	23	784,26	784,26
301-110		2.190,00	1	1	2.190,00	2.190,00
Plant	1100	2.190,00	1	1	2.190,00	2.190,00
40-200C		797.297,92	14	14	56.949,85	56.949,85
40-200F		544.579,74	0	9	60.508,86	0,00
40-200R		270.540,35	0	9	30.060,04	0,00
40-200V		287.403,92	0	9	31.933,77	0,00
40-210		3.987.788,04	14	14	284.842,00	284.842,00
80-210		6.021.246,56	1	10	602.124,66	6.021.246,56
YY-210		10.945.414,12	0	9	1.216.157,12	0,00
Plant	1200	22.854.270,65	29	74	308.841,50	788.078,30
Vendor	300	22.874.498,63	53	98	233.413,25	431.594,31
		495.785,61	35	35	14.165,30	14.165,30
100-431		133,33	1	1	133,33	133,33
101-110		1.871,57	14	14	133,68	133,68
1300-340		8.066,71	3	4	2.016,68	2.688,90
1300-350		28.000,13	0	3	9.333,38	0,00
1300-370		2.000,01	1	2	1.000,01	2.000,01
1300-550		0,00	1	1	0,00	0,00
1300-780		1.666,67	0	1	1.666,67	0,00
60-100F		344,02	1	2	172,01	344,02

CSO [1] (800) ▾   compsof0   INS   01:30PM

Start   Wi   Ex   Mi...   S...   S...   S...   S...   P...   Ex...   ch...   1:30 PM

▶ **Figure 11–3**   Order Value Analysis Report

12

Procurement Information Delivery

Many business managers believe that the reporting process ends with the Presentation stage. Having put together a well organized, useful report, they conclude that their work on it is finished. This is a typical mistake, especially in companies that haven't yet established good reporting processes. As any IS staff can corroborate, the number one reporting request is for new reports that have already been implemented! Most reports, often some of the best that a company designs, are never used because no one knows about them.

In the MAPP process, Publishing is designed to improve awareness, knowledge, and circulation of a given report within the company. The main objective of the publishing strategy is to get a report into the hands of the end users who can make the best use of the report information.

This chapter draws upon our experience with procurement professionals in a wide range of industries, and provides information on creating a publishing system especially suited for procurement reports.

Areas covered in this chapter include:

- R/3™ procurement publishing with Microsoft® Exchange
- Procurement report circulation plan
- Rollout issues for procurement reports
- Strategies for training and feedback
- Permissions and authorizations
- Creating discussion forums
- Publicizing procurement reports

12.1   PUBLISHING WITH MICROSOFT EXCHANGE

Choosing an appropriate medium is the first step in creating a publishing strategy for a report. Throughout this chapter we recommend Microsoft Exchange as the primary medium for collaboration. Exchange is easy to use and is fully integrated with all Microsoft products. Just as important, it uses Internet technology as its model for corporate communication. Internet communication is especially important for procurement professionals, who are constantly on the road and often need to communicate via a remote connection. In addition, Exchange can be used to develop solutions without programming, a feature that allows custom solutions to be built quickly, easily, and outside of the IS department. Finally, applications developed with Microsoft Outlook (Microsoft's mail and organization system) have access to the administration, security, and Internet features of the Microsoft Exchange Server. For these reasons, we believe that Microsoft Exchange is a very good choice of medium for creating a procurement publishing system.

The basic model for our publishing strategy is illustrated in Figure 12–1. Here, we imagine an R/3™ report has been created in Excel with ActiveSheets. The report administrator places the report in a public folder in Exchange. The public folder is designed to include all the targeted consumers of the report. Any user who needs the report can access the file simply and easily as a mail attachment.

Exchange Public Folders

Microsoft Exchange public folders provide a useful platform for easy collaboration within a company. Public folders are storage areas held on Exchange servers where information can be organized and grouped according to company-specific criteria—by workgroups, for example. This information can then be shared among the target users. There are many forms that information can take, including:

- Email messages
- Graphics
- Sound bites
- Bulletin boards
- Web browsers
- Discussion forums
- Customer tracking
- Electronic help desks

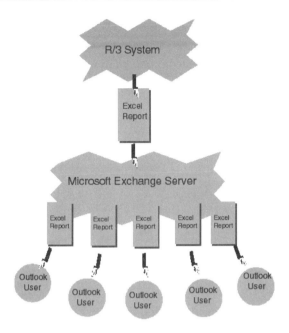

▶ **Figure 12–1** Exchange Publishing Scenario

Microsoft Exchange and Microsoft Outlook have rich capabilities for customization. Companies can use the Outlook forms designer or Outlook's standard templates to build their own collaborative solutions. Figure 12–2 shows a typical public folder setup in which email and bulletin board messages are posted for group information.

Once the application designers have set up the public folders, users can freely customize how the information is viewed, sorting and grouping specific characteristics of the public folder contents according to their particular needs.

Exchange Public Folders Purchasing Scenario

In the past, the purchasing department of a company has had to create, monitor, and distribute reports for their users. Both the users and the department find this to be an inefficient system. Using Exchange, the department switches to a "purchasing self-service" business process. In this system, users can monitor orders made against the purchase requisitions that they place from an Excel-based report in Exchange. This process removes the need for the purchasing department to monitor and produce reports for the users, and the people ulti-

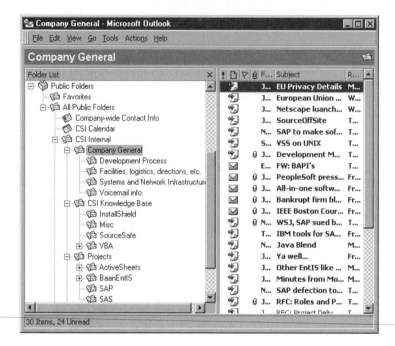

▶ **Figure 12–2**   Public Folders in Outlook

mately responsible for the purchase can monitor it themselves and even make their own reports.

12.2   KNOWLEDGE TRANSFER

After an appropriate medium such as Exchange has been decided upon, it is time to devise a strategy for how rollout, training, and feedback will be conducted for the report. The rollout plan should focus on creating and maintaining the rollout schedule, from initial training to the implementation of the report. To facilitate training, all materials should be located in a central area or folder where they can be easily accessed by the report's consumers. In addition, all training activities need to be publicized and coordinated with training personnel. Finally, there should be a feedback system created for the continuous improvement of the report's content and use.

Rollout

The rollout schedule should consist of three components: time, audience, and materials. Time establishes the logistics of the rollout schedule— that is, when and where the training will take place. Ramp up time until the report is fully utilized should also be taken into account.

When examining the audience for a rollout, it is best to consider what the "roles" are for the report. Understanding the roles entails listing all of the report's consumers and grouping them by user types. Many times during a rollout, the administrator doesn't know exactly who the users are, but they do have a profile that tells them what the user roles are. These roles are defined by asking such questions as: If a variety of users need the report, how will their differing needs be addressed? Will some users require updates? Will others need full training? Do users outside the company need the report? What will they require?

The final component, materials, describes all information that exists outside the report itself. Examples of materials include: documentation, announcements, training materials, video, email, and posters—all of which need to be implemented.

The following is a list of typical questions that the rollout plan should consider:

- What is the process for the rollout?
- What is the training schedule?
- Where will training be conducted?
- Who needs to be involved in the rollout?
- What materials need to be written?
- How will materials be transmitted?
- How will documentation be handled?
- Who is responsible for documentation/materials?

Assigning Tasks in Exchange

The administration of reports necessarily involves collaborating with a number of people, ranging from the original producers of the report, to application developers, to training personnel. The task feature of Outlook/Exchange allows administrators to itemize the tasks that need to be performed by various team members and to monitor their progress. This same feature can also be used to track the routing of the report, as illustrated in Figure 12–3.

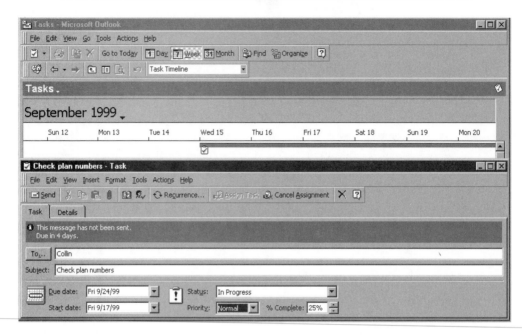

▶ **Figure 12–3**   Task in Exchange

Training

In the Publishing phase, all training activities among the various levels of consumers for the report should be coordinated and publicized. Typically, training
is a weak area in the reporting process, in part because it requires collaboration
between and among different parts of the organization. But training is the key to
the effective communication of the ideas in the report. When devising a training
plan for the report, the following types of questions should be addressed:

- What training materials must be created?
- Who will require training?
- Where will training take place?
- What training materials will be available and where?
- After the rollout, what is the plan for training new end users?
- How will changes to the report be transferred?

The training system should be integrated so that producers, training personnel, and consumers are all in sync. Again, effective communication is key among all the groups involved. Department heads, report producers, or even HR personnel will need to make report administrators aware of new users of the report.

Remote Training in Exchange

In order to facilitate training and collaboration among procurement personnel who might not be able to attend on-site events, the "discussion application" feature in the Outlook Forms Designer is a particularly useful option. With this application, an administrator can build features like on-line bulletin boards for remote users that can be used to post answers to frequently asked questions, or simply to maintain a database of information related to a specific report. This application can also be designed to respond directly to questions by specific users. In Figure 12–4, a specific report question is answered by a trainer and posted to the discussion forum. In this example, the history of responses to a particular request or issue is also available.

Feedback

All business processes, including the reporting process, need to adapt to continuous change. Feedback is one of the primary tools for improving the reporting process. A good feedback system is important not only for troubleshooting, but for making sure that the report stays useful and relevant. In all stages of the MAPP process, there is a feedback "loop," in which appropriate personnel are periodically consulted for approval. When Managing, for example, we submit a "scoping" document to get necessary input from managers and business sponsors of the report. In the Publishing stage, feedback from all consumers and producers of the report should be solicited. In order for all parties involved in the process of the report to voice their concerns, report managers need to consider carefully the medium through which feedback will be solicited and delivered. Other feedback issues to consider are:

- Should a formal feedback document be created?
- Is a feedback forum appropriate?
- Who will be responsible for logging and responding to feedback?
- What is the routing procedure for types of feedback?
- How will common feedback concerns be converted into change?

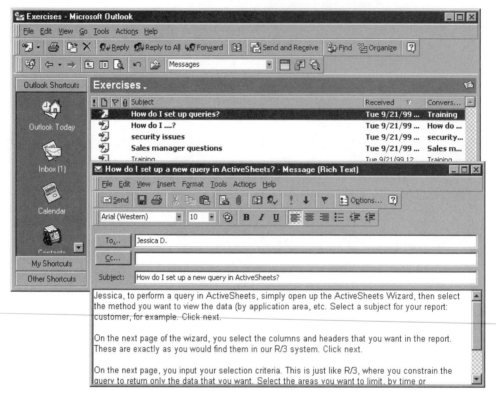

▶ **Figure 12–4**   Exchange Discussion Application

Finally, we also recommend that a formal post-implementation assessment be conducted among the business users. This assessment should actively solicit feedback from users on issues such as deployment, training, and support. Our goal is to achieve immediate improvements in the initial stages of the report deployment.

Feedback Forum in Exchange

As business-to-employee communication moves from the server to the Internet, Web-based forums for feedback will become increasingly important. Remote discussion forums are especially effective for procurement professionals. Using the Web access feature in Exchange, you can enable "threaded" discussion groups in Outlook or standard Web browsers (see Figure 12–5). Web-

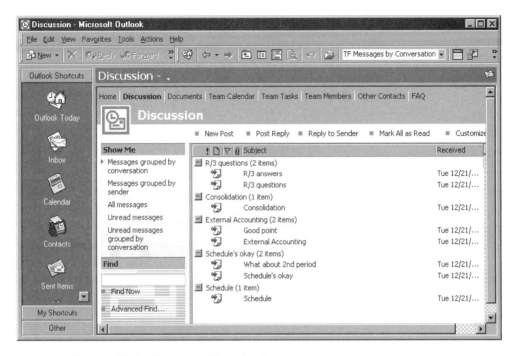

▶ **Figure 12–5**   Web-based Discussion Forum

based discussion groups allow both users and consumers alike to monitor and participate in a range of issues such as content, technology, and process. In addition, application developers can use the Web-based data objects (HTML library, Outlook Web Access) that are available in the Microsoft Exchange Server. These can be developed to allow access to email, calendar, directory, and public folder information over the Internet or Intranet.

12.3   CIRCULATION

Once a strategy for rollout and training has been devised, the next step to consider in the Publishing phase is information delivery. A good circulation plan takes into account such issues as:

- What permissions are necessary for which users?
- What media will be used to circulate the report?

- Is there a routing procedure?
- When and how often does the report get used?
- Who gets the report and when?

The first priority of a circulation plan is, of course, that the report gets to the target user groups. A secondary goal, however, is to make sure that there is an effective communication strategy for the report. Ongoing updates and pertinent information should be circulated to the many constituencies involved in the creation and delivery of the report. A system needs to be in place to channel this information to the appropriate members of the organization. Information may include:

- Updates to business sponsors of the report
- Summaries to users
- General updates to the organization
- Correspondence to IS management
- Communications among implementation team members
- Administrative updates and reports

Following are examples in Exchange for distributing and sorting information to various members of the reporting community.

Permissions and Authorizations in Exchange

In Exchange, access permissions can be set on specific folders so that specific users can author certain documents while others can have read-only privileges. In Microsoft Exchange 5.0, moderating public folders is also possible. This feature allows companies to establish a process for approving the content of public folders. By selecting the properties of a given folder, you can monitor and approve what gets published in public folders.

Tracking in Exchange

Exchange also offers tracking applications that allow companies to record, view, and respond to information that is constantly changing. If routing is a high priority in the process of the report's use, a tracking system can be devised so that all are aware of where the report currently resides, who has ownership, and what action has or needs to be taken.

Another option for tracking changes is to develop custom applications using the Microsoft Exchange Scripting Agent. The Agent can be used to design applications for workflow purposes as well as for routing and tracking reports.

12.4   *INCREASING AWARENESS*

After all the logistics of the delivery of the new report are in order, the last step in the Publishing phase is to devise a "marketing" plan to increase awareness about it. Increasing awareness is really nothing more than finding effective ways to publicize the activities surrounding the rollout, training, and continuous use of the report.

Certain facts of the report will need to be on hand to design an effective publicity campaign. A list of the users must be created, as well as a grouping by user types (for future users of the report). All matters relating to the reporting schedule must be clear. For example: When does the report need to be delivered? When is the rollout? When will training begin? Other useful facts to gather are:

- Who are the sponsors of the report?
- What purpose will the report serve?
- Where can people go to find out more?
- What are the important dates to remember?

After all the facts are collected, they will need to be documented and approved by the report producers and all others involved in the transmission of the report (IS, for example). Then, public relations documents will need to be written and distributed via appropriate channels. Media possibilities for distribution might include:

- Emails
- Web link
- Posters
- Presentations
- Meetings

Publicizing in Outlook

Highly effective tools for increasing awareness in a company are the public folders, bulletin boards, and other forum capabilities in Exchange. As illustrated in

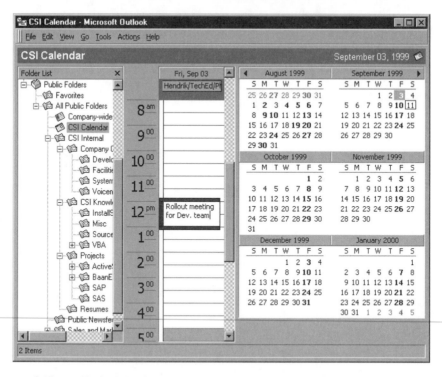

▶ **Figure 12–6**   Calendar in Outlook

Figure 12–6, the Outlook Calendar also has rich capabilities for scheduling and making announcements. The Calendar can be used for:

- Making group schedules available
- Posting significant events
- Listing training class schedules
- Sharing information
- Arranging online training events

Specific messages, appointments, or schedules can be copied to the user's personal calendar.

13

Business-to-Business Reporting for R/3™ Procurement

$\mathbf{T}$his chapter presents a sample scenario on how to implement reporting solutions for purchasing using standard desktop tools and the SAP™ R/3™ system. First, we describe typical procurement business processes that span the boundary between your organization and its suppliers. Then, we show how the MAPP methodology can be used to gather the requirements for reporting, define the reports, and define a strategy for distributing the information to people in both your company and your vendor's organization.

In this chapter we examine a reporting environment that is common to all supply chain management environments. In the sample scenario presented here, we show you how to create reporting solutions that span system, departmental, and organizational boundaries.

13.1   THE CASE OF *MRO.COM*

MRO.COM is an online purveyor of maintenance, repair, and operating supplies (MRO) for small- and medium-sized companies. MRO.COM's business model is simple: Their goal is to act as a go-between with MRO.COM suppliers and business purchasing departments. MRO.COM builds online purchasing "communities" for particular product lines, such as office furniture. By consolidating orders within an MRO.COM community, it can negotiate the best price with distributors. What's more, MRO.COM leaves the distribution up to the suppliers; that is, MRO.COM does not carry a physical inventory or maintain delivery facilities.

MRO.COM's success depends on its ability to establish a Web presence and to operate with buying efficiency. Their reporting solution must span business processes from the customer to the supplier. The system must process tens of thousands of customer orders per day. Manage-by-exception must be the rule. Expediting should be necessary only when the vendors have not delivered orders on time or when a source of supply must be found for a new product or item.

Business-to-Business Procurement at MRO.COM

Figure 13–1 provides a high-level overview of the buy-to-order process at MRO.COM.

As shown in Figure 13–1, the MRO.COM B2B scenario involves both procurement and sales. It represents an integrated, virtual business process that spans multiple systems and organizations. This process consists of four parts:

1. *Order processing:* Orders are placed on the Web and input into the SAP™ R/3™ system, which automatically generates requisitions. Buyers aggregate these requirements by product line.
2. *Sourcing:* Potential sources of supply for these orders are identified via the order history information from the R/3™ system as specified for a given

1. Order placed online

Order

Business-to-Business Procurement

Source

SAP™R/3™

4. Orders are filled directly from vendor to MRO.COM customer

2. Orders are consolidated and sourced

Deal

3. Buyers negotiate terms with suppliers

▶ **Figure 13–1** MRO.COM Business-to-Business Scenario

product line in the purchasing info records. If no vendors are found, a Web search for potential vendors is carried out. If an arrangement exists with a vendor for a specific product line, orders are placed automatically with the vendor.

3. *Negotiating:* Buyers negotiate terms and conditions with suppliers.

4. *Fulfillment:* The orders placed by MRO.COM are sent directly to the customer.

13.2 *MAPPing Phase I: Managing Information for the Procurement Environment*

As described in Chapter 2, the goals of Phase I are to identify the:
- Business problem the reporting solution needs to solve
- Business process(es) on which the reporting solution will focus
- Existing reporting tools that the solution can leverage (e.g., existing analyses in R/3™)
- Reporting tools that will need to be built or customized

The Situation at MRO.COM

B2B procurement at MRO.COM faces the challenge of how to effectively identify sourcing problems for specific product lines, given the number of transactions the system must process per day. MRO.COM management recognized early on that, to succeed, they would have to do more than just build a Web presence. Rather, they must efficiently manage the buyer-seller relationship because their mission is to match buyers with sellers of a product or commodity. Management knew that they would also need to be able to deal effectively with external suppliers. This meant that suppliers would need up-to-the-minute information about orders processed through MRO.COM.

MRO.COM assigned Joe Morgan as the Director of Customer Fulfillment. Although Joe's primary responsibility was managing MRO.COM purchasing agents and external vendors, the job title kept focus on the mission: identifying sources of supply for their customers and processing their orders in the shortest possible time. Joe's mandate was to manage an integrated intercompany business process—B2B Procurement—rather than a set of independent functional departments.

Business Needs Analysis for MRO.COM

Working with an outside consultant, Joe developed a plan for a management reporting solution that integrated the disparate islands of information at MRO.COM. Indeed, data had been stored in a variety of systems, including:

- An array of Internet information servers feeding data into a central Oracle database
- An SAP™ R/3™ system for operational data
- An on-line Web catalog system developed by MRO.COM
- A customer profiling data mart developed with the Data Warehousing Software from the SAS Institute, Inc.

A key business need for MRO.COM was to provide seamless access to each of the data sources in the system. Another important requirement was to provide a "business process view" of the data in the report. For example, customer inquiries would need to be able to track customer orders through procurement to the vendor and delivery. Being able to measure each step in the process was crucial for MRO.COM's ability to adjust its business model as well as increase customer satisfaction. The ability to forecast future requirements was also important because it affected future negotiations with vendors.

Identifying Business Processes

Using the Visio Business Modeler from Visio Corp, Joe Morgan described the core business processes used at MRO.COM for filling customer orders from its outside suppliers. After consulting with the SAP™ Project Team at MRO.COM, he identified the third-party order processing business process as the one that best described how their business was run.

In third-party order processing, sales orders fed into the R/3™ system from the MRO.COM Oracle database are flagged with a special item type called "third-party orders." In R/3™, purchase requisitions are automatically created, which initiates a series of activities in purchasing, including:

- Automatic source determination, a facility provided by R/3™ that automatically funnels requisitions to available sources of supply (vendors) described in R/3™
- RFQ processing, if bids are required for a product

- Aggregation of requirements for different products. Purchasing agents can view the requisitions generated for a particular product. This is a key R/3™ feature that is critical to MRO.COM's business, since it allows buyers to quickly consolidate the requirements for a product. The greater buying power, in turn, means better terms with suppliers and greater savings for customers.

- Automatic generation of purchase orders. If an agreement already exists with a preferred vendor, then orders are automatically generated for the suppliers. This activity requires little to no human intervention.

Identifying Roles

The next step for MRO.COM in building its reporting solution was to identify the reporting roles in the procurement activities. Here, Joe Morgan concentrated on the critical touchpoints between the organizations involved in the process. For third-party order processing, these roles are:

- **Requirements controller.** The requirements controller is responsible for monitoring all incoming customer requirements. The requirements controller prepares weekly forecasts for each major product line. The requirements controller needs access to the customer profiling database as well the operational R/3™ data.

- **Product line specialist.** Product line specialists provide information to customers online about products offered through MRO.COM. Their job is critical for helping customers "order the right stuff." The product line specialists need information from the online product catalog and the R/3™ operational data, particularly the material master data that identifies the available stock at vendors for a product line. Product lines at MRO are office furniture, computer equipment, cleaning supplies, paper products, business forms, software, and cleaning services.

- **Expeditor.** The expeditor monitors orders for key customers and expedites any problem deliveries.

- **Purchasing agent.** The purchasing agent negotiates contracts with suppliers. Purchasing agents are organized by product line; that is, each purchasing agent, defined as a purchasing group in the R/3™ system, does all the buys for a specific product line.

- **Vendor.** The vendor is a key player in MRO.COM's business. Vendors need to manage the delivery process and must have access to the operational SAP™ R/3™ data.
- **Customer.** MRO.COM is a complete self-service environment. Customers need to check the status of their orders, make changes, etc. They also need access to the R/3™ system.

As-Is Analysis

In the case of MRO.COM, the as-is reporting analysis consisted of:

- Ad-hoc reporting facilities provided by SAP™ and Oracle.
- Decision support interfaces created in a data mart provided with the SAS system. These included facilities for data mining on raw customer data in the customer database. The data mart integrated customer information from a variety of sources, and was provided as a service of Dun & Bradstreet.
- SAS tools were primarily used by the Requirements Controller to study customer demand. This approach, however, made the data mart isolated from other reports provided in SAP™.
- Excel reports. Virtually all of the existing reports used by managers, vendors, key customers, and buyers were created in Excel. The reason for this is that Excel represented the most understandable and easiest-to-learn interface of the alternatives. Since the people interpreting the reports were not in the same company, it made little sense to standardize on an ERP reporting tool.
- Some personnel required notification when an exception occurred. For expediters, notification came best over wireless phones, since they were usually on the vendors' premises when checking the fulfillment of orders.

Reporting Needs Analysis

From the business needs and the as-is analysis, it was clear that MRO.COM needed a reporting environment that could:

- Assimilate data from multiple sources
- Provide real-time access to operational data

- Use standard desktop reporting tools such as Microsoft Excel, and a Web browser such as Netscape® Navigator or Microsoft Internet Explorer
- Allow data to be published to wireless devices

Analyzing MRO.COM's Reporting Data Requirements

Joe Morgan took a long, hard look at the available data sources, and derived a series of reports that would be key to each of the roles that would need the information. These are described in the "scoping" document in Table 13–1.

Table 13–1   Scoping Document

Report	Data Source	Role Supported	Description
Incoming Orders	Oracle database	Product line specialists	Incoming orders by product line, broken down for customer. Reports are run in real-time against Legacy Oracle database application.
Customer Forecast	SAS Datamart	Requirements planner	Forecast customer demand based on trends identified by product line.
Open-to-Buy Report	SAP™ R/3™	Vendor	Allows vendor to identify what products need orders. Vendors are allowed to then create their own purchase orders based on the open-to-buy budget.
Buyer's Negotiation Sheet	SAP™ R/3™; Oracle Database; Web site	Purchasing agent	Compares the vendor's average price with the market price.
Deliveries in Pipeline	SAP™ R/3™	Vendor; Expeditor	Orders ready for shipment from vendor.
Vendor Hit List	SAP™ R/3™	Purchasing agent	Top vendors by order value.

13.3   MAPPING PHASE II: ANALYZE THE PURCHASING REPORTING SOLUTION

Good reports need good data. In phase two of MAPPing, we analyze the data required to build meaningful reports. By analyzing business information available within the SAP™ system or accessible elsewhere in other systems, you can produce a detailed description of the reporting solution(s) you need to provide. In this phase, we define the:

- Business objects used in the report
- Time (periods) to cover in the report
- Organization entities, or units, for which the report is valid
- Characteristics, key figures, and ratios that we use in the report

Business Objects

A business object can be a valuable source for organizing information in your report because it identifies the report's main data point. The business object gives a high-level, aggregate view of the data required in the report, an important advantage in building reporting solutions.

Time Periods

In enterprise reporting, performance is usually measured in relation to a particular time period, whether by month, quarter, or fiscal year. Identifying an appropriate time period can answer important questions about performance, such as: are we performing better than last year/last month?

It is important to identify the time periods for which the report is valid. While a typical report contains month-to-month comparisons, your users may need access to data that is more current, down to the week, day, or minute.

For the most part, SAP™ provides you with access to up-to-the-minute data. However, for performance reasons, your site may decide to update the records at less frequent intervals.

You also will need to determine how many previous years' data you require. Many SAP™ installations store one prior year of data, with summary records for previous years. While this is sufficient for most business needs, you may need to reach further back into the past if, for example, you are asked to develop a trend analysis.

Organizational Units

In R/3™ procurement business processes, the following organizational entities are important:

- **Purchasing organization.** Responsible for negotiation and contractual obligations with supplier. The form of procurement is defined by the assignment of purchasing organizations to company codes and plants. A purchasing organization is responsible for one or more plants, buys services or materials, and negotiates conditions of purchase with vendors.
- **Plant.** The site that produces or provides an order, goods, or service and that is responsible for goods after delivery. A plant can contain one or more storage locations, allowing stocks of materials to be organized according to predefined criteria (e.g., location and materials planning aspects). The plant is usually the organizational unit for material valuation. The preferred (default) shipping point depends on the shipping condition and the loading condition. A storage location is assigned to a plant for the placement of materials in storage (stock put-away).
- **Company code.** The legal entity responsible for payment for the goods or service. The company code is used to record all relevant transactions and generate all supporting documents for the legally required financial statements such as balance sheets and profit and loss statements. A company code can be assigned to one or more purchasing organizations.
- **Purchasing group.** The department, buyer, or group responsible for purchasing a class of materials. The purchasing group is internally responsible for the procurement of a material or a class of materials. The purchasing group acts as the main channel for a company's business interactions with its vendors.
- **Storage location.** The physical location, such as a storage area, where the received goods are stored. The storage location is an organizational unit that allows the differentiation of material stocks within a plant.

Organizational Units at MRO.COM

Figure 13–2 shows how two of MRO.COM's most lucrative product lines, office supplies and office furniture, are defined as purchasing organizations in the R/3™ system.

At MRO.COM, purchasing groups were assigned to a purchasing organization. A purchasing group consisted of a purchasing agent, material controller, and one or more expeditors. These teams were responsible for the execution of sourcing projects for their respective purchasing organization. This cross-functional approach ensured that all business processes were managed together and

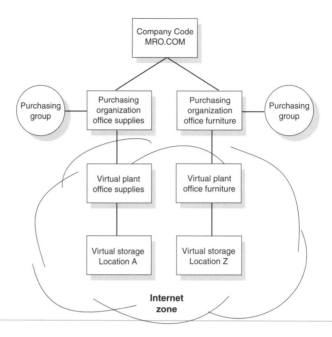

▶ **Figure 13–2**   Organizational Units at MRO.COM

in place to bring the product to the customers. The material controller identified the demand for the purchasing agent, and the purchasing agent and expeditor worked closely together to ensure that shipments from vendors arrived on time.

The company code MRO.COM of North America, Inc. is the legal entity responsible for the purchasing transactions carried out by MRO.COM.

Because MRO.COM carried no inventory on its premises, inventories were managed as "virtual" plants. The plant was used to collect demand from sales orders entered by customers on the MRO.COM Web site. The resulting requirements were then assigned automatically to the appropriate vendor. For office furniture, ten vendors were assigned orders based on a quota system. Based on the prior period on-time delivery and price performance and other incentives, vendors could expect to get a greater share of the total dollar value of orders processed through MRO.COM. The quota arrangement tools in R/3™ purchasing were used to determine which vendor received a higher or lower share in which period.

Storage locations were based on the vendor's distribution area for products. This allowed MRO.COM expeditors to quickly view the status of orders ready to ship to customers. When vendors were ready to ship product to MRO.COM customers, they could post a goods receipt in the R/3™ system, which would automatically show the "inventory" available to MRO.COM and the distribution area that had the inventory. Because MRO.COM did not actually own the inventory, the inventory was managed by quantity only, not by value.

Characteristics

Characteristics tell us what needs to be analyzed in the report. Characteristics are used to summarize different types of information, such as "Material."

Business objects and organizational units are actually two examples of the characteristics you can use in your reports. In purchasing, for example, the purchase order and the purchasing organization are both examples of characteristics.

Key Figures and Ratios

Key figures and ratios are the statistical values used to forecast or measure performances, such as "total value of ordered material by plant." They normally take the form of a quantity or value and are expressed in a currency or unit of measure or as a percentage.

The Procurement Report Analysis at MRO.COM

Joe Morgan, MRO.COM's Director of Customer Fulfillment, used the information from the Manage phase to determine the requirements for building the procurement report solution. After analyzing the available data, he summarized the information in the report in Table 13–2.

Table 13–2   Data for Procurement Report

Business Object	Organizational Unit	Ratio/Key Figure	Time
Purchase Order	Purchasing organization	Order value, invoice value, quantity delivered	Weekly
Purchase Requisition	Purchasing group; Plant	Order quantity	Daily
Material	Plant	Purchased material value	
Outline Agreement	Purchasing groups	Open-to-buy value/quantity	Monthly
Stock	Plant, storage location	Quantity	Daily
Vendor	Purchasing organization	Order value, invoice value, quantity delivered	

The next step was to make sure that the data was appropriately organized into an information structure in SAP™. The infostructure assembles the raw data used in the report, and provides the report with the data summarized by characteristic (business object and organizational unit), ratio, and time.

13.4 *MAPPING PHASE III: PRESENT THE REPORT SOLUTION*

|MAPP▶ In this phase you create the report, using the raw data and report definitions defined in the Analyze phase. This is the point where you actually create and validate the reports with your users.

Creating the Procurement Info Structure

The next piece in the procurement information system at MRO.COM is the R/3™ infostructure. As we have seen, the infostructure serves as a staging point for the transactional information in the R/3™ system. In this section, we will show you—step by step—how to create a procurement infostructure based on the information specified.

We will build the infostructure to meet the informational requirements of the characteristics and key figures listed in Table 13–2. This data will be the source of all reports we show in this chapter.

1. Run transaction MC21 or select the following path from the Implementation Guide (IMG):
   Logistics – General —▷ Logistics Information System —▷ Data Basis —▷ Information structures —▷ Maintain self-defined information structures
2. Enter the infostructure code and the application id for purchasing as shown in Figure 13–3.
3. Enter a description for your report.
4. Enter the application number ("01" for Sales).
   If a similar infostructure exists, enter the name of the infostructure in the Copy from Infostructure field.
5. Press Enter to display the Enter Characteristics screen.
6. Press the Select Characteristics button. The characteristic selection screen appears.

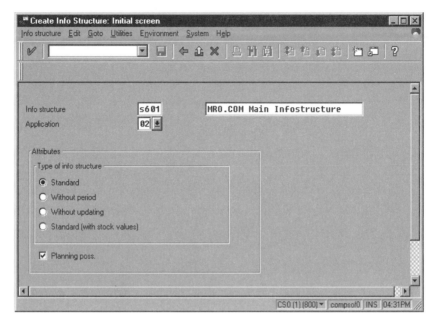

▶ **Figure 13–3** Info Structure with Application Code

7. Press Enter to enter the characteristics and key figures.

8. Select the "Choose characteristics" function.

9. Select the field catalog for "Material," "Vendor," and "Purchasing Organization" since these contain information about the primary business objects in your report.

   When you double click on a field catalog entry, a list of the fields contained within the catalog appears on the left as shown in Figure 13–4.

10. Press Copy and Close to enter the characteristics in the infostructure.

11. Press the Select Key Figures button.

   A list of the available key figures appears. Select the key figures from the quantities and values field catalogs for purchasing.

12. When you have finished, the infostructure should appear as in Figure 13–5, with the characteristics on the left, and the key figures on the right.

13. Select Infostructure —▷ Check to have the system check the validity of the info structure.

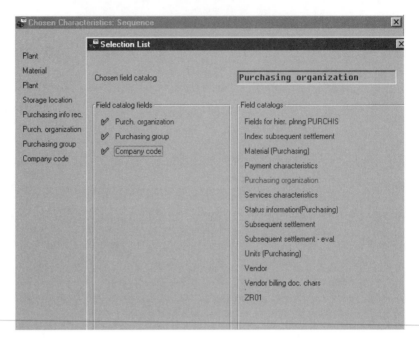

▶ **Figure 13–4**   Selection List Screen

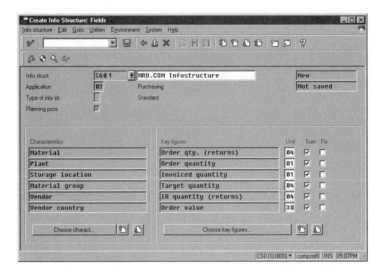

▶ **Figure 13–5**   Infostructure Fields

14. Select Infostructure —▷ Generate to save and activate the infostructure in your system.

    If the Correction and Transport system is active, you will need to enter the development class in your system (see your system/project administrator for the development class and correction number to enter).

15. When the infostructure is active, review the log for any errors.

In this phase, you will use the raw data and report definitions developed in the Analysis phase to create the report. In the Presentation phase, you are finally able to transform data into a valuable document for the end users that have been waiting for the information you've assembled. Not only do these users need timely and accurate data, they also need to be able to use that information efficiently. To help you present your reporting solutions advantageously, we have divided the Presentation phase into two processes:

1. Creating templates in order to validate your report design with selected users, and

2. Creating appropriate formats for your final presentation.

Creating the Report Template

Think of the report template as the prototype of your report. While the actual report may be created in a variety of media—such as an SAP™ report, an Excel spreadsheet, a Web page in HTML, or a presentation in hard copy—we recommend that you design a template in electronic form because you will constantly return to the template as you make changes and improvements to the report.

Sample Report Template: MRO.COM

In Chapter 8 we defined the report template using Microsoft Excel. At MRO.COM, we will show you how to define the template in the R/3™ system. MRO.COM uses the Flexible Reporting feature of the R/3™ Logistics Information System because it needs central output control over online and hard copy reports. In addition, it is most convenient for the requirements planners to work in the R/3™ system, since they require access to a broad range of information online.

Reporting in the Logistics Information system has two parts: Standard Analyses and Flexible Analyses. Standard reporting provides interactive drilldown functionality based on the infostructure and helps you better analyze the data as defined in the infostructure. Flexible reporting gives you more options for formatting the display of a report and allows you to access data in more than one infostructure.

Using the infostructure for MRO.COM completed in the previous section as the data source, here is how we create the standard analysis drilldown for the base MRO.COM.

1. Select transaction OMOL or choose the following from the Implementation Guide:

   Logistics Information System —▷ Reporting —▷ Standard Analyses —▷ Change Settings

2. Choose Purchasing as the application

3. Press Enter to display the drilldown characteristics for the standard analysis. The system proposes the characteristics from the infostructure. Select Choose Characteristics to limit the drilldown to vendor, purchasing organization, and month (fewer drilldown characteristics will enhance performance).

4. Select Goto —▷ Key figures to determine how the key figures in the report should be displayed. For each key figure you can determine whether the display should be in tens, thousands, etc., or the number of decimal places to display, as illustrated in Figure 13–6.

5. Select GoTo —▷ parameters to determine the layout characteristics of the report. Here you can determine the overall layout of interactive reports created with the infostructure.

> **TIP** You should always specify a default currency and translation method for the analysis. You should also make sure to specify the exchange rate type. This will make your reports more consistent and will also ensure that the values will be displayed in one currency only.
>
> Also, the number of periods field should be standard across all infostructures, since it specifies the default number of periods (quarter, month, weeks) to analyze.

6. Select Settings —▷ Save to save your report.

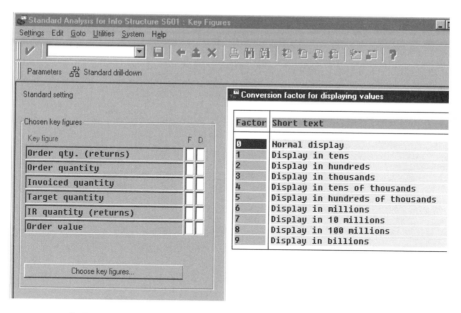

▶ **Figure 13–6**   Key Figures Display

Running the Report

Now we will run the interactive R/3™ report used by MRO procurement teams to analyze purchasing transactions.

1. Select Tools —▷ Self-defined Analysis from the Purchasing Information System menu.

2. Select the infostructure containing the data you want to analyze (see Figure 13–7).

3. Enter the selection criteria as shown on the selection screen in Figure 13–8.

4. Press F8 to execute the report. The results display appears in Figure 13–9.

NOTE The characteristic material is in the left column, and the key figure "Invoice amount" is on the right.

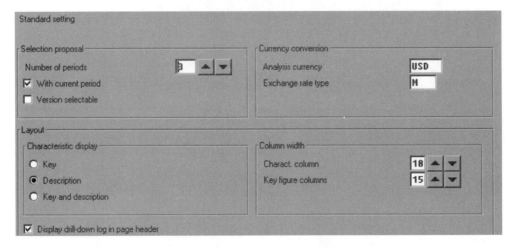

▶ **Figure 13–7**   Infostructure Data

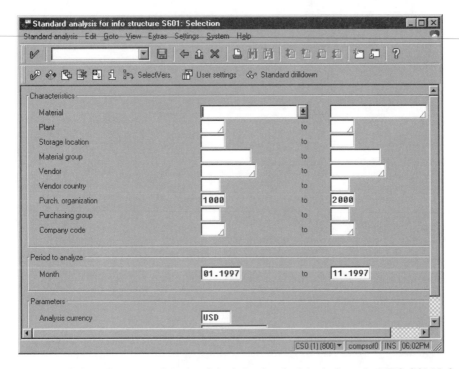

▶ **Figure 13–8**   Infostructure Selection Criteria for Standard Analysis on the MRO.COM Info Structure

No. of Material: 153

Material	Invoice amount
Bulb A 60/33x128 f	15.339,62 USD
Bulb A 60/33x128 r	7.317,17 USD
Bulb A 60/33x128 y	8.198,76 USD
Coil 220-235V 60-w	12.298,14 USD
220-235V 80-watt c	868,87 USD
220-235V 80-watt f	720,53 USD
220-235V 80-watt y	305,16 USD
220-235V 80-watt y	1.642,38 USD
Bulb A 80/33x128 c	93.374,92 USD
Bulb A 80/33x128 f	14.986,98 USD
Bulb A 80/33x128 r	6.347,43 USD
Bulb A 40/33x128 y	661,19 USD
Coil 220-235V 80-w	11.504,71 USD
Hub (LP)	0,00 USD
CATALYTIC CONVERTO	0,00 USD
Air conditioning	0,00 USD
Onboard computer	0,00 USD
Twisted Pair Cable	10.596,00 USD
Shielded Twisted P	11.655,60 USD
Braided Cable	12.715,20 USD
Harddisk 1080 MB	142.015,94 USD

▶ **Figure 13–9**   Standard Analysis with Material Description and Invoice Amount

5. From the results display you can:
   - Choose which characteristic to drill down by (View —▷ Drill down by).
   - Get a breakdown of all by period (select a key figure and then View —▷ Time series).
   - Perform an automatic ABC classification of the results (GoTo —▷ ABC Analysis). This is handy for analyzing which of the vendors are responsible for the most order value—that is, the "A" class).
   - To sort the list, select View —▷ Ascending/Descending.
   - To view key figure comparisons, such as planned vs. actual values, select Edit —▷ Comparisons, Planned vs. Actual.
6. To display a graphic, press GoTo —▷ Graphics. The R/3™ Logistics Information System displays the information as shown in Figure 13–10.

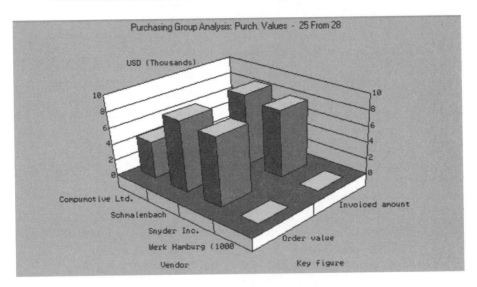

▶ **Figure 13–10**   Graphic Display of Report Results

Creating the Update Rules for the Infostructure

The R/3™ Logistics Information System allows you to control how characteristics and key figures are updated from R/3™ business transactions. The methods that control how this information is updated are called update rules. In this section, we show you the ins and outs of update control using the procurement example of MRO.COM.

Normally, you need to change update rules in R/3™ only if you have special requirements. Usually the only task you would need to do here is activate the update for an infostructure. This function allows transaction data to be updated into the infostructure when the transaction occurs or at a later time interval. This means that your reports could then have access to the data in real time or monthly, depending on the policy at your site.

To create or change update rules, perform the procedure that follows. In this example, we want to make sure that the net value for each order item is calculated for the date of the requisition, which is the day the sales order was created in R/3™ from the MRO.COM Web site. Otherwise, the order value calculated would be calculated on the date of the purchase order, which could actually be made some days later.

1. Select Logistics Information System —▷ Logistics Data Warehouse —▷ Updating —▷ Updating Definition —▷ Specific definition using update rules —▷ Maintain update rules —▷ Create from the Implementation Guide or enter transaction MC24.

2. Enter the name of the infostructure and the update group used. The usual value here is "SAP™," unless your company has created its own update group. You can also copy the update rules from an existing infostructure, which we would almost always recommend.

3. Press Enter to list the available update rules for the infostructure.

4. Place the cursor on a key figure and select the function "Rules for Key figures."

5. The screen shot in Figure 13–11 shows the update rule for "Net order value."

   The left portion of the figure shows the key figures for the infostructure and the right side shows the rule for updating net order value. The date field indicates that we will update the net order value based on the field MCEKPO-BADAT, which is the requisition date.

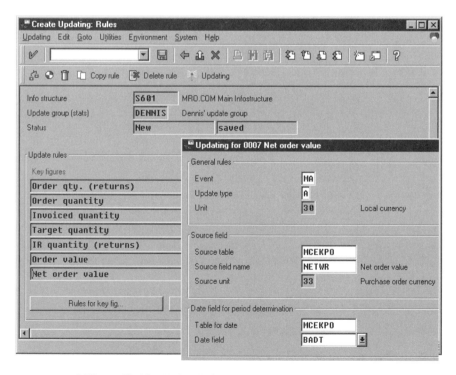

▶ **Figure 13–11**   Update Rules

Purchasing Report in Excel

At MRO.COM, vendors and buyers need to access information in the purchasing report using Microsoft Excel. They need to access a subset of the information in the procurement report created previously. To achieve this, they use ActiveSheets to define Excel workbooks for the vendor and buyer reports.

Creating the Vendor Open to Buy Report

The vendor open to buy report shows the open quantity to purchase from existing vendors for materials with long-term contracts. MRO.COM encourages its vendors to monitor their positions in these contracts to ensure that adequate advance warning is given when the target quantity is reached.

In this report, we assume that the key figures target quantity, order quantity, and net order value are in an infostructure in your R/3™ system.

The following procedure shows you how to create the OTB report.

1. Start the ActiveSheet Wizard.
2. Log on to your R/3™ system.
3. Select the Purchasing Report with the key figures above and press Next.
4. Select Columns for Target quantity, Order quantity and Order value then press Next.
5. Make your selection criteria, then select Finish.

The report displays as shown in Figure 13–12.

Creating the Buyer's Negotiation Sheet

The buyer's negotiation sheet at MRO.COM is an Excel report that allows purchasing agents to compare the vendor's pricing with the market average price performance. In this example, the order price paid to the vendor is compared with the actual invoice price (that is, the amount the vendor billed) and the market average price for the material. The market price for all products purchased at MRO.COM is stored in a SAS data warehouse and linked to a column in the Excel worksheet, as shown in Figure 13–13.

NOTE In Figure 13–13, the market price is from a SAS Data Warehouse. The vendor, material, purchase order, and invoice price columns are from SAP™. The market price is from SAS, and the discount is from Excel.

MRO.COM Open to Buy report for:	Dell System Services		
Position:		11/11/99 10:48 EST	

Material	Target quantity	Order quantity	Net order value
Flatscreen MS 1775P	9000	1028	897691.01
Harddisk 2113 MB / ATA-2	2500	3322	623955.88
Harddisk 4294 MB / SCSI-2-Fast	1500	898	575022.79
Harddisk 2149 MB / SCSI-2-Fast	1500	1839	571769.23
Harddisk 1080 MB / SCSI-2-Fast	17000	3526	559591.88
Flatscreen MS 1785P	7500	421	367802.54
Flatscreen MS 1585	8000	390	304643.48
Flatscreen LE 50 P	1900	791	227639.8
MAG DX 15F/Fe	5000	442	227146.47
Flatscreen MS 1460 P	4000	394	220702.07
MAG DX 17F	5000	402	216919.73
Flatscreen LE 64P	4000	353	201363.8
Sunny Sunny 01	4000	364	198285.5
Flatscreen MS 1575P	17000	262	192540.01
Processor 166 MHz	29000	579	114765.63
Professional keyboard - NATURAL Model	10000	2728	97112.09
SIM-Module 16M x 32, 70 ns	1500	906	88463.8
Professional keyboard - MAXITEC Model	2300	2744	71748.85
Standard Keyboard - EURO Model	1000	4246	70916.43
Standard Keyboard - EURO-Special Model	1700	3520	58410.95
Professional keyboard - PROFITEC Model	2900	2809	57785.8
SIM-Module 8M x 32, PS/2-72 Pin EDO-RAM	17000	1098	56020.62
Processor 133 MHz	30000	1551	47162.55
Software set for office	900	300	46021.82
SIM-Module 4M x 36, 70 ns	10000	1094	41637.51
SIM-Module 8M x 36, 70 ns	2900	603	41168.27
Processor 100 MHz	30000	1721	40683.89
Desktop Standard Case	5000	100	9250.31

▶ **Figure 13–12** Vendor Open to Buy Report

The last column shown in Figure 13–13, discount over market, represents the discount the vendor offers over the market price. It is calculated from the order price using the following formula: Order price/market price. In Excel, this formula could be represented as:

$(H1 - G1)/H1$

Vendor ID	Vendor Name	Material ID	Material Description	Purchase Order Price	Invoice Price	Market Price	Discount Over Market
1010	Sunny Electronics GmbH	M-06	Flatscreen MS 1460 P	$3,492.00	$3,600.00	$3,899.00	$ 407.00

▶ **Figure 13–13** Buyer's Negotiation Sheet

where H1 is the cell containing the market price and G1 is the cell containing the order price. If the order price field contains a 0 or the market price field contains a 0, we can avoid the Excel "zerodivide" error by first using the Excel IF function to test for 0 in the cells. This would mean that the cell function would expand to:

=IF(OR(H1=0, G1=0),0,(H1 – G1)/H1

This function does nothing if H1 or G1 contains a 0.

13.5   *MAPPING PHASE IV: PUBLISH THE REPORT SOLUTION*

In this section we examine how procurement reports are distributed to the decision-makers along the procurement business process at MRO.COM. In the Publishing phase of the MAPP process the following sorts of questions need to be addressed:

- Are there special media concerns?
- What is the most effective media, given the audience and the uses of the report?
- What information needs to go to what users?
- Who needs what authorizations?
- When must the report be delivered?
- What is the routing schedule?
- In what order will the report be received?
- What's the process for the rollout?
- What is the training schedule?

Media

Crucial to the success of report publishing is the choice of medium. The medium must take into consideration all the users as well as possible uses of the report. If the report will be employed differently by different users, more than one medium may be needed to fulfill all the report requirements. For example, some users may need the report delivered in Microsoft Office, or others may need remote access capabilities. Whatever the case, the earlier stages of the reporting process will have identified who needs the report, for what purposes, and when.

Publishing Media for MRO.COM

As we indicated earlier, MRO.COM's reporting requirements have two main components. The first is that the majority of the existing reports used by managers, vendors, key customers, and buyers were created in Excel. Moreover, an ERP reporting tool was not desired because the people using the reports were often not in the same company. Thus, Excel was chosen as the presentation medium. This led MRO.COM to consider the option of using Microsoft Exchange as the primary publishing medium. However, the second requirement led the company to consider a different option. One of the main requirements for the procurement reporting solution was real-time data. As you recall, some personnel required notification when an exception occurred. For expeditors, notification came best over wireless phones, since they were usually on the vendors' premises when checking the fulfillment of orders. Hence, the publishing medium needed to be able to distribute Excel reports efficiently, and it needed to be able to deliver real-time data over wireless connections. For this reason, Joe Morgan, the Director of Customer Fulfillment at MRO.COM, chose the Enterprise Information Portal as its delivery mechanism. Not only could they easily deliver the ActiveSheets/Excel reports, the EIP's wireless capabilities would ensure that the expeditors got up-to-the-minute, real-time data.

As shown in Figure 13–14, the EIP delivers e-business intelligence as real-time indicators in a secure and personalized wireless environment. With the EIP, Joe saw that remote users who needed immediate, real-time enterprise data could access it from a pager, laptop, or a microbrowser. Up-to-the-minute reports of sales orders, profit and loss statements, or customer analyses were available. Directories of information located in enterprise applications, such as lists of customers, vendors, or employees, were also available as public information in a standard Web format.

Since the EIP's synchronous information delivery solutions are compliant with Microsoft Office, MRO.COM found that live enterprise data could be served in several text-based formats, including HTML, HDML, RTF, or ASCII. This information could then be accessed or delivered to a variety of output devices that run MS Windows CE, Palm OS, or any number of devices that support the Wireless Access Protocol (WAP). The EIP also allowed MRO.COM business users to publish documents such as sales reports, profit and loss state-

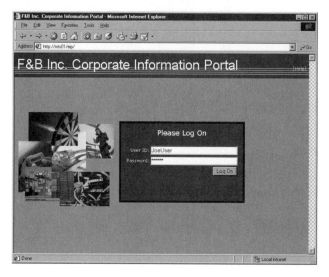

▶ **Figure 13–14**   EIP and Wireless

ments, or customer analyses to colleagues across the organization, increasing collaboration and information sharing.

Circulation Plan

The circulation plan concentrates on the actual information delivery. A good circulation plan needs to take into account such issues as:

- What are the roles or views that need to be set up?
- What permissions are necessary for which users?
- Is there a routing procedure?
- When and how often does the report get used?
- Who gets the report and when?

The Circulation Plan at MRO.COM

Given the many different types of procurement reports and different users of the reports, Joe Morgan decided to implement a role-based publishing plan. In role-based information delivery, the business information is organized and structured according to "views." The views represent user types or profiles set up so

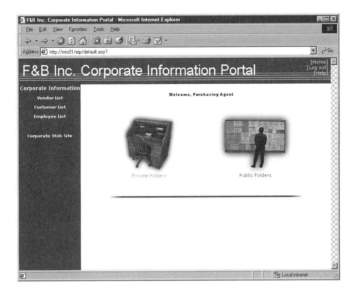

▶ **Figure 13–15**   Purchasing Agent Profile

that the user gets only information that is fitting with his or her roles in the company or in the reporting process. Once a role associated with the user's position and responsibility has been assigned, he or she can access the data in various self-created directories. Figure 13–15 shows a typical user profile with "public" and "private" views of business information.

Using the role-based method, Joe came up with the circulation plan as shown in Table 13–3.

Training

The last consideration of the Publishing plan is to devise a schedule and system for the rollout and training of the report's users. When devising a training plan for the users, the following types of questions should be addressed:

- What training materials must be created?
- Who will require training?
- What groups need which kind of training?
- How will the rollout training be scheduled?

Table 13–3   Circulation Plan

User	Role	Report	Frequency
Joe West	Product Line Specialist	Incoming Orders	Daily
Kim Fellini	Product Line Specialist	Incoming Orders	Daily
Liz Hatley	Requirements Controller	Customer Forecast	Weekly
Ray Watters	Requirements Controller	Customer Forecast	Weekly
Tina Tryon	Vendor	Open to Buy Report	Weekly
Frank Turner	Vendor	Open to Buy Report	Weekly
Shelley Warner	Vendor	Open to Buy Report	Weekly
Mary Hartwell	Purchasing Agent	Buyer's Negotiation Sheet	Weekly
Linus Cowley	Vendor; Expeditor	Deliveries in Pipeline	Daily
Wes Nestman	Vendor; Expeditor	Deliveries in Pipeline	Daily
Frederica Ho	Purchasing Agent	Vendor Hit List	Monthly

- Where will training take place?
- What training materials will be available and where?
- After the rollout, what is the plan for training new end users?
- How will changes to the report be transferred?

The training system should be integrated so that all members of the reporting team are in sync. Again, effective communication is key among all the groups involved.

Training at MRO.COM

Having isolated the basic needs for training of the report's users, Joe puts together the plan shown in Table 13–4 that will eventually be submitted for final approval.

Table 13–4 Training Plan

User	Role	Report	Rollout Group	Training
Joe West	Product Line Specialist	Incoming Orders	Group C	Hands on
Kim Fellini	Product Line Specialist	Incoming Orders	Group C	Hands on
Liz Hatley	Requirements Controller	Customer Forecast	Group C	Hands on
Ray Watters	Requirements Controller	Customer Forecast	Group C	Hands on
Tina Tryon	Vendor	Open to Buy Report	Group B	SAP™ CBT /Video
Frank Turner	Vendor	Open to Buy Report	Group B	SAP™ CBT /Video
Shelley Warner	Vendor	Open to Buy Report	Group B	SAP™ CBT /Video
Mary Hartwell	Purchasing Agent	Buyer's Negotiation Sheet	Group B	SAP™ CBT /Video
Linus Cowley	Vendor; Expeditor	Deliveries in Pipeline	Group A	Hands on
Wes Nestman	Vendor; Expeditor	Deliveries in Pipeline	Group A	Online
Frederica Ho	Purchasing Agent	Vendor Hit List	Group A	Online

SECTION 4

Financial Accounting

The SAP™ R/3™ accounting system is geared toward meeting the ever-increasing demands on accounting departments. Accounting must not only be integrated with all company processes, but it also must become more of a management tool for all company departments. In the R/3™ system, accounting is divided into key areas, such as financial accounting, asset management, and management accounting (controlling). All three areas not only facilitate the storage and recording of data but allow management to monitor, control, and plan key business transactions on the basis of up-to-date accounting information. The R/3™ accounting system allows access to information in each phase of a corporate organization—from development to key logistical operations. It also provides important links to and from vendors, customers, and financial institutions.

To be most effective, financial accounting must satisfy both internal and external accounting requirements. Internal requirements—that is, profit center accounting or profitability analysis—are handled by controlling. External accounting processes—such as providing accounting disclosures and information to shareholders, creditors, and the public—are the primary elements of financial accounting.

This section describes the main elements in financial accounting. It also provides the business background of external accounting with the high-level business rules governing financials in R/3™.

We focus on the following areas:

- Financial business drivers
- R/3™ financials reports
- Financials value chains and business processes
- External accounting tasks and activities
- External accounting business objects
- R/3™ financials organizational units
- Financials performance measures
- R/3™ information system
- Decision support tools
- Financials characteristics, key figures, and ratios

14

Understanding R/3™ Financial Accounting Information

|MAPM ► The management stage of the MAPPing method entails identifying what needs to be measured in the process of the successful deployment of a report. That includes providing the following types of management assessments:

- Business drivers
- "As Is" assessment
- Business processes
- Audience (company specific)[1]
- Priority (company specific)

In this section, we examine business background and decision support requirements from a financial accounting perspective. We take a look at the data that is available for financial reporting in the R/3™ system and map out the key areas for managing activities. These areas include:

- Business drivers analysis
- Business needs assessment
- "As Is" assessment
- Value chain analysis
- Business process analysis
- Tasks and activities analysis

1. Both the audience and priority will be specific to your company's needs, usages, and requirements. Thus, they cannot be dealt with adequately here.

14.1   TYPICAL BUSINESS DRIVERS IN FINANCIALS

A large portion of the managing phase has to do with assessing reporting needs. To identify those needs, you must examine the common business drivers for financials. Understanding the business drivers behind the report will ultimately help you define the necessary content of the report.

Table 14–1 categorizes the key business requirements that drive financial activities in the SAP™ R/3™ system. It also includes some of the typical questions that users of financials reports might ask.

Table 14–1   Key Financial Business Requirements

Key Business Driver	Questions Addressed
Manage fixed assets	What are the fixed assets expenditures, given total assets?
	What is the fixed asset growth as compared to total assets?
	Does the organization have too much capacity or too little for a given sales volume?
Determine liabilities	How much total debt can an organization incur and still remain financially fit?
	How do total assets compare to long-term debt?
Improve cash position of the company	What are the sources for cash receipts?
	Which items are considered for cash disbursements?
	How do cash-flow ratios compare to industry standards or the organization's annual figures?
Monitor receivables and rate of collections	What is the accounts receivable turnover?
	How do quarterly figures project for the year?
	How does accounts receivable turnover compare to sales trends over X time periods?
	How do prior period billings compare to total collections?
	What is the average collection period?
Maximize profitability	What is the PE ratio?
	What is the capitalization rate?
	What is the net asset or "book" value?
Manage debt-paying capability	How quickly can a company pay off debt if its assets are liquidated?
	How does income from operations compare to interest from debt?

The business drivers considered here are:

- Managing fixed assets
- Controlling liabilities, total assets, and debt
- Improving cash position
- Monitoring receivables and rate of collections
- Maximizing profitability
- Managing debt-paying capability

Once you have a good idea of what the business drivers are for the company report, you should document these in a report or spreadsheet. The goal of this document should be to help you determine exactly what the report is supposed to accomplish.

14.2   ASSESSING R/3™ FINANCIAL INFORMATION

Table 14–2 indicates the main external accounting information available in R/3™. This information will be useful in assessing what standard reports are currently available in the R/3™ system.

Table 14–2   External Accounting Data

Report Type	Description
Balance Sheet/P&L	Financial statement of assets, liabilities, and stockholders' equity. Includes company code, business area, reporting period, comparison period, absolute difference, and relative difference.
Balance Sheet, P&L from Cost of Sales Ledger	Time period comparison by balance sheet. Contains company, company code, financial statement version, currency type, balance sheet type, financial statement item, fiscal year comparisons, and variance.
Cash Flow	Cash flow by direct method. Analyzes sales collections, material disbursement, personnel disbursement, financial collections, other operating collections, other operating disbursements, and taxes by income.
List of Account Balances	General ledger account balances. Lists company, company code, account number, cash forward balance, previous months, reporting debit, reporting credit, total debit balance, and total credit balance.

Table 14–2 External Accounting Data (Continued)

Report Type	Description
Account of Lists	Lists and directories. Includes chart of accounts, company codes, general ledger account list, account assignments, account statements, and average balance.
Tax on Sales/Purchases Return	Tax reports, including advance return for tax on sales/purchases, transfer postings for deferred taxes, tax subsequent debit, input tax for parked documents, and reports specific to country.
Accounts Receivable Evaluations	Customer standard evaluations. Offers due date analysis, payment history, currency analysis, overhead items, DSO analysis, terms offered/terms taken, interest calculation, bill of exchange processing, and credit management.
Consolidation	Financial reporting data. Includes the following standards reports: list of ownerships, investment in companies, investments, equity, hidden reserves, eliminated hidden reserves, retained earnings, IC profit: inventory and supplier data, asset transfers, and asset transfer depreciation.
Cost of Sales Reporting (Special Ledger)	Analysis of cost of sales reporting. Contains profit and loss statement item, plan version (stored planning data for comparative analysis), and reporting period.
Asset Accounting	Analysis of fixed assets. Reports by individual assets, asset portfolio, balance sheet, profit and loss, cost accounting, depreciation forecasting, special valuation, closing, day-to-day activities, and taxes.

14.3 *UNDERSTANDING FINANCIAL ACCOUNTING BUSINESS PROCESSES*

We should now consider the business process scenarios that cover all the business areas that were identified in the business drivers document. Reviewing the business processes will provide us with a better understanding of how the financial accounting data can be derived from R/3™. The business process scenarios will also help us identify which areas will be measured in the report, how the report will be used, and where (that is, what organizations, people, etc., will be affected by the report).

To understand R/3™ financials business processes, we take you through the main processes and then single out one, the consolidation business process scenario, as an illustrative example.

SAP™ R/3™ Financial Accounting

SAP™'s integrated financial application components encompass all aspects of financial accounting, including controlling, investment management, treasury management, and enterprise controlling.

In the following, we examine the FI-LC module, which is SAP™'s process for external accounting and the consolidation of subsidiaries (legal consolidation). We begin by detailing a scenario from consolidation, and then explain its sub-processes, tasks, and activities.

Consolidation Business Process Scenario

Figure 14–1 represents an illustrative R/3™ financials value chain, the consolidation business process. Each link in the chain represents the interaction of key R/3™ external accounting components from a high-level view.

Represented in Figure 14–1 is a general outline of how a typical financials process flows. The value chain depicts how the individual financial statements of companies in a corporate group are combined to create consolidated financial statements. The consolidation process involves eliminating certain trading partner and financial relationships among group companies.

R/3™ consolidation deals with the ways in which companies summarize financial information from different subsidiaries and joint ventures in various currencies and countries. The consolidation business process scenario is designed for companies with multiple legal entities that want to create consolidated financial statements for statutory and management reporting purposes. R/3™ consolidation is especially applicable to diversified multinational companies.

Master Data

In the R/3™ system, local financial systems are structured along corporate guidelines. Data in local systems is reconciled for intercompany balances, local currency translation, and valuations/adjustments required by group accounting rules. Consequently, local management possesses financial statements of the

▶ **Figure 14–1** Consolidation Value Chain

company from both a local and a corporate group view. Seldom are all related data available in R/3™. Due to local infrastructure characteristics and the fact that some entities in a company may not have an R/3™ system, business data can be taken from local databases and such spreadsheets as Microsoft Excel. After the data are collected, they are then transferred to consolidation.

Step and Simultaneous Consolidation

The consolidation of a multi-level corporate group is performed using either step or simultaneous consolidation. Step consolidation refers to the process by which individual companies are consolidated step-by-step according to a multi-level corporate hierarchy of defined subgroups. (Subgroups are defined according to meaningful categories such as region or business unit, or by individual hierarchy levels of a multi-level enterprise.)

In simultaneous consolidation, no hierarchies of ownership relationship are required. The total percentage of ownership of a consolidation group's investee is computed, and the percentage of group ownership is used to identify the total group's portion of the investee equity. Since the percentage of ownership of a full consolidation group is used to compute the group consolidation adjustment for any one investee, consolidation of the total group is made simultaneously.

Consolidation Analyses

In consolidation, companies report their individual financial statements to a consolidated entity that treats each company as a unit of consolidation. Consolidation is the process of collecting and reconciling the financial statements of companies into a single consolidated financial statement that accurately portrays the financial circumstances of all companies as a whole. Companies carry out consolidations to merge financial statements for meeting certain legal requirements, as well as to aid in internal decision-making. Consolidation scenarios allow for the following types of business analysis:

- Intercompany payables and receivables
- Intercompany expense and revenue
- Income from investments
- Intercompany profit/loss in inventory
- Intercompany profit/loss in transferred assets
- Consolidation of investments

Actual consolidation can be performed once the following are available to the consolidation system:

- Individual financial statements
- Currency translations
- Intercompany balance verification

Once all necessary standardizing or reclassification entries (e.g., reclassification of finished goods into unfinished goods for purposes of corporate group reporting) are recorded, they can be applied to the above categories.

Eliminations

Once the preceding information is made available, intercompany eliminations may be performed. Eliminations include payables and receivables, expenses and revenues, income from investments, profit/loss inventory, and transfer of fixed assets.

Table 14–3 lists the main types of eliminations supported in the FI-LC module.

Table 14–3   Intercompany Eliminations

Elimination Type	Description
Payables and receivables	Eliminate the payables and receivables and revenue and expense that originate from goods and service transactions among group companies.
Intercompany profit and loss	Eliminate intercompany profit and loss in both transferred assets and inventory.
Consolidation of investments	Eliminate the investment holdings of parent companies in a group against the proportional equity of subsidiaries and associated companies in the same group.

Numerous aspects of consolidation of investments are covered in R/3™, which are reflected in Table 14–4.

Reporting

Consolidation information supports a general understanding of how a business is working. This business process shows how the legal requirements are ful-

Table 14–4   Consolidation of Investments

Business Case	Definition
First consolidation	The first inclusion of a company in the consolidated financial statements.
Step acquisition	An increase of an investment in a company by directly acquiring additional shares.
Change in indirect investment	The group's share in a company changes without a change in the direct investment percentage. (This is usually the case when additional shares are acquired in the company's parent as a result of step acquisition.)
Increase/decrease in capitalization	The capital stock and the investment's book value increases or decreases without a change in the investment percentage.
Transfer	A parent company sells all or some of its shares in a subsidiary to another company within the group.
Subsequent consolidation	Reflects the adjustment of the minority shares and/or the amortization of good will and hidden reserves that need to be made because of changes in capital structure.

filled. From a management perspective, it's important to see the trees as well as the forest; hence, the emphasis is on extensive reporting functions. Reports are generated with multiple versions defined to compare the results of different consolidation scenarios. These scenarios may be driven by alternative consolidation methods or currency simulations.

Standard reports are available once consolidation activities have been implemented and approved. In addition, user-defined reports are also available.

15

Analyzing R/3™ Financial Accounting Information

MAP
In the analysis phase of reporting, the most important activity is to identify all the relevant information available for the report. Here, you need to match up the business needs defined in the last stage of the game with what is available in the R/3™ system. This analysis will entail examination of the business information contained in the system, including knowledge of ratios used to measure performance, organizational dimensions used, and the source data. An analysis of the following areas will help us access this information in R/3™:

- Business objects
- Performance measures
- Decision support applications
- Information sources (characteristics, key figures, and ratios)

15.1 UNDERSTANDING FINANCIAL BUSINESS OBJECTS

Business objects help us identify the characteristics that are important for reporting purposes and locate what characteristics are available in R/3™. A business object encapsulates the business logic of a certain data source, for example, a sales order. The object contains various levels of information, such as the possible header types, available organizations, item data, object types, and other information useful for reporting purposes.

The primary business objects for R/3™ Financial Management are represented in the following:

- General Ledger accounts
- Customer account
- Ledgers
- Accounts Payable (vendor) account
- Accounting documents
- Chart of accounts

General Ledger

The business object General Ledger represents the values that are used for the preparation of the balance sheet, profit and loss statements as shown in Table 15–1.

Table 15–1   The General Ledger

Characteristic	SAP™ Technical Name	Description
Average balance	RLDNR1	The average balance ledger used to calculate average balances
Consolidation type	LC_TYP	The type of consolidation used
Valuation	DE G_VALUTYP	Legal, group, or profit center valuation
Allocation method	SPLITMETHD	The assignment of a distribution method to the ledger, used to determine how documents posted in the system are updated in a ledger
Balance carry forward	VORTR	Set up for automatically carrying balance forward for the ledger
Client	MANDT	The unit that is legally and organizationally independent

Customer Account Business Object

As described in Table 15–2, the Customer Account contains records of receivables or payables information for a debtor. The data is recorded in the company code and provides an illustration of business transactions with the customer in terms of value.

Table 15–2   The Customer Account

Characteristic	SAP™ Technical Name	Description
Customer number	KUNNR	A number that uniquely identifies the customer
Record date	ERDAT_RF	The date a master record, or part of the master record, was created
Accounting clerk	BUSAB	Identification code used by accounting clerk for reporting or correspondence
Authorization group	BRGRU	The group defined for authorization protection
Payment method	ZWELS	List of payment methods defined for a customer or vendor
Block payment	ZAHLS	The block of an open item or an account during payment transactions
Interest calculation	VZSKZ	Entered interest calculation for automatic interest calculation
Payment terms	GUZTE	The payment terms used for credit memos, including cash discount percentages and payment dates
Amount insured	VLIBB	Total amount that is covered by insurance
Head office	KNRZE	Head office account number for branch accounts

Credit Control Business Object

The Credit Control business object represents the areas of responsibility for managing and granting credit to customers (Table 15–3). It corresponds organizationally to one or more company codes. Credit information per debtor can be monitored and managed.

Table 15–3   Credit Control

Characteristic	SAP™ Technical Name	Description
Client	MANDT	A number that uniquely identifies the customer
Credit control area	KKBER	The credit limit established for customers
Risk	CTLPD_CM	The risk category created for a new customer, and used for credit management
Currency	WAERS	Currency key for selected amounts in the system
Credit group	DSBGR_CM	Credit management representatives group for new customers
Credit update	STAFO_CM	Credit update for an open order, delivery, or billing document

Fixed Asset Accounting

The Fixed Asset Accounting business object records the value transactions that pertain to fixed assets within a company code (Table 15–4). For each depreciation area, there is one fixed asset account for each fixed asset. The fixed asset account establishes the valuation of assets, depreciation methods, and other depreciation terms.

Table 15–4   Fixed Asset Accounting

Characteristic	SAP™ Technical Name	Description
Main asset number	ANLN1	The number that uniquely identifies the fixed asset
Depreciation area	AFABE_D	Real depreciation area such as tax, group, cost accounting, or book depreciation
Beginning/end validity	ADATU/ BDATU	Beginning and end dates for validity period
Group asset	ANLGR	The combination of a number of assets for the purpose of evaluating them uniformly
Revaluation	AUFWTG	The appreciation measure defined in the system
Asset scrap value	SCHRW	The amount that cannot be depreciated in a given depreciation area
Life cycle	NDPER / NDJAR	Time period that asset is to be used and depreciated
Investment support	INVSL	The definition of the investment support measure

Vendor (Accounts Payable) Business Object

The vendor is a business partner that supplies your company with goods and services. In R/3™, Vendors can be *internal* or *external*. This means that an organization within your company can also be your supplier. (Note: the terms "vendor" and "supplier" are used interchangeably in R/3™.)

The vendor information is maintained by both the purchasing and accounts payable departments. Purchasing is responsible for the vendor pricing and business communication information. Accounts payable is responsible for recording the financial transactions with the vendor and therefore needs to maintain information such as the bank account information needed for direct wire transfers.

The vendor account number is required for most activities in purchasing. For example, all purchase orders require a vendor account number in R/3™. However, requisitioning activities do not include vendors. The Vendor business object holds the data you need for reporting on business partners in accounts payable (Table 15–5).

Table 15–5   Vendor Characteristics

Characteristic	SAP™ Technical Name	Description
Vendor number	LFA1-LIFNR	Number that uniquely identifies a supplier in the R/3™ system
Vendor communication	(multiple fields in R/3™ table LFA1)	Includes such information as the state, province, country, and postal code of the vendor, as well as the Internet address (Uniform Resource Locator or URL) of the vendor
Vendor account group	KTOKK	Classification of vendor account group in vendor master record
Posting block	SPERB_X	Block on all posting for a certain vendor account for all company codes
Tax type	J_1AFITP_D	Classification of companies according to tax areas
Jurisdiction	TXJCD	Tax jurisdiction code for determining tax rates in US
Trading partner	RASSC	Company ID for a trading partner
Authorization group	BRGRU	The group defined for authorization protection

Ledgers

The business object Ledger (Table 15–6) records and represents the movements of values or quantities for a certain sub-area of accounting. The Ledger business object is a source for other ledgers, including:

- Accounts payable
- Accounts receivable
- Consolidation
- Fixed asset
- General ledger
- Reconciliation
- Additional ledgers

Table 15–6 Ledger Characteristics

Characteristic	SAP™ Technical Name	Description
Client	MANDT	Number that uniquely identifies client
Ledger class	LDCLS	Ledger class
Debits/credits	SHKZ	Credit/debit indicator set at direct posting
Average balance	RLDNR1	The average balance ledger used to calculate average balances
Consolidation type	LC_TYP	The type of consolidation used
Valuation	DE G_VALUTYP	Legal, group, or profit center valuation
Line items	GLSIP	Line items written for master data
Ledger name	LDTXT	Name of ledger
Language	SPRAS	Language keys
Allocation method	SPLTMETHD	Assignment of a distribution method for ledger updates

15.2   *UNDERSTANDING FINANCIAL ORGANIZATIONAL STRUCTURES*

As a reporting analyst, you will need to understand how typical organizations are defined in R/3™ financials. The reason for this is that your reports will necessarily have an organization dimension. For example, if your report is relevant to a particular region and distribution channel, you will need to understand the relationship between these organizational entities in R/3™ and how they have been configured in your R/3™ system.

Organizational Entities in Financials

Organizational units describe the entity designated to perform a certain set of functions within a company. Financial business processes in R/3™ involve the following organizational units:

- Company
- Company code
- Business area
- Financial management area
- Cost center
- Profit center

Company

Companies are the base units used in Financial-Legal Consolidation, for which individual financial statements are prepared for legal consolidation. In external accounting, a company typically is an independent legal entity.

In financial accounting, a company represents the smallest organizational unit for which individual financial statements can be drawn up according to the relevant commercial law. A company can consist of one or more company codes.

Company Code

The company code is used in all financial transactions. It contains the chart of accounts and thus is the organizational unit referenced for all statutory reports, such as the balance sheet and profit and loss statements. In R/3™ purchasing, the purchasing organization is assigned to a company code.

Business Area

A business area is an organizational unit within financial accounting which represents a separate area of operations or responsibilities within an organization. Financial accounting transactions can be allocated to a specific business area.

Financial Management Area

The financial management (FM) area is the organizational unit within a company for which budgets and financial resources are planned. An FM area can cover one or more company codes. Where you are taking advantage of the integration with investment accounting, the controlling areas involved must be assigned to an FM area.

Cost Center

An organizational unit within a controlling area that represents a separate location of cost incurrence, cost centers can be set up based on functional requirements, allocation criteria, activities or services provided, location and/or area of responsibility.

Profit Center

A profit center is a subdivision of a business organization which is set up for internal management control purposes. Operating profit can be calculated for profit centers on the basis of the cost-of-sales and/or the period accounting methods. By incorporating certain balance sheet account values into the calculation, a profit center can be extended to become an investment center.

15.3 UNDERSTANDING FINANCIALS PERFORMANCE MEASURES

Performance measures are the main source of content for the report and contain the most important information for analysis purposes. They provide the key figures and ratios that are used to measure performance. R/3™ has a number of information sources built into the system that provide you with standard ratios that measure performance in an R/3™ Financials system.

Balance Sheet Ratios

The key performance measures are:

Vertical Analysis
Balance sheet analysis, in which each entry within a total (e.g., cash) is divided by the total itself (e.g., total assets)

$$\text{Vertical analysis} = \frac{\text{Individual entry on balance sheet}}{\text{Total}}$$

Fixed to total assets
Estimate fixed assets expenditures given total assets

$$\text{Fixed to total assets} = \frac{\text{Fixed assets}}{\text{Total assets}}$$

Fixed asset turnover
Comparison of annualized sales to average of fixed assets

$$\text{Fixed asset turnover} = \frac{\text{Sales}}{\text{Fixed assets}}$$

Liabilities
Average total of liabilities divided by average total assets

$$\text{Liabilities} = \frac{\text{Total debt}}{\text{Total assets}}$$

Capital structure
Portion of a company's capitalization to its total capitalization

$$\text{Capital structure} = \frac{\text{Preferred stock or Long-term debt or Common stock}}{\text{Total capital}}$$

Capital employed
Measures how well capital is being used to produce revenue

$$\text{Capital employed} = \frac{\text{Sales}}{\text{Capital} - \text{Nonoperational assets}}$$

Average working capital
Measures the amount of liquidity

$$\text{Average working capital} = \frac{\text{Beginning working capital} - \text{End working capital}}{2}$$

Acid test
Compares a company's current liabilities with quick assets

$$\text{Acid test} = \frac{\text{Cash + Marketable securities + Accounts receivable}}{\text{Current liabilities}}$$

15.4   PROFITABILITY

Earnings per common share
Net income divided by number of common shares issued and outstanding

$$\text{Earnings per common share} = \frac{\text{Net income}}{\text{Issued and outstanding shares}}$$

Price earnings (PE) ratio
Describes the relationship between market price and earnings per share

$$\text{Price earnings ratio} = \frac{\text{Market price per share}}{\text{Earnings per share}}$$

Times interest earned
Number of times interest is covered by operating profits

$$\text{Times interest earned} = \frac{\text{Income from operations}}{\text{Interest expense}}$$

15.5   ACCOUNTS RECEIVABLE

Cash flow
Difference between disbursements and receipts

$$\text{Cash flow} = \text{Cash receipts} - \text{Cash disbursements}$$

Receivables turnover
Ratio of total credit sales to receivables

$$\text{Receivables turnover} = \frac{\text{Total credit sales}}{\text{Receivables balance}}$$

Receivables to sales
Average age or level of customer accounts outstanding

$$\text{Receivables to sales} = \frac{\text{Average receivables}}{\text{Net credit sales}}$$

16

Understanding the R/3™ Financial Information System

|MAP▶| **I**n this chapter, we examine some options that are available for presenting R/3™ data to end users. The first we examine is the Financial Accounting Information System (FAIS), SAP™'s primary financial accounting reporting tool. Next, we take a look at a specific report that can be created using the FAIS as the primary presentation application.

16.1 FINANCIAL ACCOUNTING INFORMATION SYSTEM

The Financial Accounting Information System is a component of the Accounting Information System (described in Chapter 3), an R/3™ reporting tool that can be used to create reports as well as to present the data that is collected. The Financial Accounting Information System accesses business information based on the underlying infostructures, which describe the data that purchasing applications can access. These infostructures are a kind of multi-dimensional data cube that contain the data that has been collected from R/3™ financial transactions.

The data is collected as characteristics, key figures, and time period. As we noted earlier, characteristics are the objects you report on, such as customer or material. Key figures are the statistical values, such as invoiced sales, used to forecast or measure performance. Key figures are usually expressed as a value or quantity. The last part of the data cube is an aggregate of the data by time period, such as by daily, weekly, monthly, or fiscal periods.

16.2   STANDARD ANALYSES IN THE R/3™ FINANCIAL ACCOUNTING INFORMATION SYSTEM

The Financial Accounting Information System contains standard reports that can be accessed with the standard analyses shipped with R/3™. Standard reports are available for such key procurement areas as:

- General Ledger
- Accounts Payable
- Accounts Receivable
- Fixed Assets
- Consolidation
- Special Purpose Ledger

The following is a list of the types of analyses provided in the R/3™ Financial Accounting Information System. You can use this list to identify the reporting analyses that you may require for your organization.

Each decision support tool provides:

- ABC analysis (Pareto)
- Top N listing (list of values based on a key figure)
- Trend analysis
- Exception analysis (based on trend or threshold)
- Ability to dynamically switch currencies
- Time-series breakdown (from year to month to week to day)
- Planned vs. actual (where appropriate)
- Display access to master data records, in the case of customer and product, respectively

General Ledger

For each company, company code, or business area, the General Ledger analysis provides information on chart of accounts, balance sheet, account balances, line items, and structured balance lists. The following types of analyses are provided:

- Balance sheet/ P&L
- Cash flow
- List of account balances
- Line items
- Structured balance list

- Chart of accounts lists
- Account statements
- Average balances
- Posting totals
- Tax on sales/purchases return
- Foreign trade regulations

Accounts Payable

The accounts payable analysis provides information on account lists, account balances, and open items. For each vendor, the following types of analyses are available:

- Balances in local currency
- Open items
- Due date forecast
- Payment history
- Master data
- Interest calculation
- Bills of exchange
- Payment transactions
- Withholding tax

Accounts Receivable

The accounts receivable analysis provides information on account lists, account balances, and open items. For each customer, the following types of analyses are available:

- Balances in local currency
- Open items
- Due date forecast
- Payment history (analysis and prognosis)
- Days overdue analysis
- Master data
- Interest calculation
- Bills of exchange
- Payment transactions
- Credit management

Fixed Assets

The Financial Accounting Information System provides analyses for asset values, asset history, and depreciation values. Fixed asset information can be found in the following types of analyses:

- Individual assets
- Asset portfolio (asset, inventory, leased assets)
- Balance sheet
- P&L
- Cost accounting
- Depreciation forecast
- Special valuation
- Closing
- Taxes

Consolidation

The consolidation analysis provides you with wide range of consolidation reporting data. The following types of standard analyses are available:

- Master data
- Financial reporting data
- Journal entries
- Totals report
- Report writer
- EIS drilldown reports
- Auxiliary reports

Special Purpose Ledger

The special purpose ledger stores user-defined summarized data for various accounting functions, such as planning, allocations, rollup, balance carry-forward, and so forth. Standard analyses provide information on totals records, local documents, global documents, planning documents, and Report Painter reports.

16.3 *Characteristics, Key Figures, and Ratios*

Each of the data elements displayed in a decision support tool can be a characteristic or key figure. Characteristics are the objects you report on, such as customer or material.

Key figures are the statistical values, such as invoiced sales, used to forecast or measure performance. Key figures are usually expressed as a value or quantity.

Ratios combine a characteristic and associated key figure that can be used as a performance measure, as described above.

Table 16–1 lists the characteristics and key figures required for each of the decision support tools described previously.

Table 16–1   Decision Support Characteristics and Key Figures

Decision Support Tool	Characteristic	Key Figure
Customer account (Accounts Receivable)	Distribution channel Division Material Sales organization Sold-to party Company code Customer number Business area Country key	Account balance Customer number Currency key Fiscal period Fiscal year Monthly sales Total of the credit posting Total of the debit posting Bank account number Bill of exchange Cash discount Clearing date Dunning area Payment method Postal code Tax amount Tax code
Vendor account (Accounts Payable)	Business area Company code Country key Vendor Customer	Account number Bank account number Bank key Bank country Bill of exchange Cash discount Debit/creditor indicator Dunning area Fiscal period Fiscal year Local currency Payment block Payment method Posting date Special G/L indicator Tax amount Withholding

Table 16–1   Decision Support Characteristics and Key Figures (Continued)

Decision Support Tool	Characteristic	Key Figure
G/L account	Company code	Chart of accounts
	G/L account number	G/L account
	Group account number	Account group
	Business area	P&L statement
	Currency type	Financial statement version
		Reporting year
		Reporting periods
		Comparison year
		Plan version
		Fiscal year
		Account currency
		Account balance
		Balances in foreign currency
Fixed assets	Company code	Depreciation area
	Asset number	Report date
	Business area	Sort version
	Cost center	Location
	Plant	Asset class
		Sub-number
		Property
		Insurance
		Asset history
		Transaction data
		General assets
		Inventory
		Leased asset
		Asset transfers
		Acquisitions
		Transfers
Consolidation	Company	Ownerships
	Version	Investee equity
	Fiscal year	Investments
	Period	Hidden reserves
	Subgroup	Equity structure
		Eliminated hidden reserves
		Asset transfers
		IC profit: inventory
		IC profit: supplier
		Retained earnings
		Transaction types

Table 16–1   Decision Support Characteristics and Key Figures (Continued)

Decision Support Tool	Characteristic	Key Figure
Special ledger	Ledger Period Company code	P&L cost of sales Period breakdown Local currency Cost center Material Unit of measure Finished products Account quantity

16.4   *EXAMPLE: FINANCIAL ACCOUNTING INFORMATION SYSTEM REPORTS*

The following examples describe how to perform a number of financial accounting reports using the Financial Accounting Information System. You will find information on the following reporting areas:

- Balance Sheet
- Accounts Receivable
- Accounts Payable
- General Ledger

Balance Sheet

The Balance Sheet report provides a financial statement for a set reporting period. A P&L statement can also be defined through this report.

To create a Balance Sheet report:

1. From the Information Systems menu, select Financial Accounting.
   The Financial Accounting Information System displays.
2. From the General Ledger menu, select Balance Sheet.
   The Balance Sheet/P&L window displays.
3. Enter the following selection criteria:
   Chart of accounts: CAUS
   Company code: 3000
   Financial statement version: BAUS
   Reporting year: 1997
   Comparison year: 1996
4. Select Execute.
   The Balance Sheet report displays, as in Figure 16–1.

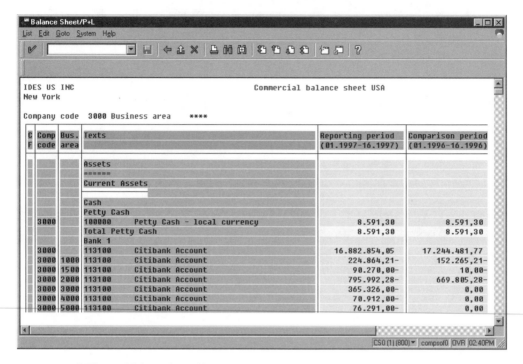

▶ **Figure 16–1**   Balance Sheet Report

Accounts Receivable (Open Items Report)

The Open Items report allows you to manage Accounts Receivable information. You can assess overdue items, and a number of different views to analyze the information are available. For example, you can assess the open items by company, account number, industry, and so forth.

To create an AR Open Items report (customer accounts summary):

1. From the Information Systems menu, select Financial Accounting.
   The Financial Accounting Information System displays.
2. From the Accounts Receivable menu, select Open Items.
   The Open Items window displays.
3. Enter the following selection criteria:
   Company code: 1000
   Open items at key date: 08/01/1998
4. Select Execute.
   The List of Customer Open Items report displays, as shown in Figure 16–2.

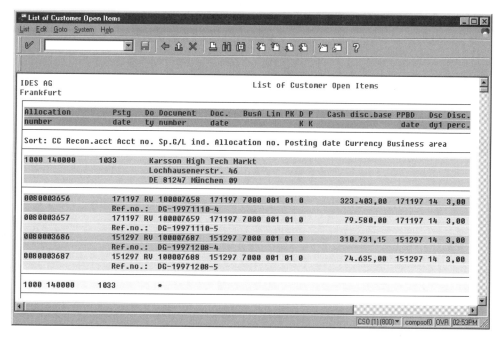

▶ **Figure 16–2**   Customer Open Items Report

Accounts Payable (Vendor Open Items)

This analysis allows you to manage Accounts Payable information by assessing overdue items from vendors for a given period. This report allows you to view debits and credits, and provides a number of different views to analyze the information. For example, you can assess the open items by company, account number, industry, and so forth.

To create an AR Open Items report (customer accounts summary):

1. From the Information Systems menu, select Financial Accounting.
   The Financial Accounting Information System displays.
2. From the Accounts Payable menu, select Open Items.
   The List of Vendors Open Items window displays.
3. Enter the following selection criteria:
   Company code: 3000
   Open items at key date: 08/01/1998
4. Select Execute.
   The List of Vendor Open Items report displays, as shown in Figure 16–3.

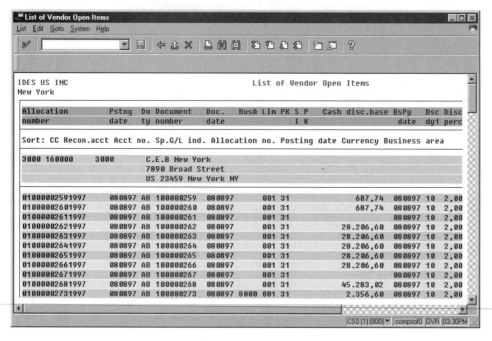

Figure 16–3　Vendor Open Items Report

General Ledger (Account Balance)

This analysis provides information on account balances in the General Ledger. You can use this report to find the debit total for the fiscal year, the debit or credit balance, the credit total for the reporting period, and the balance carried forward.

To create a General Ledger:

1. From the Information Systems menu, select Financial Accounting.
   The Financial Accounting Information System displays.
2. From the General Ledger menu, select Account Balances.
   The Balance Sheet/P&L window displays.
3. Enter the following selection criteria:
   Chart of accounts: CAUS
   G/L account: 1000
   Company code: 3000
   Reporting year: 1996
4. Select Execute.
   The G/L Account Balances report displays, as shown in Figure 16–4.

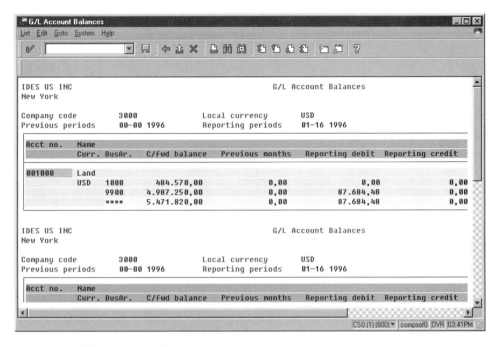

▶ **Figure 16–4**   G/L Account Balances

17

Financial Information Delivery

MAPP **T**he information delivery plan is too often an overlooked aspect of the reporting cycle. Many reports, often some of the best that a company designs, are never used because they never make it to their intended target audience.

In the MAPP process, Publishing is designed to improve awareness, knowledge, and circulation of a given report within the company. The main objective of the publishing strategy is to get a report into the hands of the end users who can make the best use of the report information.

This chapter draws upon our experience with financial professionals in a wide range of industries, and provides information on creating a publishing system especially suited for financial reports.

Areas covered in this chapter include:

- R/3™ financial publishing with Microsoft Digital Dashboard™
- Financial report circulation plan
- Rollout issues for financial reports
- Strategies for training and feedback
- Permissions and authorizations
- Creating discussion forums
- Publicizing financial reports

17.1   *PUBLISHING WITH MICROSOFT DIGITAL DASHBOARD*

Choosing an appropriate medium is the first step in creating a publishing strategy for a report. We recommend Microsoft Digital Dashboard as the primary mechanism for collaborative reporting. However, all of the publishing methods that have been covered in this book are equally appropriate.

The basic model for our publishing strategy is illustrated in Figure 17–1. Here, we imagine an R/3™ report has been created in Excel with ActiveSheets. The report administrator posts the report on the company server. The report is delivered according to roles in the organization that have been set up in the Microsoft Digital Dashboard. The report appears in the dashboards of all end users with that role.

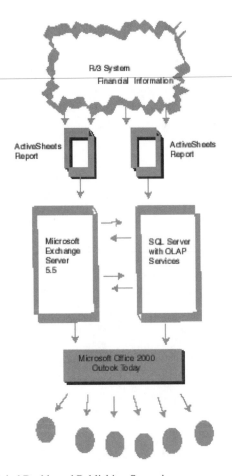

▶ **Figure 17–1**   Digital Dashboard Publishing Scenario

Microsoft Digital Dashboard Overview

The Microsoft Digital Dashboard is a customization of the Microsoft Office 2000 work environment. It consolidates in a single view information from many sources, using various analytical and collaborative tools. Key business information is localized on the individual desktop, enabling access to an integrated view of company information and knowledge sources. The strength of the Digital Dashboard (DD) lies in its ability to control information for users by filtering out unnecessary information while retaining and organizing data they need.

On its simplest level, the DD is a Web page running within the Microsoft Outlook client. The Outlook Today page is the jumping off point, acting as a kind of portal within the Office 2000 environment. Your company's IT development staff builds the dashboards and determines the content and the level of customization that will be available in the Outlook window. Content can be configured according to user or, better for reporting purposes, to role. Typically, the base content is configured according to the business role, and then customization options are available for the user to build a personalized dashboard.

Figure 17–2 illustrates a possible Outlook Today dashboard configuration.

▶ **Figure 17–2**   Microsoft Digital Dashboard

Information sources called "nuggets" determine the information displayed in the dashboard. These sources can consist of a wide range of sources, including:

- Calendars and tasks
- Links to Outlook folders
- Internet content
- Web components
- Document libraries
- Business data
- Personal content
- Information resources and tools
- Multimedia

Digital Dashboard Financial Reporting Scenario

Over the years the financial department of Acme Products, Inc. has created several thousand reports, which have been created in numerous information systems, mostly legacy reports and SAP™ R/3™. The district managers have decided that they would like to consolidate the reports by weeding out the extraneous reports, keeping the ones that are used, and in some cases, creating new ones that better indicate financial performance. After painstakingly choosing the right reports, the district managers now want to distribute these reports to their financial managers. They are concerned that the new reports will just be added to the pile of reports in use, and that they will not be used exclusively, which was the original intent of the project.

To handle the distribution and use problem, the district managers have decided to implement Microsoft Digital Dashboard as the mechanism of information delivery. Working with IT development, they customize the Outlook Today environment according to various profiles. The report administrator is made responsible for making sure the reports are delivered to the right user. For example, the financial managers responsible for external accounting have their own profile. When they open Outlook, they have a new Outlook Today page with links to categories most common to their areas of responsibility, including reporting, projects, resources, investments, and so forth. This setup is illustrated in Figure 17–3.

Now, when the financial managers choose the Reports category, they will have links to the financial reports they need for accrual, reconciliation, and currency reporting. By selecting Financial Reports in their Digital Dashboard, they receive a report tree, which is illustrated in Figure 17–4.

Now, when the period reports need to be accessed, the financial managers merely have to select the report. Since these Excel reports have been created with ActiveSheets, the information is dynamically updated whenever they open the report. The ActiveSheets report is shown in Figure 17–5.

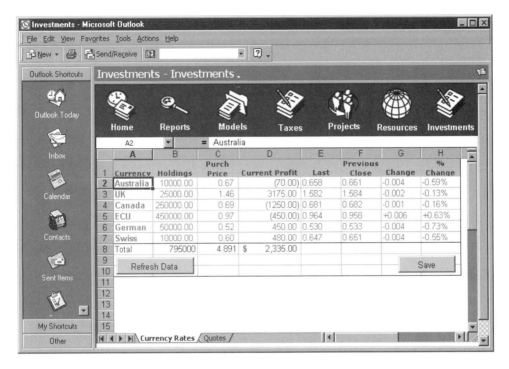

▶ **Figure 17–3**   Financial Manager User Profile

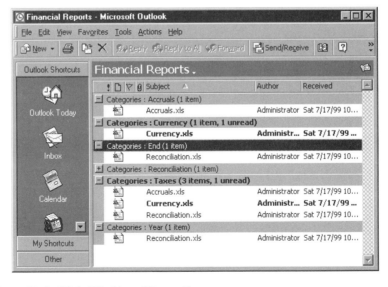

▶ **Figure 17–4**   Digital Dashboard Report Tree

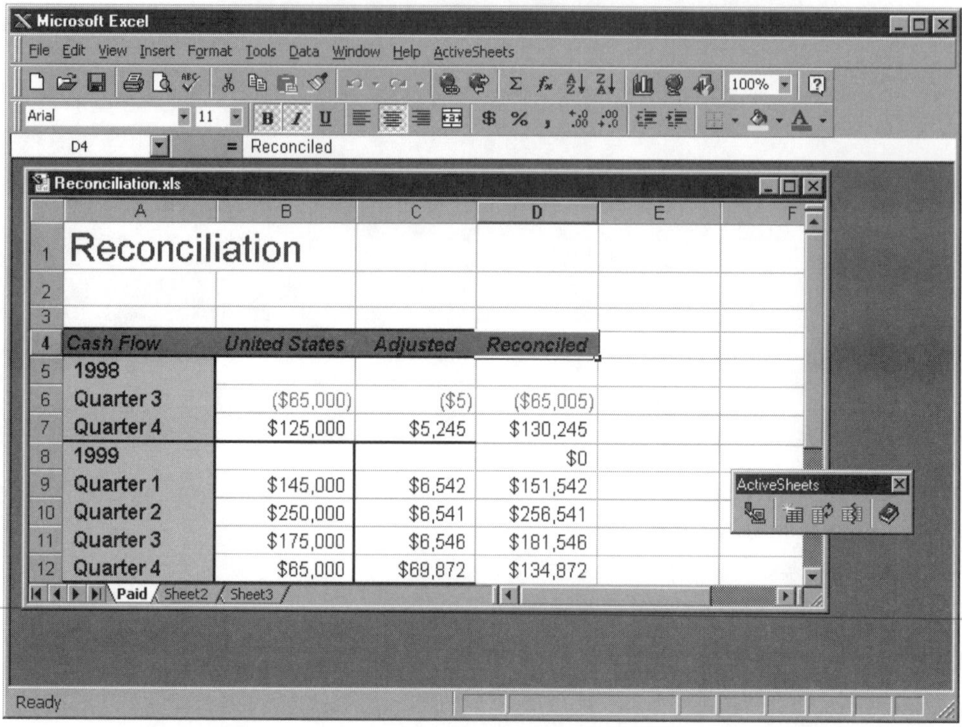

▶ **Figure 17–5**   ActiveSheets Report in Digital Dashboard

The advantage of this delivery system is that now the end users of the report have it localized in the dashboard area. They can modify or customize the views as they like, but the content will remain the same. This way, the district managers have tighter control over the new reporting process, and the end users are better focused on which reports to use.

17.2   CIRCULATION

Once a mechanism for distribution is decided upon, the logistics of information delivery is the next step to consider in the Publishing phase. A good circulation plan takes into account such issues as:

• What permissions are necessary for which users?
• Is there a routing procedure?

- When and how often does the report get used?
- Who gets the report and when?
- What are the roles or views that need to be set up?

The first priority of a circulation plan is, of course, that the report gets to the target user groups. An effective communication strategy for the report also needs to be created. Ongoing updates and pertinent information should be circulated to the many constituencies involved in the creation and delivery of the report. A circulation plan needs to be in place to channel this information to the appropriate members of the organization. Information may include:

- Updates to business sponsors of the report
- Summaries to users
- General updates to the organization
- Correspondence to IS management
- Communications among implementation team members
- Administrative updates and reports

Role-Based Reporting with the Microsoft Digital Dashboard

As discussed earlier, in role-based information delivery, the business information is organized and structured according to "views." The views represent user types or profiles set up so that the user gets only information that is fitting with the user's role in the company or in the reporting process. Once a role has been assigned, associated with each user's position and responsibility, data can be accessed in various folders or directories that have been created for the user. These also should be customizable according to user preferences.

The Digital Dashboard can be configured according to user profiles. For each profile, a new Web page can be created to customize the content for various types of business users. While this can be a time-consuming process and heavy on IT development, once implemented the profiles can be easily administered. In this respect, other methods, such as an Information Portal, are better in defining profiles, because they only have to determine authorizations for certain kinds of content. Also, this method doesn't have the user-driven report capabilities of portals.

Figure 17–6 illustrates a potential user profile. Note that once again the categories of information have been conveniently ordered in Outlook Window Pane (Home, Reports, Resources, etc.). In this user profile example, a financial manager has important tax reports made available via the Taxes link. These reports

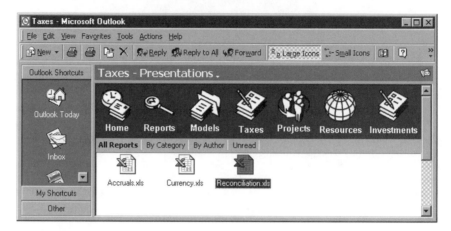

▶ **Figure 17–6**   Reports Available in User Profile

have been set up in Outlook folders and distributed to all financial managers with tax responsibilities.

17.3   *KNOWLEDGE TRANSFER*

The next step in the delivery process is to devise a strategy for how rollout, training, and feedback for the report will be conducted. The rollout plan should focus on creating and maintaining the rollout schedule, from initial training to the implementation of the report. To facilitate training, all materials should be located in a central area where they can be easily accessed by the report's consumers. Typically, this will be a menu item, in the Digital Dashboard screen, for example. In addition, all training activities need to be publicized and coordinated with training personnel. Finally, there should be a feedback system created for the continuous improvement of the report's content and use.

Rollout

The rollout schedule should consist of three components: time, audience, and materials. Time establishes the logistics of the rollout schedule— that is, when and where the training will take place. Ramp up time until the report is fully utilized should also be taken into account.

When examining the audience for a rollout, it is best to consider what the roles are for the report. Understanding the roles entails listing all of the report's consumers and grouping them by user types. Many times during a rollout, the administrator doesn't know exactly who the users are, but does have a profile outlining the user roles. These roles are defined by asking such questions as: If a variety of users need the report, how will their differing needs be addressed? Will some users require updates? Will others need full training? Do users outside the company need the report? What will they require?

The final component, materials, describes all information that exists outside the report itself. Examples of materials include documentation, announcements, training materials, video, email, and posters—all of which need to be implemented.

The following is a list of typical questions that the rollout plan should consider:

- What is the process for the rollout?
- What is the training schedule?
- Where will training be conducted?
- Who needs to be involved in the rollout?
- What materials need to be written?
- How will materials be transmitted?
- How will documentation be handled?
- Who is responsible for documentation/materials?

Collaboration with the Digital Dashboard

The administration of reports necessarily involves collaborating with a number of people, ranging from the original producers of the report, to application developers, to training personnel. Using the Digital Dashboard, developers can create a platform for this sort of collaboration. Figure 17–7 illustrates a "Team Folder" configuration, in which all of the main aspects of the project can be localized on a single Web page with links to important project folders.

The advantage of the approach just described lies in the clear focus of the team and project goals, as well as the localization of the information and improvement in communication among team members.

Training

In the Publishing phase, all training activities among the various levels of consumers for the report should be coordinated and publicized. Typically, training is a weak area in the reporting process, in part because it requires collaboration between and among different parts of the organization. But training is the key to the effective communication of the ideas in the report. When devising a training plan for the report, the following types of questions should be addressed:

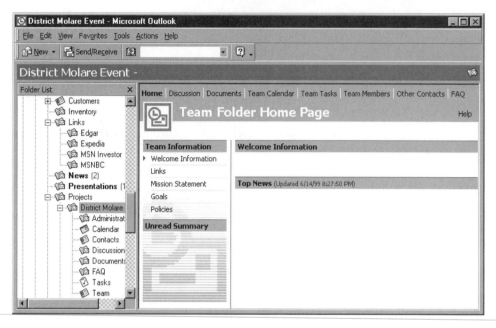

▶ **Figure 17–7**   Digital Dashboard Team Folder

- What training materials must be created?
- Who will require training?
- Where will training take place?
- What training materials will be available and where?
- After the rollout, what is the plan for training new end users?
- How will changes to the report be transferred?

The training system should be integrated so that producers, training personnel, and consumers are all in sync. Again, effective communication is key among all the groups involved. Department heads, report producers, or even HR personnel will need to make report administrators aware of new users of the report.

Training Libraries in the Digital Dashboard

One of the key advantages of the Digital Dashboard lies in its ability to easily link, consolidate, and organize documents. For training purposes, entire libraries of useful information can be collected and distributed according to user profile, project, team, or report subject.

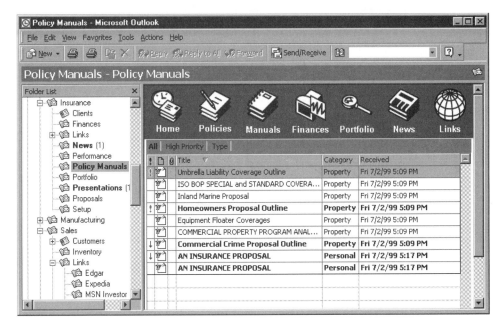

▶ **Figure 17–8** Digital Dashboard Training Library

Figure 17–8 illustrates a library of insurance-related documents and can be used to demonstrate models for various types of documents.

Feedback

All business processes, including the reporting process, must adapt to continuous change. Feedback is one of the primary tools for improving the reporting process. A good feedback system is important not only for troubleshooting, but for making sure that the report stays useful and relevant. In all stages of the MAPP process, there is a feedback loop, in which appropriate personnel are periodically consulted for approval. When Managing, for example, we submit a "scoping" document to get necessary input from managers and business sponsors of the report. In the Publishing stage, feedback from all consumers and producers of the report should be solicited. In order for all parties involved in the process of the report to voice their concerns, report managers must consider carefully the medium through which feedback will be solicited and delivered. Other feedback issues to consider are:

- Should a formal feedback document be created?
- Is a feedback forum appropriate?

- Who will be responsible for logging and responding to feedback?
- What is the routing procedure for types of feedback?
- How will common feedback concerns be converted into change?

Finally, we also recommend that a formal post-implementation assessment be conducted among the business users. This assessment should actively solicit feedback from users on issues such as deployment, training, and support. Our goal is to achieve immediate improvements in the initial stages of the report deployment.

Feedback Forum Using the Digital Dashboard

As business-to-employee communication moves from the server to the Internet, Web-based forums for feedback will become increasingly important. The Digital Dashboard can utilize the Web access feature in Exchange to enable "threaded" discussion groups, as shown in Figure 17–9. Web-based discussion groups allow users and consumers alike to monitor and participate in a range of issues such as content, technology, and process.

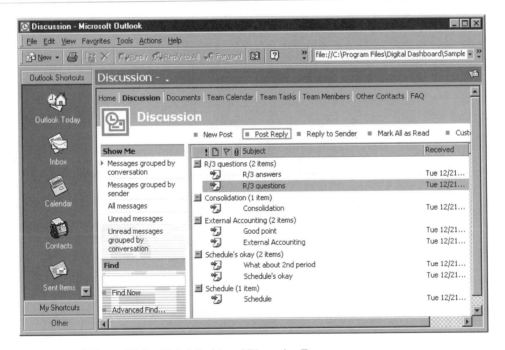

▶ **Figure 17–9**   Digital Dashboard Discussion Forum

17.4 INCREASING AWARENESS

After all the logistics of the delivery of the new report are in order, the last step in the Publishing phase is to devise a "marketing" plan to increase awareness about it. Increasing awareness is really nothing more than finding effective ways to publicize the activities surrounding the rollout, training, and continuous use of the report.

Certain facts of the report will need to be on hand to design an effective publicity campaign. A list of the users will need to be created, as well as a grouping by user types (for future users of the report). All matters relating to the reporting schedule must be clear. For example: When does the report have to be delivered? When is the rollout? When will training begin? Other useful facts to gather are:

- Who are the sponsors of the report?
- What purpose will the report serve?
- Where can people go to find out more?
- What are the important dates to remember?

After all the facts are collected, they will have to be documented and approved by the report producers and all others involved in the transmission of the report (IS, for example). Then, public relations documents will need to be written and distributed via appropriate channels. Media possibilities for distribution might include:

- Emails
- Web link
- Posters
- Presentations
- Meetings

Publicizing in Outlook

Perhaps the greatest single attribute of the Digital Dashboard is its ability to publicize information within and outside the organization. That users begin their browsing for information in the Outlook Today page allows for a high profile access to company information. Company news can be posted daily, hourly, or up to the minute.

Figure 17–10 demonstrates a potential news page for a healthcare company. This approach can be a very good use of building awareness of a report in a

▶ **Figure 17–10**   Company News

company. You can post information on the report to all constituencies according to their profile.

In addition, the Digital Dashboard can access the Outlook Calendar for team scheduling and announcements. Figure 17–11 illustrates the use of a team calendar to coordinate project activities. The Outlook Calendar can also be used for:

• Making group schedules available
• Posting significant events
• Listing training class schedules
• Sharing information
• Arranging online training events

▶ **Figure 17–11**   Digital Dashboard Calendar

18

Business-to-Business Reporting for R/3™ Financials

This chapter presents a business scenario that illustrates the importance of reporting in the financial management of a company in accordance with public accounting rules. We also examine the communication of that information to third parties, who either evaluate the information for their constituents or explain and compare the data for a particular industry or market.

First, we look at a business process for financial management and determine which kinds of information are needed to make decisions in the consolidation process. Next, we examine the requirements for reporting, define the reports, and delve into the strategy for distributing the information electronically to people within or outside the company.

18.1 THE CASE OF DASAUTO AG

DASAUTO AG (www.dasautoag.com) is a traditional manufacturing company of racing cars and high-performance street cars. The company targets its products to an exclusive audience of motor sport enthusiasts worldwide in the high-end auto market. The company's goals are to create a multinational network of distributors and to increase its production of cars targeted toward the consumer market by 25% a year over the next five years. The company has undergone considerable expansion in the last two years, which has led to problems in the consolidation of financial information. This information is needed to support its multinational management team and to explain the production and financial aspects of the company to employees and third parties. A public company traded in the US and Germany, DASAUTO AG must communicate information about the company to third parties in accordance with the accounting principles of both countries. Third parties such as banks, investment analysts, and specialized reporting companies then take the information about the company and share it with the company's constituents, private investors, and others who need to compare DASAUTO financial information with similar information collected from competitors and peers in the industry.

Consolidation in external accounting is a critical business process for DASAUTO AG. What's more, the company sees a unique opportunity to leverage the ebusiness environment created by the Internet and wireless networks to inform its investors and third-party business partners in a much more fluid and efficient manner. In order to do this, the company needs to have a state-of-the-art ebusiness reporting infrastructure for external accounting.

One of management's goals is to continue to increase stock price and performance in public equity markets. In order to do this, management needs to have a flexible reporting structure. In the past, DASAUTO AG has only been able to provide financial information on an end-of-quarter basis. The difficulties in collecting, consolidating, and sharing information has hindered the communication of accounting information greatly. The new system must enable management to see real-time information and share that information on a daily basis. Obviously, that information needs to be shared and processed in accordance with a set of security standards. Moreover, the company must have a better idea of which role the consumer has in the overall information supply chain. Managing this complexity presents a tremendous challenge to the SAP™ R/3™ team that has been chartered with creating a reporting infrastructure.

Financial Consolidation at DASAUTO AG

The diagram in Figure 18–1 illustrates a high-level overview of the financial consolidation process at DASAUTO AG.

Figure 18–1 illustrates the activities needed so that the DASAUTO management team can provide information for internal support purposes and sharing with third parties. The process consists of four main parts. The first part consists

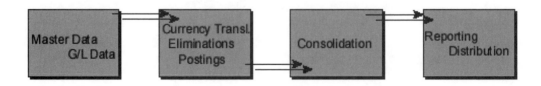

▶ **Figure 18–1** DASAUTO AG Consolidation Business Process

of collecting master data and general ledger data. The second involves preparation of the information, especially the process of incorporating the master data into the system for consolidation. This process has three main elements: translating the currency, posting the information (bringing new data into the general ledger system as a transaction), and making sure that the transactions are eliminated from the overall result. The next area is the actual consolidation. Consolidation entails bringing together similar types of information from a number of different subsidiaries and the currencies of those subsidiaries into one consolidated system. The last activities are the reporting and distribution processes, which involve creating standard reports and ad hoc reports. These reports help the management team and third parties to access and analyze the information that has been consolidated.

18.2 *MAPPing Phase I: Managing Information for the Financials Analysis Environment*

The goals of Phase I are to identify the:

- Business problem the reporting solution needs to solve
- Business process(es) upon which the reporting solution will focus
- Internet communication infrastructure the company will exploit
- Existing reporting tools that the solution can leverage (e.g., existing analyses in R/3™)
- Reporting tools that will need to be built or customized

The Situation at DASAUTO AG

When the new management team began two years ago at DASAUTO AG, the worldwide auto industry was depressed, and especially the market for high performance and luxury automobiles. Management not only had to deal with a difficult market, but also had to cope with an infrastructure that was based on a traditional manufacturing reporting environment and not geared toward communicating the financial results of the worldwide operation internally and externally. Furthermore, the management team needed to address the depressed value of the company in the stock market, which was at an all-time low, and needed to regain the confidence of the financial analysts who evaluate company performance. Lastly, the implementation of an improved manufacturing information technology from SAP™ AG brought better process optimization, but the system still left a gap in internal and external information delivery.

DASAUTO consists of 24 subsidiaries and sales offices scattered throughout the world, and these companies produce separate balance sheets in their own currency. The group's currency, however, is in US dollars. Exchange rates played an important role in the group's overall earnings of US dollars (196.6 million for the 1998 fiscal year). For management, these issues not only created a challenge for communicating the financial results quickly, but also created a barrier in understanding the pulse of the market in terms of foreign exchange and the exposure of the company to foreign exchange fluctuations. These fluctuations on a day-to-day and even hourly basis could have a tremendous impact on the company's bottom line.

Fritz Hoffmann, the CEO of the company for the past two years, had his yearly review of the company's financials and the internal infrastructure available to support the company's goal of growing top line revenue at a 25% a year clip. He called together his top financial analysts and his internal IT management team to understand the new SAP™ R/3™ system. The financial analysts very quickly pinpointed the financial consolidation process as one of the key barriers to information. The failure to provide this information in a very timely manner to top management and to other sources and targets in the market was seriously affecting the organization. For its part, IT was frustrated by the fact that the duration and difficulty of implementing the SAP™ R/3™ system in manufacturing made it difficult for IT to solve the financial reporting problems. In order to achieve the company goals, it was obvious to all that the financial analysts would have to have a greater role in creating the information that they needed for managing, sharing, and distributing that information among themselves and with third parties.

Business Needs Analysis for DASAUTO AG

Fritz decided to augment his internal resources with outside agencies to help him create the types of information that he could use for internal and external purposes. Many of the company's original SAP™ R/3™ implementation consultants have moved on to other projects, leaving an SAP™ knowledge gap behind. However, he wanted an information and knowledge management system that better reflected the business process optimization his company had experienced due to the introduction of SAP™ R/3™. He also wanted the information to reflect the surge of interest in the company's products that was coming from their very modern Website. One of the traditional weaknesses of enterprise intelligence reporting is that it fails to integrate information from the Internet into the ERP infrastructure. Hence, Fritz also wanted to introduce an outside perspective into the information development. He decided to work more closely with the company's investor relations agency and the financial accounting firm that creates and audits the balance sheet and financial report that DASAUTO shares with the financial community.

The data that Fritz needs is stored in a number of areas throughout the company. The SAP™ R/3™ system contains performance indicators and comprehensive results and information about the company and items that have material effects on the operation. These include the liquid funds, receivables, inventories, fixed assets, liabilities (short term and long term), and information about the equity structure. SAP™ is the primary general ledger system for the company.

The second source of information is an array of proprietary software products and database systems that are used in markets where the company has no manufacturing, but only a sales infrastructure. These include sales force automation, customer tracking, and sales supports systems. It also includes smaller financial accounting packages and some homegrown applications built in Microsoft Office's Visual Basic for Applications (VBA) programming environment. Through the introduction of an automobile configuration software, the company has been able to attract consumer interest to its Web site, plus collect information about the desires of these customers for certain products. It has also helped the company to determine which types of affiliations are important for the consumers. Although this is not a traditional financial reporting item, Fritz and his team feel it is an important indicator of future financial performance and a sales indicator. Hence, the company would like to find a way to explain this Website business information alongside its traditional financial reports.

Finally, there are a number of data sources that provide information about the market and DASAUTO competitors such as BMW and Ferrari. This information would also need to be included in a consolidated fashion so that DASAUTO can compare itself to other companies in the industry.

The communication of information is a critical business need that drives the effort to create a more efficient financial consolidation in DASAUTO. Fritz was able to identify two areas that have been having a great impact on the company's bottom line:

- Safeguarding the company against exchange rate fluctuations
- Creating a better understanding of the company's risk management on a day-to-day basis due to investments in a number of short term, high yield instruments in the company portfolio

Under the old system, exchange rate fluctuation and risk management created great dangers for the management team because the ability to get information about both was on a month-to-month basis. Often the fluctuations of currency exchange rates were such that the companies had to react without any pertinent information about the effects of exchange rates on the bottom line.

Creating an information system that better aligns the needs of the company with the business process for financial consolidation is one way of addressing the issues facing Fritz and his management team.

Identifying Business Processes

Using the SAP™ R/3™ ASAP Business Engineer, Fritz's team was able to get a graphical description of the business processes that are related to the financial consolidation process, and which are contained in the R/3™ Reference Model. (For a detailed discussion, see SAP™ R/3™ Business Blueprint, 2e.) After working with his financial advisory team, Fritz was able to determine how the financial consolidation was done in the system. In financial consolidation, data is taken from the general ledger in the R/3™ system and processed in a specialized data table which contains summary information of all parts of the business. In addition, other information related to the company that may or may or not be in the general ledger must also be added so that summary information reflects the true financial health of the company.

Creating the right master data for homogeneous information reporting entails setting up the consolidation rules. This business logic is critical to the entire information creation and delivery process. The team at DASAUTO will have to face a number of complex challenges. For instance, they will have to understand and respond to the financial performance of the company by geography, different organizational units, and sales channel opportunities. In doing this, they will be able to identify trends and respond better to the risks that have been having a large impact on the balance sheet.

The financial consolidation rules are the core framework for the business logic that the management team will use for preparing the information. Consolidation is crucial for two reasons:

- Communicating company financials for external accounting purposes
- Communicating company financial performance for managerial (internal) accounting purposes

The main things to be done in this area include setting up a chart of accounts, reporting on the list of companies, reporting validation checks, checking to see whether the data is completely integrated into the SAP™ R/3™ system, making rules for currency translations, and valuations and adjustments. Adherence to a number of different accounting standards is also important. In particular, the Financial Accounting Standards Board (FASB) and the International Accounting Standards Committee (IASC) have a number of rules and requirements that are especially important when DASAUTO AG prepares the financial information for external sources. In other words, this system has to keep track of the changing environment and the legal and statutory accounting requirements.

Because the SAP™ R/3™ system contains much of this business logic, the consolidation scenario is used to optimize this business process at DASAUTO. The currency exchange rates are very important to the system, especially in the context of understanding currency exposure risks. The reporting system will need to carefully handle the currency Euro, which is an amalgamation of currencies in the European market that was thrust upon the management team this year. Because the Euro has witnessed an exchange rate fluctuation to almost parity with the US dollar over the past six months, the management team has looked at a potentially larger than 10% change in the value of their inventory in Euro.

Two other key aspects of this business process are:

- Currency translation method
- Data from subsidiaries or companies and sales offices that don't have direct access to R/3™

In order to facilitate the data entry, the headquarters financial team at DASAUTO has allowed the individual countries to input information in their own language. This could further complicate the consolidation process, but the financial team feels that they have the resources with SAP™ R/3™ to tackle a number of different languages, including French, English, German, Japanese, and Spanish.

Having the real-time "pulse" of the company, along with the ability to have ad hoc information about the entire company's financial exposure and financial health, is a critical requirement for the new reporting system. DASAUTO AG made a decision early on to work with MS Excel and the Internet as a way of facilitating the real-time data access. In addition, Fritz would like to use some of the abundance of telecommunications capabilities to help deliver summary information to key employees throughout the world. The main parts of this business process, which is called Active Reporting, include:

- Loading the appropriate programs into MS Excel and the Internet
- Logging onto the R/3™ system so that a live connection can take place
- Selecting the information that needs to be included in the report
- Selecting a standard business template from a central Internet server
- Defining the areas which need to be handled in the report
- Determining different methods of calculations
- Distributing the information to a number of different people and products such as MS Excel, MS Outlook, and HTML versions of these reports.

Identifying Roles

DASAUTO AG realized there would be different audiences for the reporting information that was to be prepared around the consolidation of financials at the company. Fritz concentrated on the areas that he felt would lead to immediate improvement in the bottom line and the communication of DASAUTO's information to third parties. The identified roles were:

- Chief Executive Officer
- Chief Financial Officer
- Country managers
- Country general managers
- Public relations and investor relations agencies
- Financial accounting company and consulting groups
- Web commerce portals that provide financial information, including Thestreet.com
- Primary financial information consolidators such as Firstcall
- Company shareholders
- Partners that help DASAUTO manage the currency exchange risk (mySAP.com and CFOWEB.com)

The resulting roles analysis is illustrated in Figure 18–2.

Reporting Needs Analysis

One of the main things that the management team would like to have is a consolidated source of information about all financials of the company so that the external accounting reports can be produced. Second, the company management would like to have access to real-time data for exchange rates and for prices of investment instruments that they have in their asset base. They want to be able to take the pulse of the company at any time, just as they are able to do with the stock market. Since the financial team in the company is made up of MS Excel users, they would like to use the product to build further analytics and understand the interrelationships of some of the information from within Excel. They would also like to publish this information over the Internet so that a number of third parties, including press and investors, can have access to it.

In particular, one of the ideas that Fritz has is to provide this information as a real-time data ticker over the Internet, WebTV, telephone network. In order to do that the company needs to have a number of interfaces to telecom providers.

From the business needs and the as-is analysis, it was clear that DASAUTO AG needed a reporting environment that could:

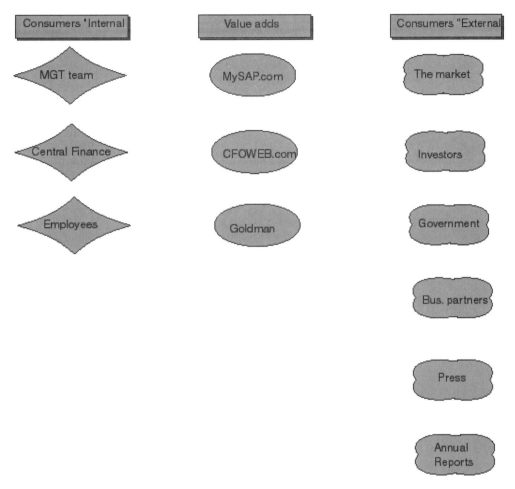

▶ **Figure 18–2** DASAUTO Roles and Profiles

- Assimilate data from multiple sources
- Provide real-time access to operational data
- Use standard desktop reporting tools such as Microsoft Excel, and a Web browser such as Netscape Navigator or Internet Explorer
- Allow data to be published to wireless devices

Analyzing DASAUTO's Reporting Data Requirements

Fritz and his team took a long hard look at the reporting requirements for the company, and were able to separate these into internal and external reports (see Table 18–1). They found that some external reports are also important for internal consumption. In particular, external accounting dictates a number of formal reports that the finance team needs to prepare and communicate. In addition, there a number of internal reports that are used to help the management team create a consistent explanation of the numbers and also make better decisions about the day-to-day operations of the company.

Table 18–1   DASAUTO Reporting Requirements

Report	Data Source	Role Supported	Description
P&L Period Costing	Consolidated G/L R/3™ External data from other G/Ls	CEO CFO Division Managers	Profit and loss statement
Payables/Receivables by Country	Consolidated G/L R/3™ External data from other G/Ls	CFO Accounting	Account payables and receivables summary
Equity Items	Consolidated G/L R/3™ External data from other G/Ls	CEO CFO Finance Investor relations	Breakdown of company equity items
Balance Sheet	Consolidated G/L R/3™ External data from other G/Ls	CFO CEO Investor relations Wall Street All key employees	Balance sheet report in public accounting standard
Balance sheet report by country	Consolidated G/L R/3™ External data from other G/Ls	CFO CEO Investor relations The market All key employees	Balance sheet report in public accounting standard according to individual country requirements

18.3   MAPPING PHASE II: ANALYZE THE FINANCIAL REPORTING SOLUTION

In phase two of MAPPing, we analyze the data required to build meaningful reports. By analyzing business information available within the SAP™ system or accessible elsewhere in other systems, you can produce a detailed description of the reporting solution(s) you need to provide. In this phase, we define the:

- Business objects used in the report
- Time (periods) to cover in the report
- Organization entities, or units, for which the report is valid
- Characteristics, key figures, and ratios that we use in the report

Business Objects

A business object can be a valuable source of information for organizing information in your report because it identifies the report's main data point. The business object gives a high-level, aggregate view of the data required in the report, an important advantage in building reporting solutions. The following business objects are important for financial accounting information:

- General ledger
- Company
- Accounts payable ledger
- Accounts receivable ledger
- Fixed asset account

Time Periods

In enterprise reporting, performance is usually measured in relation to a particular time period, whether by month, quarter, or fiscal year. Identifying an appropriate time period can answer important questions about performance, such as, "Are we performing better than last year/last month?"

It is important to identify the time periods for which the report is valid. While a typical report contains month-to-month comparisons, your users may need access to data that is more current, down to the week, day, or minute.

For the most part, SAP™ provides you with access to up-to-the-minute data. However, for performance reasons, your site may decide to update the records at less frequent intervals.

You also will need to determine how many previous years' data you require. Many SAP™ installations store one prior year of data, with summary records for previous years. While this is sufficient for most business needs, you may need to reach back further into the past if, for example, you are asked to develop a trend analysis. Reporting periods may be defined for:

- Fiscal year
- Fiscal period
- Calendar week
- Calendar month
- Calendar day

Organizational Units

In R/3™ financial business processes, the following organizational entities are important:

- Company
  An independent legal entity. The company is the base unit for which financial statements are prepared for legal consolidation. Companies might include subsidiaries, joint ventures, and affiliates. For internal consolidation, the company might have further subsets, such as a division or region.
- Company code
  The legal entity responsible for payment for the goods or service. The company code is used to record all relevant transactions and generate all supporting documents for the legally required financial statements, such as balance sheets and profit and loss statements.
- Business area
  An area utilized for flexible financial reporting purposes, such as reporting across company code boundaries. Business areas are consolidation units, which are necessary for consolidation and rollup. A business area is used for performing eliminations and generating closing statements.
- Subgroup
  A consolidated entity whose consolidation units represent companies. Subgroups are used to eliminate a parent's investment against an investee's equity. Typically, subgroups are used for reclassifications on a group level or consolidation of investments.
- Consolidation group
  Business organization consisting of two or more companies. Consolidation groups are grouped and defined according to an organization's individual needs. Any of the organizational units listed here may serve as units of a consolidation group.
- Trading partners
  A legally independent company belonging to a group. A trading partner may be an organizational unit of the consolidation group.

Organization at DASAUTO AG

Figure 18–3 illustrates the organizational structure of DASAUTO AG, split into subgroups and companies.

The management team at DASAUTO AG organized the worldwide company operations into five groups including North America, Asia, Europe, Latin America, and Rest of World. The North America and Rest of World groups run their balance sheet in US dollars. Each of the other groups uses a different currency.

With the exception of North America and Europe, both of which have fully operational R/3™ systems, many of the sales offices input data into MS Excel and subsequently upload the data into R/3™. Fritz would like to see this process automated, possibly using the Internet, so that he can have the whole picture at any point in time. Sharing the information with the entire sales team and country management creates a "pull" effect for information, because everyone in the company wants to be part of the information curve.

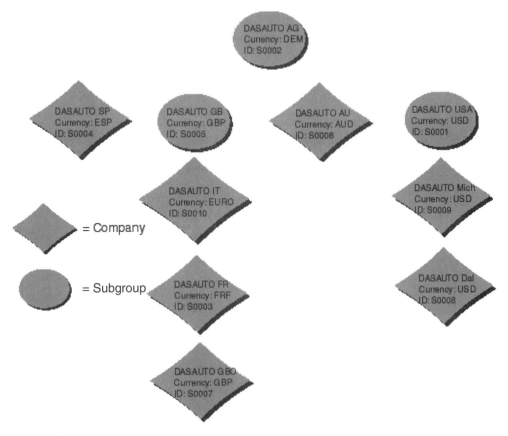

▶ **Figure 18–3**   Organization at DASAUTO AG

Characteristics

Characteristics tell us what must be analyzed in the report. Characteristics are used to summarize different types of information, such as "Material."

Business objects and organizational units are actually two examples of the characteristics you can use in your reports. In purchasing, for example, the purchase order and the purchasing organization are both examples of characteristics.

Key Figures and Ratios

Key figures and ratios are the statistical values used to forecast or measure performances, such as the "total value of ordered material by plant." They normally take the form of a quantity or value, and are expressed in a currency or unit of measure or as a percentage. Key figures and ratios might include:

- Book value
- Price/earnings ratio
- Dividend yield
- Earnings per share
- Current ratio
- Acid test ratio
- Debt ratio
- Net income return on sales
- Rate of return on total assets
- Accounts receivable turnover
- Inventory turnover
- Inventory to working capital
- Current liabilities to inventory

The Financial Report Analysis at DASAUTO AG

The financial reporting team at DASAUTO AG used the information from the Manage phase to determine the requirements for building the financial consolidation report solution. After analyzing the available data, they summarized the information in the report in Table 18–2.

The next step was to make sure that the data was appropriately organized into a report by assembling the raw data used in the report, and providing the report with the data summarized by characteristic (business object and organizational unit), ratio, and time.

Table 18–2   Data for Report

Business Object	Organizational Unit	Ratio/Key Figure	Time
General ledger	Company code	G/L account	Weekly
Consolidation	Master data	Statements	Monthly
Customer account	Customer	Account balance	Weekly
Accounts payable	Vendor	Bill of exchange	Monthly
Accounts receivable	Customer	Customer account	Daily
Reconciliation	Company code	Account balance	Quarterly

18.4   MAPPING PHASE III: PRESENT THE REPORT SOLUTION

In this phase, you create the report using the raw data and report definitions defined in the Analyze phase. This is the point at which you actually create the reports and validate them with your users.

Creating the Report Template

Think of the report template as the prototype of your report. While the actual report may be created in a variety of media, such as an SAP™ report, an Excel spreadsheet, a Web page in HTML, or a presentation in hard copy, we recommend that you design a template in electronic form because you will constantly return to the template as you make changes and improvements to the report. The following reports are defined in the SAP™ R/3™ system.

To create an R/3™ Balance Sheet report template:

1. From the Information Systems menu, select Accounting, then Financial Accounting.
   The Financial Accounting Information System window opens.
2. From the Consolidation menu, select Totals Report.
   The Restrictions window opens.
3. Enter subgroup, version, and year. If using the IDES system, enter `SWW`, `101, 1995`.
4. From the Totals report hierarchy tree, select Standard reports > External reports > Balance sheet

5. If using the IDES system, navigate to the following report: Balance sheet w/ structure pct. > Scherenz World Wide > FI-LC simulation – Exch.rates > Year 1995, prd: 012, LT 123. This is illustrated in Figure 18–4.

6. Enter the subgroup, fiscal year, period, and version, as shown in Figure 18–5.

7. Click Execute.

A balance sheet report is created. A sample balance sheet for DASAUTO AG is shown in Figure 18–6.

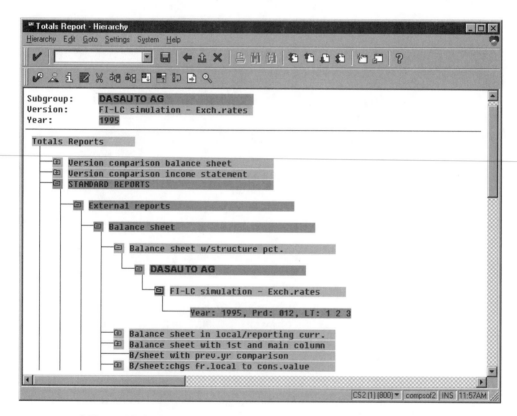

▶ **Figure 18–4**   Totals Report Hierarchy

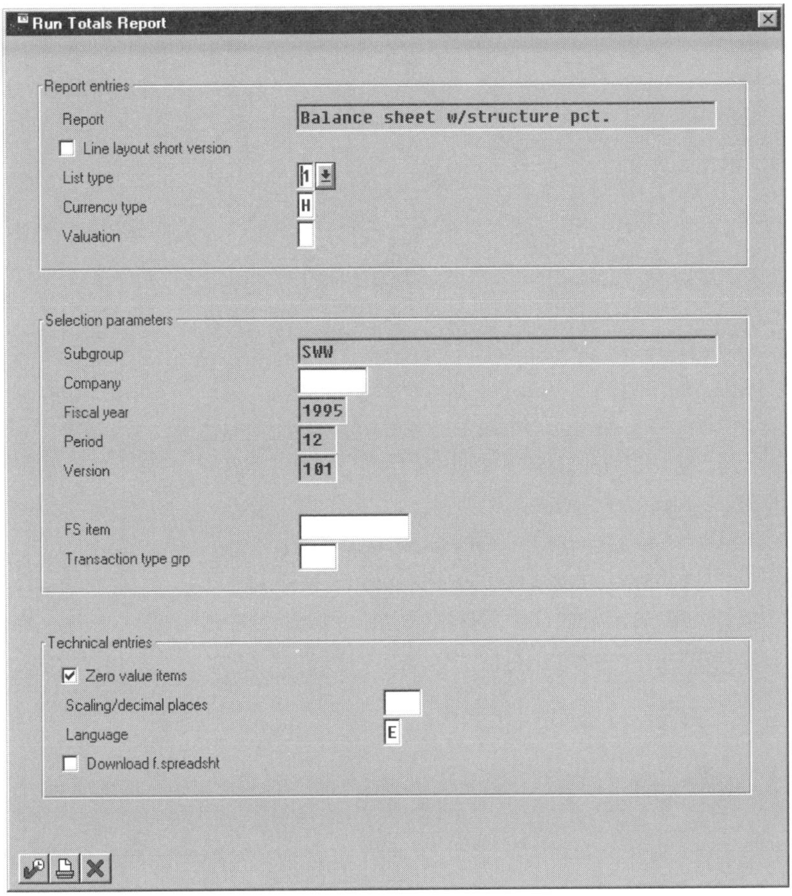

Figure 18–5 IDES Data for Balance Sheet Report

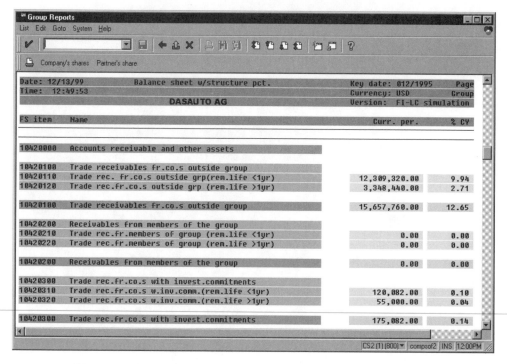

▶ **Figure 18–6**   DASAUTO Balance Sheet Report

To create an R/3™ Changes in Investee Equity report template:

1. From the Information Systems menu, select Accounting, then Financial Accounting.
   The Financial Accounting Information System window opens.
2. From the Consolidation menu, select Select report.
   The Application report tree window opens.
3. Select Financial reporting data, then select Equity, as in Figure 18–7.
4. If using the IDES system, run the Changes in Investee Equity Report.
5. Enter the subgroup, fiscal year, period, and version, as shown in Figure 18–8.
6. Execute the report.
   Figure 18–9 illustrates a sample Changes in Investee Equity report template.

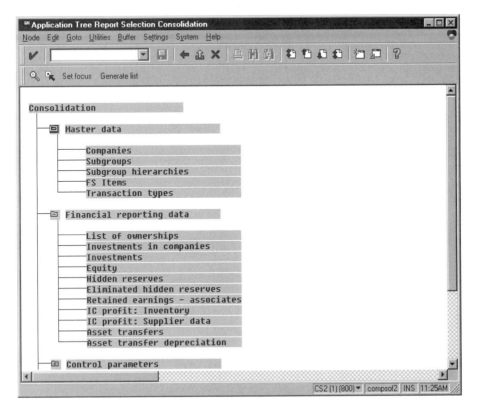

▶ **Figure 18–7**   Application Tree Report Selection

Excel Reports

At DASAUTO AG, internal and external constituents need to access information in the purchasing report using Microsoft Excel. To achieve this, they use Active-Financials to define Excel workbooks for financial reports.

To create the P&L Report:

1. Open Excel, with the ActiveFinancials menu and toolbar displayed.
2. From the Financials menu, select Launch QuickReports.
3. Logon to your R/3™ system.
4. A version/year dialog displays.

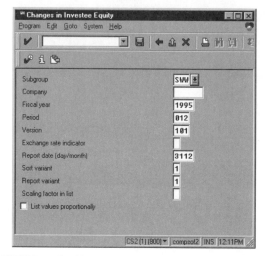

▶ **Figure 18–8**   IDES Data for Changes in Investee Equity Report

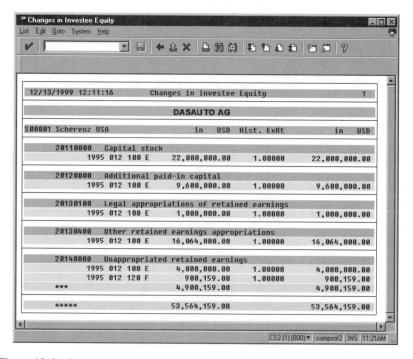

▶ **Figure 18–9**   DASAUTO AG Changes in Investee Equity Report Template

5. Select the version and year of the report you are creating. If using the IDES System, select FI-LC simulation – Exch. Rates as the version and 1995 as the year.

6. Choose Scherenz Germany from the Hierarchy view.

7. Select the Reports tab.

8. From the Report Selection pane, select the Inc. Stmt- period costing 2010 report.

9. Drag the report and drop it into a Microsoft Word document.

10. The P&L Report displays, as in Figure 18–10.

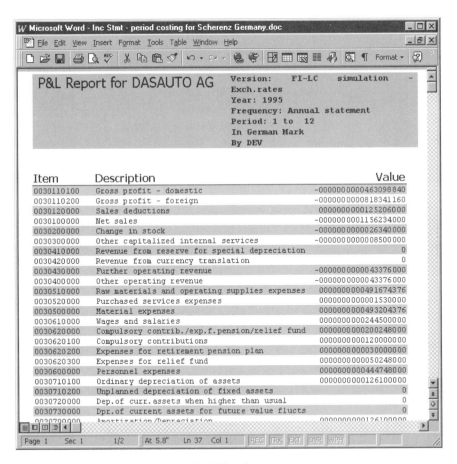

▶ **Figure 18–10** P&L Report for DASAUTO AG

To create the Balance Sheet by Country Report:

1. Open Excel, with the ActiveFinancials menu and toolbar displayed.
2. From the Financials menu, select Consolidation Wizard.
   The Consolidation Report Wizard displays.
3. Click Next.
   The next page of the Wizard displays.
4. Select the Balance Sheet radial button and click on Next.
   The next page of the Wizard displays.
5. Select the year and version. If using the IDES system, select year 1995 and FI-LC simulation – Exch. Rates. Then click Next.
   The next page of the Wizard displays.
6. Select the company and subgroup. If using IDES, select Scherenz Germany, then Click Next.
   The next page of the Wizard displays.
7. Select the following information: period 12, annual statement, local currency, and As Values. Click Next.
   The next page of the Wizard displays.
8. Click Finish.
   The Wizard places the report in Excel, as illustrated in Figure 18–11.

To create the Payables/Receivables Report:

1. Open Excel, with the ActiveFinancials menu and toolbar displayed.
2. From the Financials menu, select Launch QuickReports.
3. Logon to your R/3™ system.
   A version/year dialog displays.
4. Select the version and year of the report you are creating. If using the IDES System, select FI-LC simulation – Exch. Rates as the version and 1995 as the year.
5. Choose Scherenz Germany from the Hierarchy view.
6. Select the Reports tab.
7. From the Report Selection pane, select the Payables/Receivables 4060 report.
8. Drag the report and drop it into a Microsoft Word document.
   The Payables/Receivables Report displays, as in Figure 18–12.

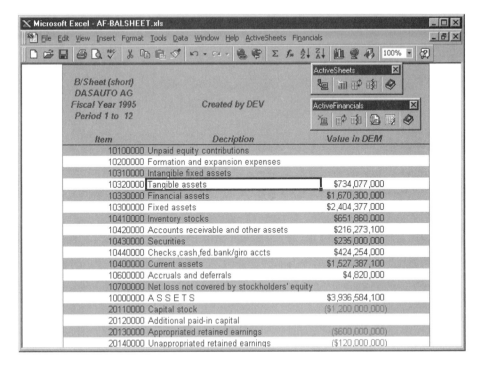

▶ **Figure 18–11**   DASAUTO Balance Sheet Report

To create the Equity Items Report:

1. Open Excel, with the ActiveFinancials menu and toolbar displayed.
2. From the Financials menu, select Launch QuickReports.
3. Logon to your R/3™ system.
   A version/year dialog displays.
4. Select the version and year of the report you are creating. If using the IDES System, select FI-LC simulation – Exch. Rates as the version and 1995 as the year.
5. Choose Scherenz Germany from the Hierarchy view.
6. Select the Reports tab.
7. From the Report Selection pane, select the Equity Items report.
8. Drag and drop the report into a Microsoft Word document.
9. The Equity Items Report displays, as in Figure 18–13.

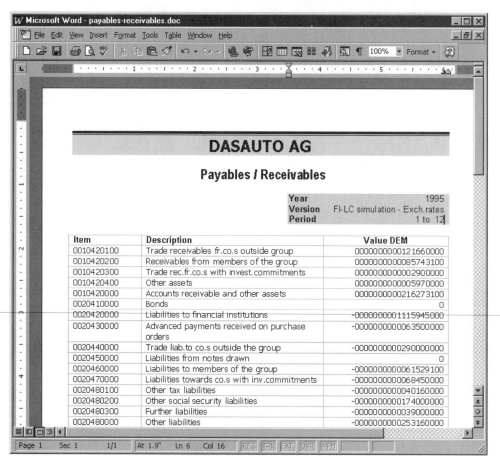

▶ **Figure 18–12**   DASAUTO AG Payables/Receivables (QuickReports)

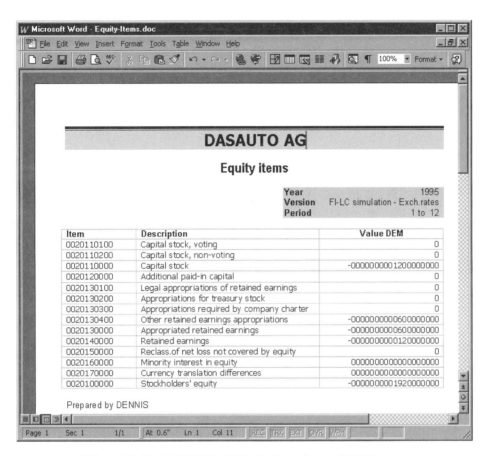

▶ Figure 18–13   DASAUTO AG Equity Items Report (QuickReports)

18.5   *MAPPing Phase IV: Publish the Report Solution*

In this section we examine how financial reports are distributed to the decision makers along the financial business processes at DASAUTO AG. In the Publishing phase of the MAPP process, the following sorts of questions need to be addressed:

- Are there special media concerns?
- What is the most effective media, given the audience and the uses of the report?
- What information needs to go to what users?
- Who needs what authorizations?
- When does the report need to be delivered?
- What is the routing schedule?
- In what order will the report be received?
- What is the process for the rollout?
- What is the training schedule?

Media

Crucial to the success of report publishing is the choice of medium. The medium must take into consideration all the users as well as possible uses of the report. If the report will be employed differently by different users, more than one medium may be needed to fulfill all the report requirements. For example, some users may need the report delivered in Microsoft Office; others may need remote access capabilities. Whatever the case, the earlier stages of the reporting process will have identified who needs the report, for what purposes, and when.

Publishing Media for DASAUTO AG

As we indicated earlier, DASAUTO AG's reporting requirements have several components. One of the main things that the management team would like to have is a consolidated source of information about all financials of the company so that the external accounting reports can be produced. Second, the company management would like to have access to real-time data for exchange rates and for prices of investment instruments that they have in their asset base. Since the financial team in the company works in MS Excel, they would like to use the product to build further analytics and understand the interrelationships of some of the information from within Excel. Moreover, an ERP reporting tool was not desired because the people using the reports were often not in the same company. Thus, Excel was chosen as the presentation medium.

Another goal was to have the capability of publishing this information over the Internet so that a number of third parties, including press and investors, could have access to it. Moreover, management was seeking to have a more flexible reporting structure. In the past, DASAUTO AG has been able to provide financial information only on an end-of-quarter basis. The difficulties in collecting, consolidating, and sharing information hindered the communication of accounting information. The new system had to enable management to see real-time information and share that information on a daily basis.

All of these challenges led DASAUTO to choose the Microsoft Digital Dashboard as the primary publishing medium. With Excel as the presentation medium and with the Internet capabilities of the MS Digital Dashboard, management felt that they had come upon the best delivery solution available in the market. Using the ActiveFinancials component, they would have real-time data available in Excel spreadsheets. They would distribute these according to roles, using the Digital Dashboard as a company Web portal. Figure 18–14 illustrates an ActiveFinancials report in the Digital Dashboard browser.

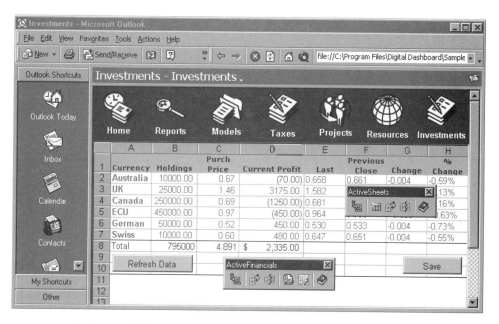

▶ **Figure 18–14**   Digital Dashboard and ActiveSheets Report

Circulation Plan

The circulation plan concentrates on the actual information delivery. A good circulation plan must take into account such issues as:

- What are the roles or views that need to be set up?
- What permissions are necessary for which users?
- Is there a routing procedure?
- When and how often does the report get used?
- Who gets the report and when?

The Circulation Plan at DASAUTO AG

Given the many different types of procurement reports and different users of the reports, DASAUTO decided to implement a role-based publishing plan. In role-based information delivery, the business information is organized and structured according to "views." The views represent user types or profiles set up so that the user gets only information that is fitting with the roles of the user in the company or in the reporting process. Once each user has been assigned a role associated with his or her position and responsibility, the users can access the data in various self-created directories. Figure 18–15 shows a user profile in the Digital Dashboard, which has been configured by role (District Manager). Note the personalization (stock ticker) and Outlook features (messages, inbox, tasks) that help make it a custom delivery solution.

Using a role-based delivery solution, the DASAUTO team came up with the circulation plan shown in Table 18–3.

Training

The last consideration of the Publishing plan is to devise a schedule and system for the rollout and training plan for the report. When devising a training plan for the report, the following types of questions should be addressed:

- What training materials must be created?
- Who will require training?
- What groups need which kind of training?
- How will the rollout training be scheduled?
- Where will training take place?
- What training materials will be available and where?

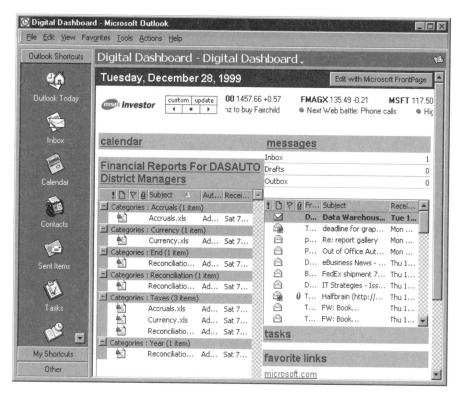

▶ **Figure 18–15**   Digital Dashboard District Manager Profile

- After the rollout, what is the plan for training new end users?
- How will changes to the report be transferred?

The training system should be integrated so that all members of the reporting team are in sync. Again, effective communication is key among all the groups involved.

Training at DASAUTO AG

Having isolated the basic needs for training of the report, the training group at DASAUTO puts together the plan shown in Table 18–4 that will eventually be submitted for final approval.

Table 18–3   DASAUTO's Role-Based Publishing Plan

User	Role	Report	Frequency
Jack Ham	CFO	P&L Period Costing	Daily
Lester Montgomery	Division Manager	P&L Period Costing	Daily
Fritz Hoffmann	CEO	Payables/Receivables by Country Equity Items Balance Sheet	Weekly
Maria Dominick	Investor	Equity Items	Weekly
Lloyd Winslow	Market Analyst	Balance Sheet	Daily
Emily Dominiani	Accounting	Payables/Receivables	Weekly
Harriet Moore	Division Manager	P&L	Daily
Greta Holzmann	Finance	Equity Items	Weekly
Conrad Dawkins	Investor	Equity Items	Daily
Frank Plasner	Market Analyst	Balance Sheet	Daily
Sara Spencer	Division Manager	P&L	Daily

Table 18–4   Report Rollout and Training

User	Role	Report	Rollout Group	Training
Jack Ham	CFO	P&L Period Costing	Group C	Hands on
Lester Montgomery	Division Manager	P&L Period Costing	Group C	Hands on
Fritz Hoffmann	CEO	Payables/Receivables by Country Equity Items Balance Sheet	Group C	Hands on
Maria Dominick	Investor	Equity Items	Group C	Hands on
Lloyd Winslow	Market Analyst	Balance Sheet	Group B	SAP™ CBT/Video
Emily Dominiani	Accounting	Payables/Receivables	Group B	SAP™ CBT/Video
Harriet Moore	Division Manager	P&L	Group B	SAP™ CBT/Video
Greta Holzmann	Finance	Equity Items	Group B	SAP™ CBT/Video
Conrad Dawkins	Investor	Equity Items	Group A	Hands on
Frank Plasner	Market Analyst	Balance Sheet	Group A	Online
Sara Spencer	Division Manager	P&L	Group A	Online

SECTION 5

eBusiness Solutions

The new Internet economy has radically altered the business landscape, transforming how businesses interact with customers, conduct core business processes, and support knowledge management across the organization. To successfully conduct e-commerce on the Web, companies need to develop business applications that effectively build a real-time collaborative environment with their customers and partners. A sales rep, for example, may want to check her quota numbers via a wireless device. A customer wants to check on the progress of an order. A partner seeks information on the availability of a product. All of these tasks need to happen seamlessly and in real-time.

The following reporting solutions are designed to help you think about the kinds of reports that can help you improve R/3™ information management in your company. All of the reports were created using the ActiveSheets software program and an R/3™ system. The advantages of such reports are their real-time data capabilities, their presentation application (Excel), and the ability to distribute the reports across the organization and beyond.

NOTE   All of these reports can be found in their Excel format in the CD enclosed with this book. Please see the appendices for working with ActiveSheets and accessing the Component Software R/3™ system.

19

Report Gallery

This chapter presents a gallery of useful report templates that can be created in Excel using R/3™ data and the ActiveSheets program. Each section contains a brief description of the template's business application and a summary of its pertinent features. All of these templates can be explored in greater detail by examining and using the Excel report templates located on the CD that comes with this book.

The following report templates are discussed:

- Budget Review
- Balance Sheet
- Commission Calculator
- Consolidated Balance Sheet
- Cost Center
- Customer
- Direct Expenses
- Human Resources
- Material
- Purchased Material
- Purchasing Negotiation
- Sales Employee
- Sales Office
- Sales Organization
- Sales Performance
- Shipping Point

19.1 BUDGET REVIEW

This report documents the budget numbers for a particular reporting group. Figure 19–1 illustrates a report that compares actual expenditures with amounts that have been allocated in the budget. Variances by dollar amount and percentage are also shown. You can get different numbers for a particular reporting group by choosing the reporting group from the drop-down menu. By selecting a different Report Type, you can also compare:

- Forecast versus Actual
- Actual versus Budgeted, year-to-date
- Actual versus Forecast, year-to-date

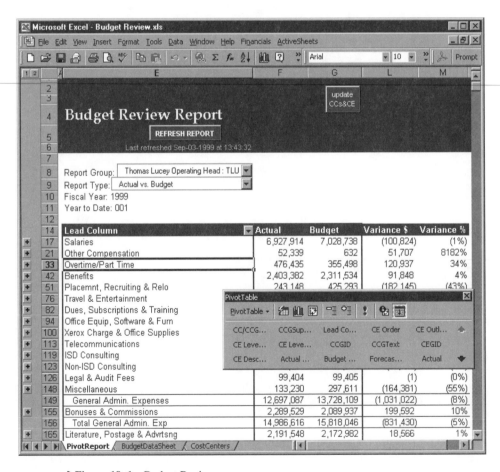

▶ **Figure 19–1** Budget Review

You can also utilize Excel's pivot table capabilities to modify the contents of the report. You can drag a button from the pivot table toolbar to the rows or columns on your report. For example, you can drag the Forecast button to a column to add the Forecast YTD column.

19.2   BALANCE SHEET REPORT

This balance sheet report template includes various worksheets related to the balance sheet that you can customize for your organization. The worksheets contain the main financial elements of a business enterprise, especially assets, liabilities, and stockholder equity. A data sheet of key financial components allows you to provide operating, expense, and financing data that link to other worksheets. The other worksheets include an Asset Chart, Balance Sheet, Income Chart, and Cash Flow Sheet. Figure 19–2 illustrates the Income Statement report.

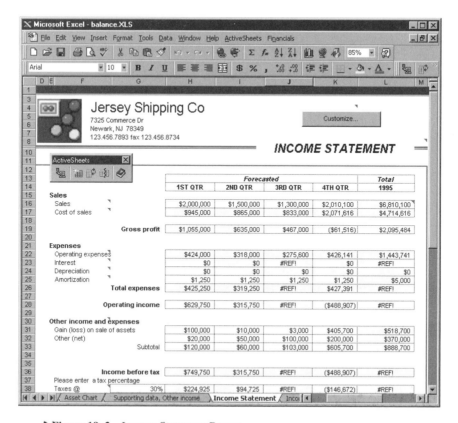

▶ **Figure 19–2**   Income Statement Report

19.3   COMMISSION CALCULATOR (WITH ODBC)

This report template calculates the sales figures per employee that are read real-time from R/3™. The commission schedule is kept in an external database, available through ODBC. By using a join inside Excel, it is possible to see all the current commissions based on up-to-date data from R/3™.

This report template includes sales commission and commission schedules workbooks. Figure 19–3 shows a report that contains tables from external data sources that are hooked into Excel via ODBC.

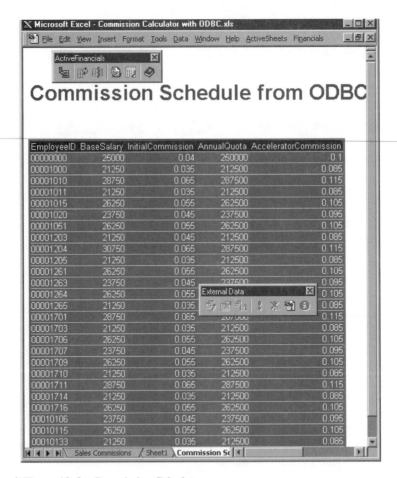

▶ **Figure 19–3**   Commission Calculator

19.4   CONSOLIDATED BALANCE SHEET

This workbook template includes various worksheets related to the consolidated balance sheet that you can customize for your organization.

The other worksheets include group shares report by region, income statement comparison (with pivot table), and company overview. Figure 19–4 shows the consolidated balance sheet report, planning data version, which contains financial statement items, subsidiary (GC), percent contribution, and subsidiary (LC).

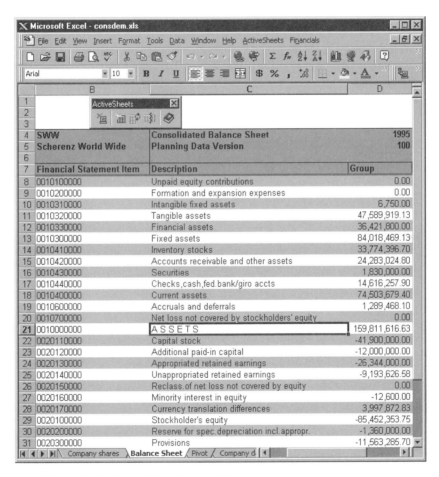

> **Figure 19–4**   Consolidated Balance Sheet

19.5   COST CENTER

This report template summarizes the cost elements that are posted to cost centers. You would use this report to view planned costs and to assess actual activity against the plan. Figure 19–5 shows the cost center detail, which contains both budgeted and actual data, and also calculates the variance and percentage of variance. You enter the controlling area, fiscal year, and posting period IDs. The cost center group may be viewed through the scroll-down menu.

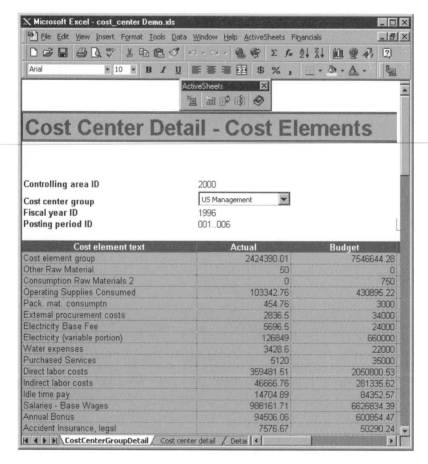

▶ **Figure 19–5**   Cost Center

19.6   CUSTOMER

The customer report template is designed to better manage customer information by enabling access to up-to-the-minute data on transactions between your company and its customers. For example, incoming orders, invoiced sales, and credit memos issued for a particular item can be viewed simultaneously for a comprehensive picture of customer activity.

Figure 19–6 illustrates a customer report assessed by gross order value, quantity, and net order value. You can analyze the customer data further by drilling down to period, sales organization, distribution channel, division, and material.

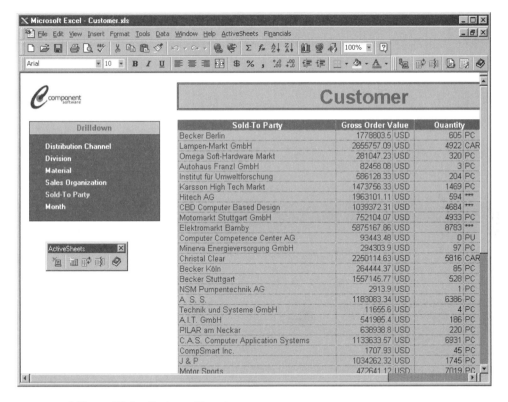

▶ **Figure 19–6**   Customer Report

19.7 DIRECT EXPENSES (CONSOLIDATED)

This report template provides an analysis of expenses accrued by each reporting group. Figure 19–7 illustrates a report that compares the expenses of each reporting group, by fiscal year and year-to-date. You can use the Excel pivot table feature to quickly sort and group the desired data for analysis.

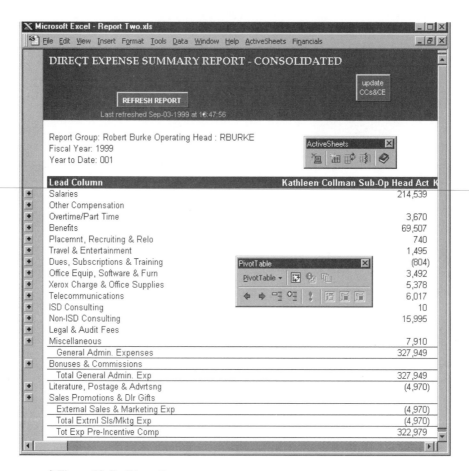

▶ **Figure 19–7** Direct Expenses

19.8 HUMAN RESOURCES

This report template analyzes employee data for an organization. Figure 19–8 shows the data used for analysis: business area, company code, employee group, employee name, position, and personnel area. This data can be sorted and analyzed by business area, cost center, company code, and controlling area.

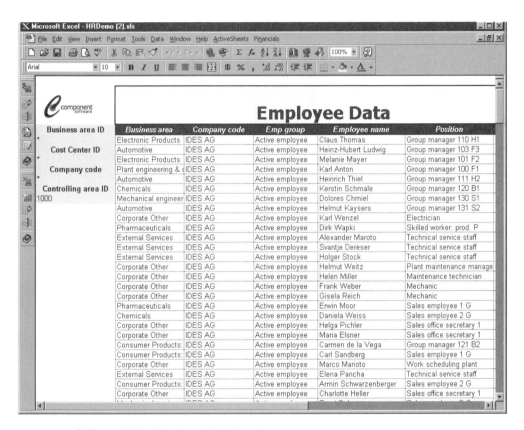

▶ **Figure 19–8**   Employee Data Report

19.9   MATERIAL

The material report template provides statistical analysis of incoming orders, displaying orders for certain materials. You can use this report to measure the performance of products and product lines.

Figure 19–9 measures material by incoming orders, quantities, and invoiced sales. With this report template, you can also drill down to distribution channel, sales organization, and date.

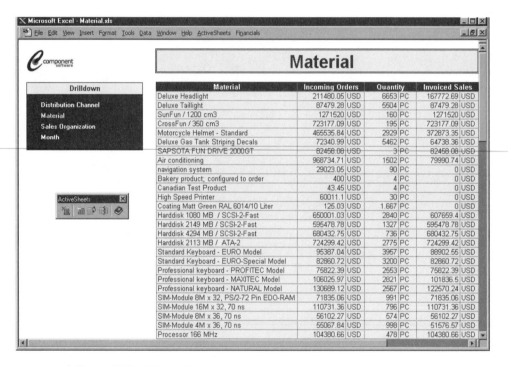

▶ **Figure 19–9**   Material Report

19.10 PURCHASED MATERIAL

This report template evaluates a purchase organization's purchases from various vendors. You can analyze each vendor according to order value and invoice value. Figure 19–10 shows an analysis of a purchasing organization's major vendors, as well as the materials and quantity of the purchases. This report encompasses raw, semi-finished, and finished materials purchased from vendors.

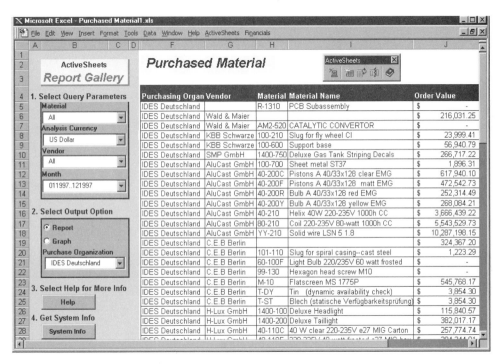

▶ **Figure 19–10**   Purchased Material

19.11 PURCHASING NEGOTIATION

This report template allows you to measure and compare the savings and discounts given by each vendor. Figure 19–11 analyzes each vendor according to the purchase order price, invoice price, market price, and discount over market for a given material. This report template also includes worksheets to analyze market price and list all purchasing materials.

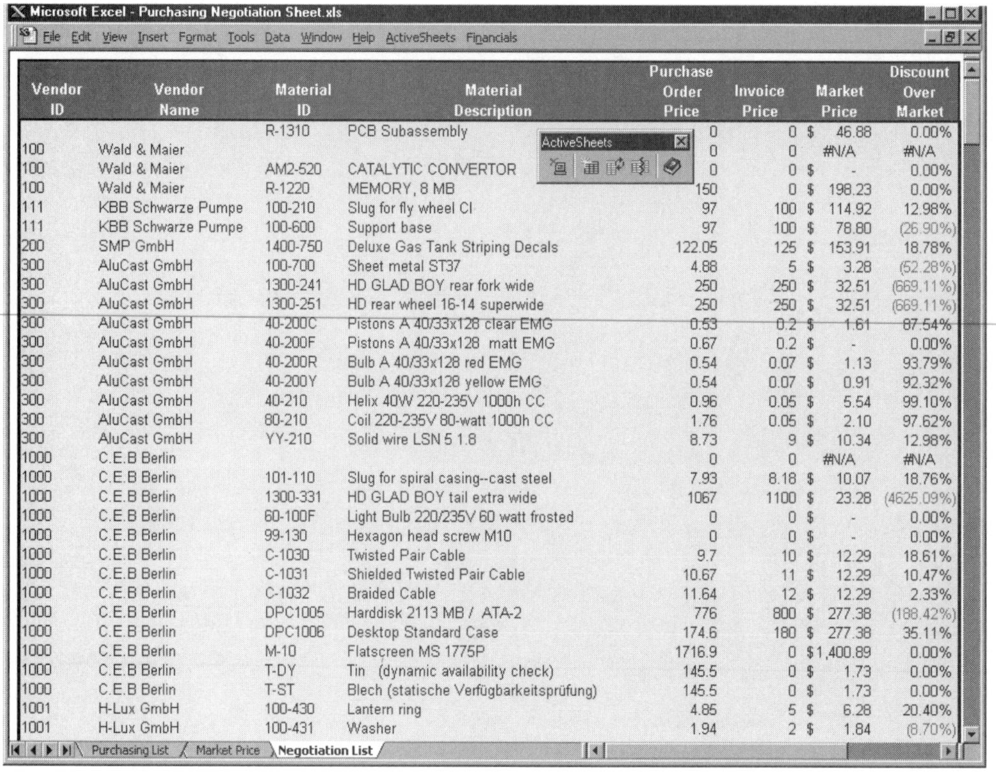

Vendor ID	Vendor Name	Material ID	Material Description	Purchase Order Price	Invoice Price	Market Price	Discount Over Market
		R-1310	PCB Subassembly	0	0	$ 46.88	0.00%
100	Wald & Maier			0	0	#N/A	#N/A
100	Wald & Maier	AM2-520	CATALYTIC CONVERTOR	0	0	$ -	0.00%
100	Wald & Maier	R-1220	MEMORY, 8 MB	150	0	$ 198.23	0.00%
111	KBB Schwarze Pumpe	100-210	Slug for fly wheel CI	97	100	$ 114.92	12.98%
111	KBB Schwarze Pumpe	100-600	Support base	97	100	$ 78.80	(26.90%)
200	SMP GmbH	1400-750	Deluxe Gas Tank Striping Decals	122.05	125	$ 153.91	18.78%
300	AluCast GmbH	100-700	Sheet metal ST37	4.88	5	$ 3.28	(52.28%)
300	AluCast GmbH	1300-241	HD GLAD BOY rear fork wide	250	250	$ 32.51	(669.11%)
300	AluCast GmbH	1300-251	HD rear wheel 16-14 superwide	250	250	$ 32.51	(669.11%)
300	AluCast GmbH	40-200C	Pistons A 40/33x128 clear EMG	0.53	0.2	$ 1.61	87.54%
300	AluCast GmbH	40-200F	Pistons A 40/33x128 matt EMG	0.67	0.2	$ -	0.00%
300	AluCast GmbH	40-200R	Bulb A 40/33x128 red EMG	0.54	0.07	$ 1.13	93.79%
300	AluCast GmbH	40-200Y	Bulb A 40/33x128 yellow EMG	0.54	0.07	$ 0.91	92.32%
300	AluCast GmbH	40-210	Helix 40W 220-235V 1000h CC	0.96	0.05	$ 5.54	99.10%
300	AluCast GmbH	80-210	Coil 220-235V 80-watt 1000h CC	1.76	0.05	$ 2.10	97.62%
300	AluCast GmbH	YY-210	Solid wire LSN 5 1.8	8.73	9	$ 10.34	12.98%
1000	C.E.B Berlin			0	0	$ #N/A	#N/A
1000	C.E.B Berlin	101-110	Slug for spiral casing--cast steel	7.93	8.18	$ 10.07	18.76%
1000	C.E.B Berlin	1300-331	HD GLAD BOY tail extra wide	1067	1100	$ 23.28	(4625.09%)
1000	C.E.B Berlin	60-100F	Light Bulb 220/235V 60 watt frosted	0	0	$ -	0.00%
1000	C.E.B Berlin	99-130	Hexagon head screw M10	0	0	$ -	0.00%
1000	C.E.B Berlin	C-1030	Twisted Pair Cable	9.7	10	$ 12.29	18.61%
1000	C.E.B Berlin	C-1031	Shielded Twisted Pair Cable	10.67	11	$ 12.29	10.47%
1000	C.E.B Berlin	C-1032	Braided Cable	11.64	12	$ 12.29	2.33%
1000	C.E.B Berlin	DPC1005	Harddisk 2113 MB / ATA-2	776	800	$ 277.38	(188.42%)
1000	C.E.B Berlin	DPC1006	Desktop Standard Case	174.6	180	$ 277.38	35.11%
1000	C.E.B Berlin	M-10	Flatscreen MS 1775P	1716.9	0	$ 1,400.89	0.00%
1000	C.E.B Berlin	T-DY	Tin (dynamic availability check)	145.5	0	$ 1.73	0.00%
1000	C.E.B Berlin	T-ST	Blech (statische Verfügbarkeitsprüfung)	145.5	0	$ 1.73	0.00%
1001	H-Lux GmbH	100-430	Lantern ring	4.85	5	$ 6.28	20.40%
1001	H-Lux GmbH	100-431	Washer	1.94	2	$ 1.84	(8.70%)

▶ **Figure 19–11** Purchasing Negotiation

19.12 SALES EMPLOYEE

The sales employee report template measures the performance of each sales person. Figure 19–12 illustrates a sales employee report that compares sales people by their incoming orders, quantities, and invoiced sales. The drilldown window at the left provides different views of the sales information available in R/3™. This allows you to keep abreast of global sales, for example, or to look up information on the productivity of your employees.

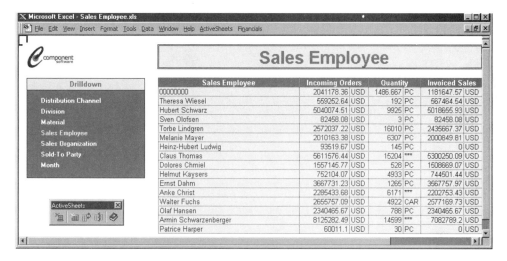

▶ **Figure 19–12**   Sales Employee

19.13   SALES OFFICE

The sales office report template measures the sales performance of an organization's sales offices. Figure 19–13 shows a report that summarizes the order history for a specific sales office or a set of sales offices. You can drill down the sales office data to distribution channel, division, sales group, sales organization, or time.

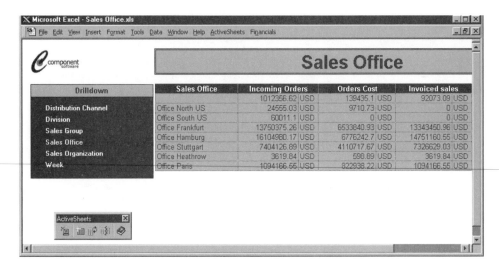

▶ **Figure 19–13**   Sales Office

19.14 SALES ORGANIZATION

The sales organization template analyzes the ordering activities and customer transactions by sales organization. The sales organization is a primary organization unit for an R/3™ sales business process. Sales organizations are used for selling and distributing products and negotiating terms of sale. Figure 19–14 compares the sales efforts of sales organizations according to incoming orders, quantity, and invoiced sales. You can drill down to distribution channel, division, material, sales district, sold-to party (customer), or date.

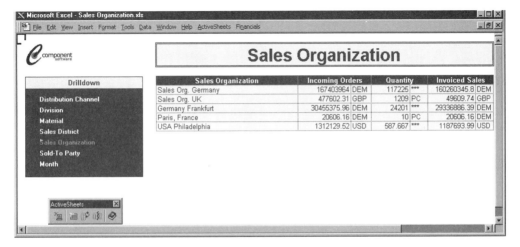

▶ **Figure 19–14** Sales Organization

19.15 SALES PERFORMANCE

This template analyzes the monthly sales performance of a number of sales reporting structures. Figure 19–15 shows the overall monthly sales by sales organization, distribution channel, and sales district. You can constrain the selection criteria by using any of the drilldown menus on the left.

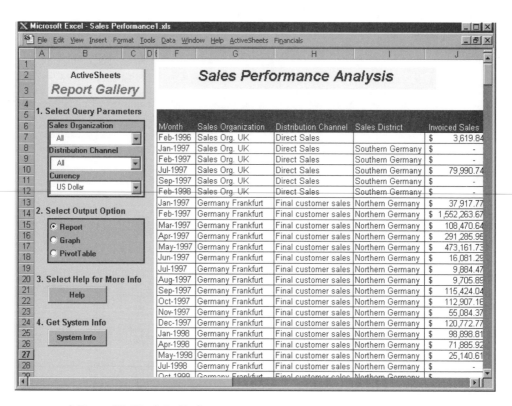

▶ **Figure 19–15**   Sales Performance

19.16 SHIPPING POINT

This report template measures the flow of goods from your company to its business partners. You can use this template to create a report that summarizes order history for a specific shipping point or a set of shipping points. You can analyze shipping points according to shipping point, route, forwarder, destination country, and/or specific period. Figure 19–16 shows a shipping point report that compares net and gross weight deliveries, volume, and the number of deliveries on hand.

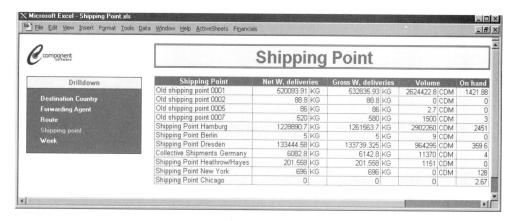

▶ **Figure 19–16**   Shipping Point

Index

R/3 Reporting
with
ActiveSheets

Part I:
Getting Started

Chapter 1:
Installing ActiveSheets

Installing ActiveSheets is a quick and easy process, but please review the following documentation for important information about your installation.

This chapter provides the following information about installing ActiveSheets:

- System Requirements
- Running the Installer
- Running the Uninstaller

Note: System administrators should consult Appendix A: R/3 Configuration, for a description of the tasks that will allow ActiveSheets users access to company information in the R/3 system.

System Requirements

The minimum system requirements for ActiveSheets are:

- Pentium-based computer running either Windows 95, Windows 98, or Windows NT 4.0 with Service Pack 3 installed
- 16 MB RAM
- 20 MB free space on local hard drive
- Connection to SAP R/3 system version 3.1G or later
- Microsoft Excel 97 with MicroSoft Office Service Release 1 installed

---

Caution: ActiveSheets requires Microsoft Office 97 Service Release 1 or later to be installed. This update is required for proper operation of ActiveSheets. ActiveSheets will not work without it. You can download the latest Microsoft Office 97 Service Release from the Microsoft website.

Running the Setup

Before you run the setup, we recommend that you close all other applications.

◆ **To install the latest version of ActiveSheets on your machine:**

1. Insert CD titled "ActiveSheets for SAP R/3" into a CD-ROM drive, or download ActiveSheets from the web.

2. Double-click on the setup icon.

   The introduction screen opens.

Note: If you are installing from a CD, the setup will launch when you insert the CD into your CD-ROM drive.

---

3. Click Next.

4. Read the End User License Agreement, then click Yes to accept the terms of the agreement.

   The setup will scan your system to make sure you have the proper software installed, and abort the installation process if required software is missing.

5. Enter your name, company, and your product serial number on the User Information page of the Setup Wizard.

Note: The serial number is located on the sleeve of your ActiveSheets CD.

6. Click Next to continue with the setup. The setup verifies the serial number you have entered. If it is not correct, the setup will return to the user information so that you can reenter your serial number.

7. Now the Setup Wizard displays the readme file. Please review the information in the readme file carefully, since it may contain late-breaking changes to the documentation, and compatibility information that may apply to you.

8. Click Next to proceed to the directory selection step.

9. You can either accept the default installation directory (recommended), or click Browse and select another folder if you wish to install ActiveSheets into a different directory. Click Next when you are ready to proceed.

   The Select Program Folder screen displays.

10. You can allow the Setup Wizard to create the ActiveSheets icons in the default program group, select another program group from the list of existing program groups, or enter a new folder name. Click Next when you are ready to proceed.

    The ActiveSheets Setup Wizard installs ActiveSheets on your machine. At the end of the installation process the Setup Wizard confirms that the installation was successful.

11. Click Finish to complete the setup process.

12. Restart your computer to ensure that all the necessary system configuration changes have taken place.

Uninstalling ActiveSheets

If you ever need to remove ActiveSheets from your system, the Uninstall utility will help you do so.

◆ **To remove ActiveSheets from your system:**

1. From the Start menu select **Settings**, then **Control Panel**.

   The Control Panel opens.

2. Double-click the Add/Remove Programs icon in the Control Panel.

   The **Add/Remove Program Properties** dialog opens.

3. Select ActiveSheets from the list of installed programs and click Add/Remove.

4. Click Yes to confirm that you wish to remove ActiveSheets from your system.

   The Uninstall deletes ActiveSheets from your system.

Chapter 2:
QuickStart Guide

If you are like most people, you prefer to read as little documentation as possible. With that in mind, we have designed a "bare bones" introduction to ActiveSheets that will help you get up and running as quickly as possible. You can refer later to the rest of the user manual (or online help) for more detailed descriptions of specific ActiveSheets attributes and functions.

To try out the steps in this chapter, you may access your current R/3 system or you may use the SAP International Demonstration and Education System (IDES). If you want to use the IDES system and do not have it installed, consult Appendix C (on this book's CD) for information on getting access to the Component Software IDES demo machine.

This chapter gives you a quick overview to:

- Getting Started
- The ActiveSheets Wizard
- Report Gallery

Getting Started

To establish a live connection to an R/3 system, you must first log on to R/3.

♦ **To log on and off to R/3:**

Logon
button

1. Click on the Logon button on the **ActiveSheets** toolbar.

   The **Logon** dialog opens.

2. Click the system you want to log on to (see Chapter 3: ActiveSheets Overview for logon procedures).

Note: If no systems appear in the list, click Add to specify one. Enter a description, the IP address or host name of the Application Server, any applicable Router String, and the System Number. Consult your system administrator to obtain the correct settings for your specific implementation.

---

3. Enter the client, your user name, password, and "E" for the language.

Note: You must have a valid logon in the target R/3 system.

---

4. Click OK to log on.

   ActiveSheets establishes a live connection to the R/3 system.

Logoff
button

5. Click on the Logoff button on the **ActiveSheets** toolbar.

   A dialog box opens, asking you if you want to log off from the R/3 system.

6. Click Yes to confirm that you want to log off.

The ActiveSheets Wizard

The ActiveSheets Wizard gives you access to management reporting in R/3. The ActiveSheets Wizard uses the R/3 Information Warehouse to extract reporting data from all SAP application areas—from financials to logistics. By referencing the data sources in your information catalog, you can use the ActiveSheets Wizard to build a report with speed, accuracy, and flexibility.

◆ **To create a report using the ActiveSheets Wizard:**

InfoAgent Wizard
button

1. Click the ActiveSheets Wizard button on the **ActiveSheets** toolbar.

   The **Logon** dialog opens.

2. Double-click the system you want to log on to. (See Chapter 3: ActiveSheets Overview for logon procedures.)

3. Enter the client, your user name, password, and language.

4. Click OK to log on.

   The first page of the ActiveSheets Wizard displays, as well as its Office Assistant (if you have enabled the Assistant).

Note: If you have not previously refreshed your Local information catalog, ActiveSheets will prompt you to do so.

---

5. Click Next.

   The next page of the Wizard displays.

Tip: The ActiveSheets Wizard provides you with a browser that helps you find the data source you need. Select the view that you would like to use for exploring the Information catalog.

---

6. Open the Sales and Distribution folder.

   Subjects related to Sales and Distribution display.

7. Open the Sales Organization subject (indicated by a circular object).

   Data sources related to Sales Organization display.

8. Select the Sales organization data source.

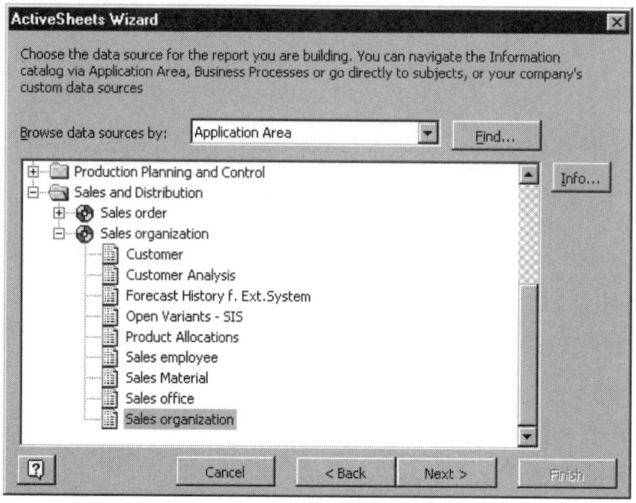

Figure 2-1   ActiveSheets Browser

9. Click Next.

    The next page of the Wizard displays.

10. Select Distribution channel Text from the Available fields column (click on the item once).

Note: Each SAP data source contains a number of fields. The ActiveSheets Wizard displays a list of all available fields in the selected data source. Select the fields that you want to insert as columns into your worksheet.

---

11. Click on the Info button.

    The Info button provides additional information on the chosen field.

12. Close the Information window.

13. Click on the Add Column button.

    The field is moved to the Selected field column.

14. Select the Net orders 1 and Sold-to party Text fields and click on the Add column button for each.

Add Column button

15. Select the Sold-to party Text in the Columns area, then click the Move Up button twice.

16. The field moves to the top of the list and now will be the first column in the worksheet.

17. Click Next.

18. The next page of the Wizard displays.

19. Select the Sales organization ID criteria and click on the Add Column button.

    The **Sales Organization Criteria Properties** dialog opens. Here you can specify the criteria placement and value properties.

Note: The Available selection criteria listbox lists the criteria available to be used as a constraining factor for your report. The Required and chosen selection criteria lists both the required selection criteria that are essential to the report and the criteria that you define for limiting the data you want to retrieve. A question mark next to criteria (in the Required and chosen selection criteria area) indicates that the criteria have not been fully defined, and that you need to set the criteria properties. To edit criteria properties, click on the criteria item and then click Properties, or double-click the criteria item.

---

20. Click cell B2 on your worksheet.

    The cell you selected is recorded in the Location text box.

21. Click in the Value text box and enter a value range. (Enter * to select all values, or, if you're using the IDES system, enter `1000` for the value.)

22. Click OK.

23. The sales organization ID is listed with a green check mark, indicating that its properties have been specified. The ActiveSheets Wizard places the criteria on your worksheet.

24. Click Next.

    The final page of the Wizard displays.

Tip: To give a more polished look to your worksheet, select any of ActiveSheets's built-in formats. The Preview area displays each format.

---

25. Select any format from the list and click Finish.

    The **Select Results Area** dialog displays.

26. Click OK to accept the default values.

    The ActiveSheets Wizard places the report into your worksheet and then reformats the data to fit properly in the columns.

	A	B	C	D	E	F
1						
2	Sales organization ID	1000		**Sold-to party Text**	**Distribution channel Text**	**Net orders 1**
3				Becker Berlin	Final customer sales	3357500
4				Lampen-Markt GmbH	Sold for resale	740044
5				Omega Soft-Hardware Markt	Sold for resale	530478
6				Autohaus Franzl GmbH	Sold for resale	103920
7				Institut für Umweltforschung	Final customer sales	968820
8				Karsson High Tech Markt	Sold for resale	804722
9				Hitech AG	Final customer sales	274802.1
10				Hitech AG	Service	0
11				CBD Computer Based Design	Final customer sales	735732.44
12				CBD Computer Based Design	Service	0
13				Motomarkt Stuttgart GmbH	Sold for resale	330000
14				Elektromarkt Bamby	Sold for resale	1127125
15				Computer Competence Center AG	Service	0
16				Minerva Energieversorgung GmbH	Final customer sales	555500
17				Christal Clear	Sold for resale	2058975
18				Becker Köln	Final customer sales	97600
19				Becker Stuttgart	Final customer sales	1490940
20				NSM Pumpentechnik AG	Final customer sales	5500

Figure 2-2   Completed ActiveSheets Report (IDES Values)

ActiveSheets Report Gallery

The ActiveSheets Report Gallery provides built-in templates for both new and experienced users. These templates work with the SAP IDES system (see Appendix C for information on the IDES system). The Report Gallery is an easy way to start using ActiveSheets without having to build individual reports. It also demonstrates what kinds of reports ActiveSheets is capable of producing, and what you can do with reports you create yourself.

Each of the reports in the Report Gallery takes data from R/3 and brings it into Excel. You can then use Excel's powerful pivot table and graphing functions to view and manipulate the data.

Note: Each report in the Report Gallery contains macros. In order for the reports to function properly, Excel must be configured to enable these macros.

◆ **To use the Report Gallery:**

1. From the **File** menu select **Open**. Find the ActiveSheets Report Gallery folder, then select the Cost Center Variance.xlt Excel template.

   The **Microsoft Excel** dialog opens and asks you whether you want to enable macros.

Note: During installation, ActiveSheets placed the ActiveSheets Report Gallery folder in your Microsoft Office templates directory.

2. Click Enable macros.

   The **EntIS for R/3 logon** dialog box displays.

3. Log on to R/3 as before.

   ActiveSheets displays the raw data retrieved from R/3.

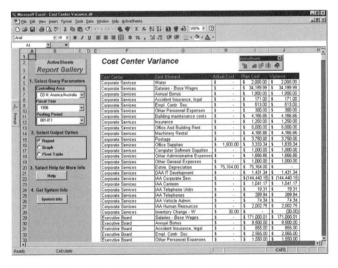

Figure 2-3 Cost Center Variance Report (IDES Values)

4. On the left side of the worksheet, under Select Query Parameters, choose a different currency from the drop-down menu.

ActiveSheets recalculates the cells.

Note: Under Select Query Parameters, you can change what data you use. For example, you might select a different fiscal year, or display monetary values using a different currency.

---

5. Under the Select Output Option, choose Graph.

ActiveSheets displays the sales performance data in a graph format.

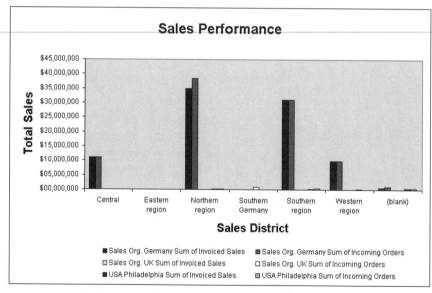

Figure 2-4   Sales Performance Analysis Graph

Tip: In addition to viewing a regular report, you can also view data in a pivot table or a graph (except for the Trial Balance report).

---

6. Under the Select Output Option, choose Pivot Table.

   ActiveSheets displays the sales performance data in a pivot table format.

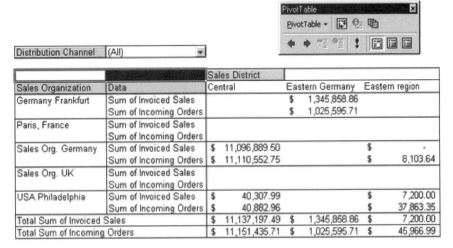

		Sales District		
Sales Organization	Data	Central	Eastern Germany	Eastern region
Germany Frankfurt	Sum of Invoiced Sales		$ 1,345,858.86	
	Sum of Incoming Orders		$ 1,025,595.71	
Paris, France	Sum of Invoiced Sales			
	Sum of Incoming Orders			
Sales Org. Germany	Sum of Invoiced Sales	$ 11,096,889.50		$ -
	Sum of Incoming Orders	$ 11,110,552.75		$ 8,103.64
Sales Org. UK	Sum of Invoiced Sales			
	Sum of Incoming Orders			
USA Philadelphia	Sum of Invoiced Sales	$ 40,307.99		$ 7,200.00
	Sum of Incoming Orders	$ 40,882.96		$ 37,863.35
Total Sum of Invoiced Sales		$ 11,137,197.49	$ 1,345,858.86	$ 7,200.00
Total Sum of Incoming Orders		$ 11,151,435.71	$ 1,025,595.71	$ 45,966.99

Distribution Channel (All)

PivotTable

Figure 2-5   Sales Performance Analysis Pivot Table

Note: The pivot table for each report is directly related to the report's graph. ActiveSheets will automatically generate a graph based on the criteria you select in the report's pivot table.

---

7. Under Select Help for More Info, click on the Help button.

   The Help button provides you with a brief description of the report.

8. Under Get System Info, click on the System Info button.

   The System Info button provides you with R/3 connection information.

That's all there is to it. As you can see, you can create a variety of R/3 reports using many different methods and accessing a wide range of R/3 information—and you don't have to have R/3 expertise. You can use a wizard to get standard reports or open a pre-built template—all from your Excel worksheets. In fact, you can bring data from any R/3 report into any Office application.

Part II:
Using ActiveSheets

Chapter 3:
ActiveSheets Overview

ActiveSheets lets you use Microsoft Excel to access financial and management information in SAP's R/3 System. Functioning as an application component in the Microsoft Windows environment, ActiveSheets delivers tremendous functionality for all R/3 users. With ActiveSheets you can build your own reports or drag and drop reports from the R/3 system directly into Excel. ActiveSheets gives you instant access to the latest information in R/3.

This chapter provides a brief overview of the ActiveSheets product, including:

- Who It's For
- What It Does
- How It Works
- What It Features

Who It's For

ActiveSheets can be used by anyone running an R/3 system and Microsoft Excel 97. If you are in accounting, operational management, finance, sales, or human resources, you will discover that ActiveSheets greatly improves information delivery in R/3. If you're unfamiliar with the intricacies of the R/3 system, ActiveSheets allows you to use Microsoft Excel rather than learn the multitude of options and screens in SAP R/3.

ActiveSheets makes it easy for you to employ R/3 reporting—you just ask for information from Excel. This shortens the learning curve, especially if you already have expertise in Excel and its easy-to-use interface. You can make your own sheets instead of depending on systems management and SAP support consultants to build them for you.

ActiveSheets will help you access and report on information. It assists in:

- Decision support for management reporting
- Ad hoc queries applied to R/3 Information Systems
- Routine tasks like printing, e-mailing a report, or making a graph
- Reports using other Microsoft Office products and tools

What It Does

ActiveSheets gives your Excel Workbooks an "active" connection to R/3. Once you choose what to put in the report, that's it. The next time you edit the workbook in Excel, ActiveSheets automatically updates the data from R/3.

ActiveSheets greatly eases the flow of information delivery in R/3. Because of R/3's complexity, reporting in R/3 presents the non-expert with several barriers to information, for example, an unwieldy graphical user interface, a confusing notation system, and an esoteric language in ABAP/4.

For decision support, ActiveSheets makes it easier for management to access and manipulate R/3 data contained in various SAP information systems and selected Business Application Interfaces (BAPIs). ActiveSheets components help you build queries and answer them even if you aren't familiar with the access paths involved in the R/3 system. Without knowing R/3 tables, programs, or reports, you can create a worksheet containing values from R/3.

How It Works

ActiveSheets works by automatically setting links to R/3 data and updating fields in your Excel spreadsheets. This gives you a seamless interface with R/3 and access to:

- R/3 Information Systems (LIS, SIS, PIS, Report Writer, etc.)
- Over 40 Business APIs
- SAP business rules and application logic
- SAP user security

Once ActiveSheets establishes an active connection to R/3, current information from R/3 instantly enters your Excel workbook. ActiveSheets also uses the Excel "Add-in" facility to extend Excel. The facility simply adds the ActiveSheets toolbar.

Tip: Add-ins are programs that add optional commands and features to Microsoft Excel.

The ActiveSheets Wizard gives you access to management reporting in R/3. ActiveSheets uses various R/3 information systems to draw reporting data from all SAP application areas—from financials to logistics.

What It Features

The main components of ActiveSheets software are:

1. Enterprise Office Start

   Provides an easy to use interface for new users.

2. ActiveSheets Wizard

   Gives you access to management reporting in R/3. You can:

   - Search R/3 Information Systems
   - Access a broad range of data in R/3
   - Create reports from all SAP application areas
   - Explore any aspect of the company being reported

3. ActiveSheets Report Gallery

   Provides a collection of prebuilt model reports for both new and experienced users.

Chapter 4:
ActiveSheets Basics

ActiveSheets creates a live connection between Excel and SAP R/3. To establish this connection, you will need to perform a few simple tasks. This chapter provides the following basic information:

- Logging On/Logging off
- Getting Help

Logging On/Logging Off

To establish a live connection to an R/3 system, you must first log on to R/3. There is a separate toolbar for ActiveSheets.

Figure 4-1   ActiveSheets Toolbar

Before following the steps below, you should have ActiveSheets installed, with the ActiveSheets for Financials add-in loaded and the **ActiveSheets** toolbar displayed.

◆   **To log on to R/3:**

Logon
button

1. Click on the Logon button on the **ActiveSheets** toolbar.

     The **Logon** dialog opens.

2. Select an R/3 system from the list and click OK.

Note: If no systems appear in the list, click Add to specify one. Enter a description, the IP address or host name of the Application Server, any applicable Router String, and the System Number. Consult your system administrator to obtain the correct settings for your specific implementation.

---

3. Enter the client, your user name, password, and "E" for the language.

Note: Your system administrator needs this information for purposes of maintaining security, adding new users, configuring the system for efficient use, and granting authorizations. Contact your system administrator if you have problems logging on.

---

4. Click OK to log on to the R/3 system.

   ActiveSheets establishes a live connection to the R/3 system.

◆ **To test your R/3 connection:**

1. From the Microsoft Excel **ActiveSheets** menu select **R/3 Connection**, then **Connection Info . . .**

   The **EntIS for R/3 Information** dialog opens.

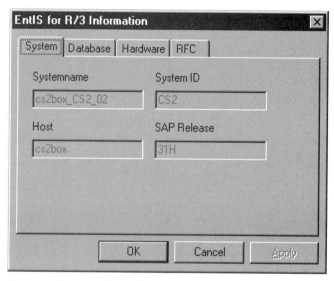

Figure 4-2   EntIS for R/3 Information Dialog

2. Click on each of the page tabs in the dialog and examine the page contents.

Note: Each tab contains information needed by your R/3 system administrator. ActiveSheets has a live connection to R/3 and the tabs reflect ActiveSheets' R/3 connection management.

---

3. Click OK or Cancel.

4. From the **ActiveSheets** menu, select **R/3 Connection**, then **Logoff**.

5. From the **ActiveSheets** menu, select **R/3 Connection**, then **Logon**.

   The **Logon** dialog opens.

Tip: The toolbar button icon will change according to your connection status.

---

6. Enter the same logon information as in step 2, but enter user name JOE.

7. Click OK to attempt to log on to the R/3 system.

   ActiveSheets prompts you that you did not log on correctly.

Tip: ActiveSheets follows the R/3 security model. All users accessing R/3 data must be authorized to do so.

---

8. Click OK twice to dismiss the error dialogs.

Getting Help

ActiveSheets comes complete with an online Help guide. The Help guide contains:

- User's Guide
- Reference
- Contents and Index

To open the Help guide, simply click the icon on the **ActiveSheets** toolbar. The ActiveSheets Help guide can also be selected from the **ActiveSheets** menu.

Chapter 5:
Using ActiveSheets

ActiveSheets allows you to create your own R/3 reports in Microsoft Excel. Primarily a decision-support tool, ActiveSheets enables you to design a report using a simple wizard. The ActiveSheets Wizard relieves you from having to learn R/3 tables, programs, or reports. You can use the ActiveSheets Wizard to create ad hoc reports for management reporting in R/3.

This chapter provides the following information:

- ActiveSheets Overview
- Running the Wizard and Logging on to R/3
- Selecting a Report
- Selecting the Fields
- Selecting Criteria
- Defining the Layout
- Generating the Report
- Editing the Report
- ActiveSheets Features
- Options

ActiveSheets Overview

ActiveSheets is a tool for building ad hoc report worksheets with SAP R/3 data. ActiveSheets is implemented as a Microsoft Excel add-in (a program that works through Microsoft Excel). When you build a report, the ActiveSheets Wizard creates a Microsoft Excel sheet formula and places it on your worksheet. The formula then retrieves the data from R/3 through the R/3 Information Warehouse or Business Application Programming Interfaces (BAPIs) and populates the cells in your worksheet, much in the same way as a SUM function in Excel populates cell(s) in Excel with a calculated result.

The ActiveSheets Wizard is the component that lets you define your report in four simple steps. First, you choose the data source of fields for your report, which can be either a BAPI or an R/3 Information Warehouse data source. Next, you choose the fields (or columns) you want in your report. After that you specify how you want to constrain your report via selection criteria. Finally, you choose the report formatting options and its placement on the sheet.

The results of your report are displayed in an area you choose on an Excel worksheet. At any time you can refresh the report in order to update data from R/3. Working directly from your worksheet, you can also enter a different selection criteria value (for example, to see a report for vendor ID "X" instead of vendor "Y") and the results will be updated immediately. If you want to share your report with colleagues who do not have access to your R/3 system, you can replace the live formulas in your worksheet with regular values, which will not be refreshed from R/3. Because the report results are placed in a standard Excel worksheet, you can use any of the standard Excel functionality, such as printing, sorting, charting, e-mailing, and Web publishing.

Running the Wizard and Logging on to R/3

As with all ActiveSheets components, the ActiveSheets Wizard establishes a live connection to an R/3 system. To do so, activate the ActiveSheets Wizard and then log on to R/3.

◆ **To activate the ActiveSheets Wizard and log on:**

InfoAgent Wizard button

1. Click on the ActiveSheets Wizard button on the **ActiveSheets** toolbar.

   The **Logon** dialog opens.

2. Select the system you want to log on to and click OK. (See Chapter 3: ActiveSheets Overview for logon procedures.)

Note: You must have a valid logon in the target R/3 system.

---

3. Enter the client, your user name, password, and language.

4. Click OK to log on.

Selecting a Report

The ActiveSheets Wizard provides a browser for selecting the R/3 data sources for your customized Excel worksheet. The ActiveSheets Wizard uses a number of views to present data sources in ways that make them easy to find.

View	Organization
Application Area	R/3 application areas > business objects > data sources
Business Processes	Business processes > business objects > data sources
Business Objects	Business objects > data sources
R/3 Open Information Warehouse Reports	Only data sources contained in the R/3 Information Warehouse
Custom Reports Only	Only custom data sources contained within the R/3 Information Warehouse

> **Note:** The R/3 Information Warehouse organizes data sources into an Information catalog that facilitates the search for and retrieval of information.

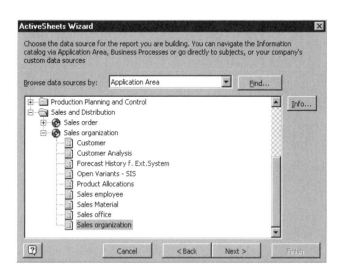

Figure 5-1 ActiveSheets Wizard Browser Page

Each data source is associated with certain business objects. The Application Area, Business Processes, and All Business Objects views display these objects, with their associated data sources shown as subitems within the business object. The Info button describes the selected business object, business process scenario, or data source. Click on any of these items and then click Info to see the description for the selected item.

You can also search for data sources containing particular text. For example, you can search for the word "Customer" to get a list of all data sources that have something to do with customers. ActiveSheets will also indicate how close a match there is between the available data source and the term you have entered. To search for a data source, click on the Find button.

◆ **To browse the available data sources:**

1. Start with a blank Excel worksheet.

2. Make sure that the **ActiveSheets** toolbar is visible.

3. Click the ActiveSheets Wizard button on the **ActiveSheets** toolbar.

   The **Logon** dialog opens.

4. Log on to R/3.

5. Click Next on the first page of the Wizard.

6. Select different Browse By options and browse the report selection tree.

◆ **To search for the report:**

1. Click Find on the ActiveSheets Wizard Select Report page.

   The **Search** dialog opens.

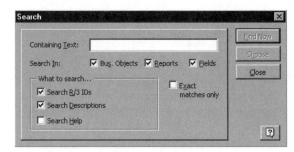

Figure 5-2   ActiveSheets Search Dialog

2. In the Containing Text box, type the text you are searching for, then click Find Now.

   Data sources relating to the text you typed are shown. The ActiveSheets Wizard will display the search results in the order of the best-matched results.

3. When you have found the R/3 data source on which you wish to base the report, simply click on it and then click Choose to proceed.

   ActiveSheets takes you to the next page of the Wizard.

Selecting the Fields

The data source you selected contains a number of possible fields. The ActiveSheets Wizard shows you a list of all available fields that you can use as columns in your worksheet. Transfer each field that you want in your report to the "Columns in your report" list. The order in which they appear in this list (top to bottom) is the order in which they will appear as columns (left to right).

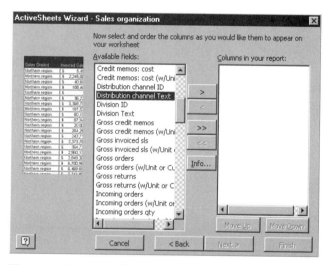

Figure 5-3   ActiveSheets Field Selection Page

Select the fields you want to use in your worksheet by double-clicking on them in the Available Fields list, or use the buttons to perform the following functions:

Button	Purpose
>	To select a field, click on it, then click on this button. The contents of the field move to the Selected Fields listing.
<	To remove a field from the Selected Fields list, click on this button.
>>	To select all available fields for your worksheet, click on this button. All fields are transferred to the Selected Fields list.
<<	To remove all of the selected fields, click on this button.
Move Up / Move Down	To change the location and order of a field on your worksheet, click on the Move Up or Move Down buttons.
Info...	To view the field's definition and use, select the field name in either list, and then click on the Info button.

Note: Due to the limitations of Excel, only 13 columns and selection criteria can be selected in a single report.

Selecting Criteria

Selection criteria constrain the data in your report by a certain type of value. Choose the desired criteria field from the available selection criteria, then specify the properties (placement and value) for the item.

The Available selection criteria listbox lists the criteria available to be used as constraining factors for your report. The Required and chosen selection criteria lists both the required selection criteria that are essential to the report and the criteria that you define for limiting the data you want to retrieve. A question mark next to a criteria item in the Required and chosen selection criteria indicates that the criteria has not been fully defined, and that you need to set the criteria properties. To edit criteria properties, click on the criteria item and then click Properties, or double-click the criteria item.

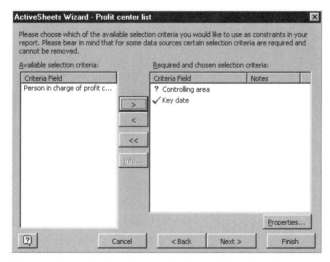

Figure 5-4   ActiveSheets Criteria Selection Page

When you add new criteria, or choose to edit the criteria properties, the **Criteria Properties** dialog prompts you to place the criteria on the worksheet you are building, and to specify the selection or constraining value for the criteria.

Note: Different reports have different criteria requirements. Some may have certain requisite criteria, while others may have no available criteria at all.

When you have finished specifying criteria, either click Finish to generate your worksheet, or click Next to configure formatting options.

Criteria Properties

In this dialog you specify how to place the criteria on the worksheet and how to assign the initial value for the criteria. By default, criteria are placed directly below the preceding criteria. You can also specify if and where to place the criteria label.

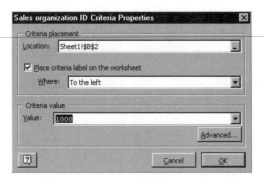

Figure 5-5   Criteria Properties Dialog

To place the criteria, put your cursor in the Location editbox and select a cell on your worksheet where you want your criteria value to go. You can place the criteria label on the worksheet, or leave it out by deselecting the Place criteria label on the sheet checkbox. The Where drop-down listbox specifies where the criteria label will go in relation to its value.

For every criteria, you must enter a value. Enter this value in the Value text box. To select all available values, enter * . Some selection criteria require a single valid value to be specified. For these criteria, the all available values option (*) is not permitted. If you try to enter * as a selection criteria where it is disallowed, you will be warned. In this instance, the Advanced button will be disabled as well.

If the selection list is enabled in the ActiveSheets **Options** dialog (General tab), you can retrieve a list of criteria values from your R/3 system. Click on the arrow to the right of the text box to view a drop-down list of all criteria values for the selected item.

You may also enter a range of values for certain criteria. If you are not sure how to specify the range, click on the Advanced button.

Tip: Time value ranges must be entered in the form: begin range..end range. For example, to get sales figures for 1997 in a report where values are aggregated to the month level, you must specify the month range as 01/1997..12/1997. Weeks are specified as week number/year. Thus, the first 13 weeks of 1998 would be written as 01/1998..13/1998. Days are reported as mm/dd/yyyy.

When you finish building your report, you can enter a new value for the criteria directly on the worksheet.

Criteria Value

The Criteria Value screen is an intuitive interface for creating the desired selection criteria. You can select either All Values or certain Specified Values.

When you select Specified Values, the rest of the dialog activates so that you can make your selections. You can specify up to three separate sets of values for your criteria. Each of these sets may be equal to, greater than, or less than the specified value, or they may contain a range of values.

The Resulting Selection Criteria text box displays the resulting value that ActiveSheets inserts into the sheet as a criteria value. This is continuously updated as you modify your selection criteria.

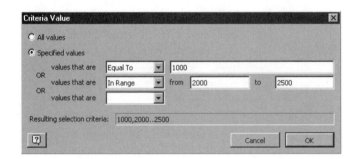

Figure 5-6   ActiveSheets Criteria Value Dialog

Defining the Layout

ActiveSheets provides a number of Excel predefined layouts that you can use to format your reports. The predefined formats include header formatting, as well as cell formatting. The formats also automatically size the columns of your report so that each column is wide enough to contain the data.

When you select the Automatically format the results option, the list of formats becomes enabled. Browse through the list items to find the desired format. As you select each format, the ActiveSheets Wizard displays a preview of the selected format in the Preview area.

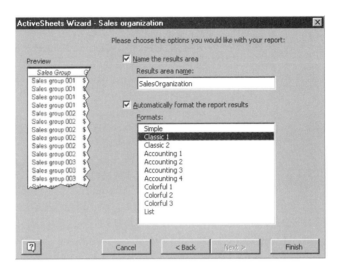

Figure 5-7   ActiveSheets Format Selection Page

Select the format of your choice and then click Finish to place your report on the worksheet.

Note: When ActiveSheets resizes the results area, it also applies or clears the formatting in order to preserve the look of the original results area.

The last page of the Wizard also includes the option to name the results area range in your new report. This is especially convenient if you use the `ASLookup` formula to compare two similar reports, such as comparing values for two different periods. To quickly select the results area, you can choose this name from the Excel name box (located to the left of the formula bar). The default name is based on the name of the data source you are using for your report.

For example, if you chose the Operations data source in your Local information catalog, ActiveSheets provides the default name "Operation" in the text box. When the results area is resized, the name is also updated (if you wish, you can change this in the **Options** dialog). This option may be turned on or off. The default option remains on unless otherwised specified.

Generating the Report

When you click Finish, the ActiveSheets Wizard will generate your report. ActiveSheets retrieves the data from the R/3 system, then prompts you to select a results area on your worksheet. ActiveSheets will not allow you to select an area that contains locked and protected cells, overlaps with a formula array, or overlaps with any selection criteria for this report. You can click on any other cell to select it as the origin.

ActiveSheets automatically calculates the size of the results area by determining the number of rows and columns in the result. If you are building a new report, ActiveSheets automatically selects an area in the worksheet on which to place the results and displays that area on the worksheet.

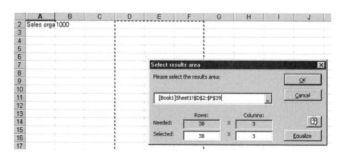

Figure 5-8   Select Results Area Dialog

You can accept the results area selected by ActiveSheets or choose your own by using the Excel cell range selection feature. The Equalize button helps you make sure that your results area is large enough to accommodate the data for your entire report. If you select another results area and click Equalize, ActiveSheets will resize the results area with the top left corner of your selection as its anchor.

When you have specified the results area range, click OK. ActiveSheets retrieves the data from R/3 and places it into the results area. If the results exceed the maximum size of array allowed in Excel, ActiveSheets will limit the number of rows to the maximum that will fit. If the prompt to resize option is selected, you will be prompted to create a value sheet (see Create Value Sheet).

Editing the Report

Once you have created a report, you may wish to make changes later on. ActiveSheets allows you to build and refine the report as needed, using the same Wizard. You can use the Wizard to add or delete columns and selections. You can also change the format of the report.

◆ **To edit the report:**

1. Click on a cell in the results area of the existing report, and click on the ActiveSheets Wizard button on the **ActiveSheets** toolbar.

   You are returned to the criteria selection page of the Wizard.

Tip: You can click Back to the column selection page, if desired.

---

2. Add/delete columns/selections as desired by proceeding through the Wizard steps.

   Change format, if desired.

3. Click Finish.

   The revised results are now displayed.

Resize Results Area

If while editing a report, you alter the number of columns and/or selection criteria, or change a selection criteria value, the size of the results area will be recalculated. If the number of rows and/or columns of the resulting data have changed, you will be asked if you want to resize the results area to the new values.

Tip: You can turn on the automatic resize option by selecting the
"Do not ask me this question again" box. If you click No (do not
resize) and select the "Do not ask…" box, ActiveSheets will not
prompt you or resize the results area in the future. If you click
Yes and select "Do not ask…", the results area will be
automatically resized as necessary without a prompt.

The new report may cause the results area to increase, in which
case ActiveSheets provides you with several resizing options. The
default option to adjust the results area allows you to insert columns
and overwrite rows. In most cases, the default option for resizing the
results area is preferable, especially when working with multiple
reports on a worksheet, but select other options as required.

Create Value Sheet

Due to the limits of the Excel array formula (about 5400 cells), at
times it may not be possible for your report to fit all the data returned
from the R/3 system. In these cases, you will be asked if you want to
create a value sheet. If you select yes, all the data returned from the
R/3 system will be placed on a separate worksheet. The data will be
saved as values only, meaning that the data in this worksheet will
not be actively linked to the R/3 system. ActiveSheets assigns the
worksheet a default name, or you can enter an original one.

The original worksheet will contain all the active data that could fit
into your report. ActiveSheets will indicate that the report is not
"complete" by inserting the text "More" at the bottom right corner of
the report (in the last row of the formula and the last column). This
feature may be turned on or off in the **Options** dialog.

Tip: Both the Create value sheet and Resize prompts may be
turned off, if desired. They can be turned back on (or off) in the
Options dialog.

Workbook Design

For optimal workbook design, you should link your R/3 report data to other worksheets and analyze them there. Create a "fact table" that has the R/3 linked data on one worksheet. Link other worksheets to this base data, then perform analyses on the linked worksheets. Use Excel features such as Link, Pivot Tables, Charts, Sorting, and Subgrouping to create "finished" reports. You can also use VB programming to automate many report features. ActiveSheets Report Gallery contains several such reports.

ActiveSheets Features

Auto Recalculation

By default, ActiveSheets recalculates formulas whenever you change any of the formula precedents (that is, any of the cells a formula references). You can change these on the Calculation tab in Excel's **Tools/Options** menu. To make this setting more accessible, you can also change via the Auto Recalculation feature on the **ActiveSheets** menu.

Note: When an ActiveSheets formula is recalculated, its values are drawn from a cache if the results have been retrieved from R/3. To reload the values from R/3, use the Recalculate Sheet option (see the following).

Recalculate Sheet: Updating With Information from R/3

Because ActiveSheets stores the last data for each ActiveSheets formula, these values are displayed when a formula is recalculated. This means that if you use Excel's Recalculate Sheet function (F9) you will see the values that were last retrieved from R/3. If the data in the R/3 system has changed in the meantime, this new data will not be shown. To force ActiveSheets to reload data from R/3, use the **Recalculate Sheet** toolbar button or menu item. This refreshes all the formulas on the active worksheet from R/3.

◆   **To update the values from R/3:**

1. Click the Recalculate Sheet button on the **ActiveSheets** toolbar.

   ActiveSheets reads the latest values from R/3 and places them on your worksheet.

Copy as Values Only: Storing Report Results Permanently

Sometimes you may want to store the worksheet as it is, and not with updated information from R/3. To do so, you must effectively eliminate the active connection between the displayed data and the queries. This can be done using the Copy as Values Only feature.

◆   **To create a worksheet without active links:**

1. Click on the Copy as Values Only icon on the **ActiveSheets** toolbar.

   The current values are placed in a new worksheet.

Tip: Copy as Values Only always duplicates the current worksheet.

Options

The **Options** menu contains the following four tabs—Prompts, General, Local Catalog, and Advanced—which will customize your ActiveSheets reports as required.

Prompts

The Prompts tab provides you with options for resizing the results area:

- Automatically resize
- Do not resize
- Prompt to resize (default)
- Resize hidden sheets
- Update results name
- Prompt to copy as values only

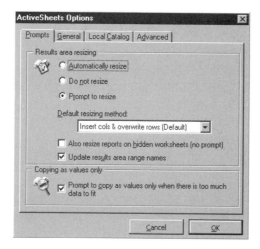

Figure 5-9   Prompts Options Tab

There are different uses for each of these options. For example, when you are creating a report, you should choose the default option, Prompt to resize, because you will want to know the amount of data being returned from your R/3 system.

On the other hand, if you are manipulating the data in an existing report, then you likely would not want the **Prompt to resize** dialog to appear every time you change the data. In this instance, the Automatically resize results area option is preferable.

Note: There are certain situations in which the Automatic resize or Prompt to resize options will fail. For instance, if ActiveSheets attempts to resize a results area that contains cells that are protected or locked, you will receive an error message.

The option not to resize is useful for special conditions, for example, if you are working with four or five separate reports on a worksheet. Typically, these reports will be positioned with some below others, leaving a limited number of rows in each report. In this case, you would not want the adjusted results area in one report to overwrite data in a report below it. The Do not resize prompt prevents this from happening by keeping the size of the adjusted results area unchanged. If your adjusted results are fewer than the original results, your report will contain the empty rows. If the adjusted results exceed the results area, ActiveSheets will insert the word "More" in the bottom right corner of the last row.

The Also resize reports on hidden worksheets option allows you to resize automatically the results area when working with hidden sheets. By default, this option is turned off, and ActiveSheets will ignore formulas if they need to be resized on hidden sheets. If the option is turned on, then ActiveSheets will automatically try to resize the data on the hidden sheet (but without prompting).

The Update results area range name option (if turned on) causes ActiveSheets to update all the names referencing the results area whenever the results area is resized. It may be turned on or off.

The last option on the prompts tab, Prompt to copy as values only when there is too much data to fit, may also be turned on or off. See the previously discussed "Create Value Sheet" for a more detailed description of this ActiveSheets feature.

Tip: All options on the Prompts tab are workbook-specific. In other words, changes made to these options are saved only in the workbook in which they are made. In new workbooks, these options are set to their default values.

General

The General tab contains the following options:

- General Options
- Result Options
- No data display

Figure 5-10 General Options Tab

When checked, the Enable loading of selection values list option allows you to use a drop-down list of criteria values within the criteria properties window.

The Automatically update links to ActiveSheets option updates the links of a formula to your ActiveSheets installation. This option is especially useful for sharing reports between different users on the network. For example, ActiveSheets reports may be placed on different drives on a company network. When the report is opened, ActiveSheets will search for the local copy of the program.

Note: When an actively linked report is opened, you will receive the following prompt: "The workbook you opened contains automatic links to information in another workbook. Do you want to update this workbook with changes made to the other workbook? To update all linked information, click Yes. To keep the existing information, click No." If you click Yes, ActiveSheets will ask you to find ActShts.xla. Press Esc and ActiveSheets will find it for you (that is, as long as you have the Automatically update links to ActiveSheets option turned on). Clicking No will leave the data in the report unchanged.

The Indicate incomplete data on the worksheet option applies to the Create Value Sheet feature. Incomplete reports may be indicated with the text "More" at the bottom row of the rightmost column. This workbook-specific feature may be turned on or off.

Tip: All General tab options, except Indicate incomplete data on the worksheet and No data display, make global changes. In other words, changes made to these options are saved in all ActiveSheets workbooks.

The last option, No data display, relates to how you want to display data that contain no values on your worksheet. Click on the drop-down list to view the No data display options. The default setting for this workbook-specific option is the #N/A error.

Local Catalog

ActiveSheets creates and stores a local catalog, or repository, of available R/3 data on your hard drive. The Local information catalog enables ActiveSheets to run the Wizard much faster than if it accesses the same information from R/3 in real time.

Local Catalog Information gives you statistics about the Local information catalog itself. Clicking on Information lists the version and size of the repository, as well as what components have been loaded to utilize this data. It also tells you when you last refreshed the Local information catalog.

Refresh Local Catalog can be used if your R/3 system is reconfigured, or if your Local information catalog becomes corrupted. When you click Refresh Catalog, you can select what information in particular you want to update or obtain. If a necessary piece of data is missing, ActiveSheets will automatically select it for retrieval. By default, all data will be refreshed.

Compact Local Catalog will compress the size of your repository file. This file can become large as a result of frequent refreshes. Compacting the local catalog will take up the least possible amount of hard drive space.

Advanced

The Advanced options are for troubleshooting purposes. If there is a need for technical support, select Log R/3 access file, and then create a name for the log file in the text box below. ActiveSheets will begin logging all calls to R/3 made from ActiveSheets and will create a "trace" file that contains all that information. If you do not specify the path for the file, by default it will be stored in your Excel Documents folder. The second option, Do not log next time ActiveSheets is loaded, is the default option. This option prevents you from leaving the log file on too long, as trace files can be fairly large. If this option is on, ActiveSheets automatically turns the trace function off when you start a new session.

Figure 5-11 Advanced Options Tab

The Troubleshooting options are designed to be used only when someone is working with a technical support professional. These options will report errors and aid in the diagnosis of the specific problem.

The Caching option allows ActiveSheets to store the results of a report in a cache. Caching greatly speeds up the reporting process. However, if problems are found with the caching feature, turn the option off.

Chapter 6:
ActiveSheets Report Gallery

The ActiveSheets Report Gallery provides built-in templates for both new and experienced users. These templates are designed for use with the SAP IDES system (see Appendix C [on this book's CD] for information on the IDES system). The Report Gallery is an easy way to start using ActiveSheets without having to build individual reports. It also demonstrates what kinds of reports ActiveSheets is capable of producing, and what you can do with reports you create yourself.

This chapter provides information on:

- Using the Report Gallery
- Cost Center Variance reports
- Customer Analysis reports
- Product Analysis reports
- Purchased Material reports
- Sales Performance reports
- Weekly Turnover reports

Using the Report Gallery

Each of the reports in the Report Gallery takes data from R/3 and brings it into Excel. You can then use Excel's powerful pivot table and graphing functions to view and manipulate the data. When you open one of the Report Gallery's reports, ActiveSheets displays the raw data retrieved from R/3. You can change what data you use under Select Query Parameters. For example, you might select a different fiscal year, or display monetary values using a different currency.

◆ **To use the Report Gallery:**

1. From the **File** menu select **Open**. Find the ActiveSheets Report Gallery folder, then select the Sales Performance.xlt Excel template.

   The **Microsoft Excel** dialog opens and asks you whether you want to enable macros.

Tip: During installation, ActiveSheets placed the ActiveSheets Report Gallery folder in your Microsoft Office templates directory.

---

2. Click Enable macros.

Note: Each report in the Report Gallery contains macros. Excel must be configured to enable these macros in order for the reports to function properly.

---

3. The **EntIS for R/3** logon dialog box displays.
4. Log on to R/3 as before.

   ActiveSheets displays the raw data retrieved from R/3.

5. On the left side of the worksheet, under Select Query Parameters, select German Mark from the Currency drop-down menu.

   ActiveSheets recalculates the cells.

Note: You can change what data you use under Select Query Parameters. For example, you might select a different fiscal year, or display monetary values using a different currency.

6. Under Select Output Range, choose Graph.

   ActiveSheets displays the sales performance data in a graph format.

Tip: In addition to a regular report, you can also look at data in a pivot table or graph (except for the Trial Balance report).

7. Under Select Output Range, choose Pivot Table.

   ActiveSheets displays the sales performance data in a pivot table format.

Note: The pivot table for each report is directly related to the report's graph. ActiveSheets will automatically generate a graph based on the criteria you select in the report's pivot table.

8. Under Select Help for more Info, click on the Help button.

   The Help button provides you with a brief description of the report.

9. Under Get System Info, click on the System Info button.

   The System Info button provides you with R/3 connection information.

Cost Center Variance

The Cost Center Variance report identifies the variance between the actual cost incurred for each cost element versus planned cost for a particular period. Essentially, the report shows you how close you are to your original cost plan. The report displays cost centers according to their controlling area. In R/3, a controlling area is the largest organizational unit in controlling. Each cost center is an organizational unit within a controlling area that represents a separate location of cost incurrence. Cost elements are the sources of cost incurrence.

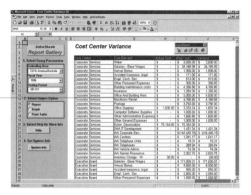

Figure 6-1 Cost Center Variance Report

By using the pivot table you can view all data, or just data related to one particular cost center or cost element. For instance, by selecting one cost center from the pivot table, you can see the total variance across all cost elements in that specific cost center. Once you have the data you want in your pivot table, click Graph to view the data in a graphical format.

Customer Analysis

The Customer Analysis report provides information on order volume, returns, and profit. This report calculates information based on gross orders, adjusted gross orders, credit memos, and operating margin to give each customer a rank from 1 to 10, from worst to best. This rank is a weighed average of the four categories. You can also display a graph showing the top customers (as many as you specify) as compared to average sales.

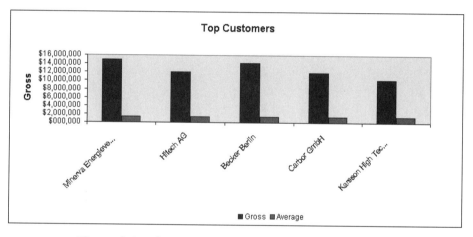

Figure 6-2   Customer Analysis Graph

Product Analysis

The Product Analysis report calculates the best-selling products
based on gross orders, adjusted gross orders, and operating
margin. ActiveSheets calculates and displays information on the
best-selling products. You can then view a graph showing the sales
of these products as compared to the average sales of all products.
To narrow down the criteria, you can specify a particular material to
display, or one particular month of sales.

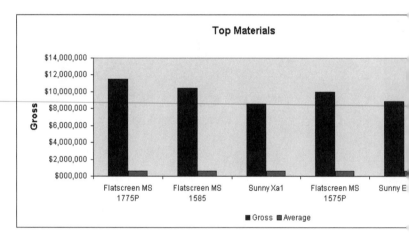

Figure 6-3   Product Analysis Chart

Purchased Material

The Purchased Material report valuates what and how much each purchasing organization has purchased from each vendor, based on order value and invoice value. You can identify each purchasing organization's major vendors, as well as the materials they purchased and in what quantity. The report encompasses raw, semi-finished, and finished materials purchased from vendors.

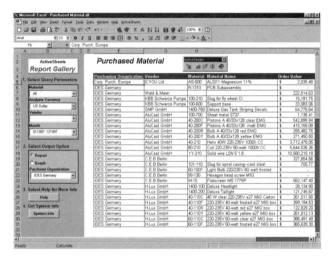

Figure 6-4   Purchased Material Report

Note: To specify a particular material in the Product Analysis and Purchased Material reports, you must enter the number for the material, not the material name. R/3 requires the actual number, and is unable to analyze data based on a name.

Sales Performance

The Sales Performance report analyzes monthly sales by sales
organization, distribution channel, and sales district. To narrow down
the sales organizations on your report, enter the sales organization
ID. The pivot table for this report is quite powerful, and provides a
number of dimensions for viewing data. You can see total sales by
sales organization, sales district, distribution channel, or
combinations of these. ActiveSheets can fully automate the Excel
pivot functions. ActiveSheets Business Application Program
Interfaces (BAPIs) deliver data from the SAP Ledger as a
dimensioned data cube. As with the other reports, the graph provides
a visual display of the data you have selected in the pivot table.

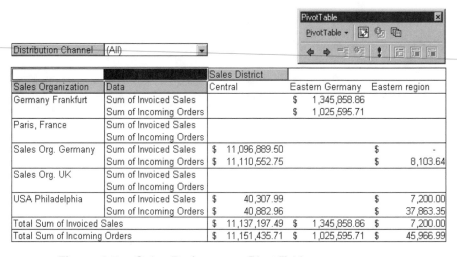

Distribution Channel	(All)			
		Sales District		
Sales Organization	Data	Central	Eastern Germany	Eastern region
Germany Frankfurt	Sum of Invoiced Sales		$ 1,345,858.86	
	Sum of Incoming Orders		$ 1,025,595.71	
Paris, France	Sum of Invoiced Sales			
	Sum of Incoming Orders			
Sales Org. Germany	Sum of Invoiced Sales	$ 11,096,889.50		$ -
	Sum of Incoming Orders	$ 11,110,552.75		$ 8,103.64
Sales Org. UK	Sum of Invoiced Sales			
	Sum of Incoming Orders			
USA Philadelphia	Sum of Invoiced Sales	$ 40,307.99		$ 7,200.00
	Sum of Incoming Orders	$ 40,882.96		$ 37,863.35
Total Sum of Invoiced Sales		$ 11,137,197.49	$ 1,345,858.86	$ 7,200.00
Total Sum of Incoming Orders		$ 11,151,435.71	$ 1,025,595.71	$ 45,966.99

Figure 6-5   Sales Performance Pivot Table

Weekly Turnover

The Weekly Turnover report analyzes weekly sales by sales organization, sales office, and sales group. The Weekly Turnover report operates much like the Sales Performance report. However, it is more specific in that you can see how each particular office, group, and individual performs on a weekly basis. The same extensive pivot table and graphing functionality of the Sales Performance report is available here.

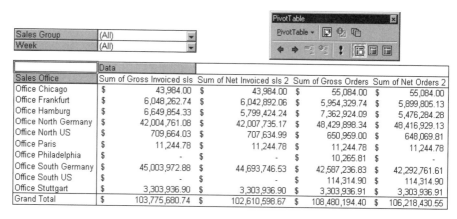

| Sales Group | (All) |
| Week | (All) |

| | Data | | | |
Sales Office	Sum of Gross Invoiced sls	Sum of Net Invoiced sls 2	Sum of Gross Orders	Sum of Net Orders 2
Office Chicago	$ 43,984.00	$ 43,984.00	$ 55,084.00	$ 55,084.00
Office Frankfurt	$ 6,048,262.74	$ 6,042,892.06	$ 5,954,329.74	$ 5,899,805.13
Office Hamburg	$ 6,649,854.33	$ 5,799,424.24	$ 7,362,924.09	$ 5,476,284.28
Office North Germany	$ 42,004,761.08	$ 42,007,735.17	$ 48,429,898.34	$ 48,416,929.13
Office North US	$ 709,664.03	$ 707,634.99	$ 650,959.00	$ 648,069.81
Office Paris	$ 11,244.78	$ 11,244.78	$ 11,244.78	$ 11,244.78
Office Philadelphia	$ -	$ -	$ 10,265.81	$ -
Office South Germany	$ 45,003,972.88	$ 44,693,746.53	$ 42,587,236.83	$ 42,292,761.61
Office South US	$ -	$ -	$ 114,314.90	$ 114,314.90
Office Stuttgart	$ 3,303,936.90	$ 3,303,936.90	$ 3,303,936.91	$ 3,303,936.91
Grand Total	$ 103,775,680.74	$ 102,610,598.67	$ 108,480,194.40	$ 106,218,430.55

Figure 6-6   Weekly Turnover Pivot Table

Part III:
Tutorial Guide

Introduction

About the Tutorial

Hello! My name is Henry Smith, and I work in the accounting department at Acme industries. In the upcoming tutorials, I take you through the ActiveSheets R/3—Excel Link to build an active vendor/invoice/order report.

Those of us in financials at Acme Industries prefer to use Microsoft Windows and Excel spreadsheets to do most of our work, but we must interact with SAP R/3 for mission-critical information. R/3 collects data from all over the world, integrating diverse business processes, currencies, legal systems, employee information and records, and financial accounting into a single information resource. We at Acme need an information retrieval process that can quickly and easily access the R/3 system. ActiveSheets provides a fast, easy-to-use tool that directly ties into SAP's client/server architecture.

Let's see how it works.

Chapter 7:
ActiveSheets Tutorial

Hi, Henry Smith here. I'm responsible for managing all accounting clerks, and my task is to revamp our internal reporting system. In this lesson I explain how to improve your reporting system and become, as they say, a power user. In this tutorial, we explore the capabilities of the ActiveSheets Wizard. You will see how ActiveSheets can be a viable alternative to R/3 reporting, one that requires less than half the time and drudgery of normal R/3 reporting procedures. To manage our distribution channels, I need a report that lists distribution channels with their net order values and sold-to parties so I can track how many sales we get for each channel, as well as who is utilizing them.

In the past our IS department required that I fill out a form containing requests for information necessary to complete this type of report. The department would then have to put the order on its already backlogged project list, or hand the request over to an SAP consultant. Not only would this cost the company a lot of money, but I'd also have to wait a few weeks for what amounts to a relatively simple report. But with ActiveSheets' capabilities, I can build this report myself and, more important, change it easily to accommodate future needs.

ActiveSheets provides a link right into the R/3 Information Warehouse. By using the ActiveSheets Wizard to arrange and select data for my report, I have it up and running in less time than it would have taken to fill out my IS request! Since I have a live link to R/3, I can run this as often as I need to. To do some really impressive reports, I can use Excel's charting capability, which I'm already familiar with. Now I know what they mean by a power user! Let me show you.

Using the ActiveSheets Wizard

◆   **To start the Wizard and log on:**

Logon
button

1. From the **ActiveSheets** toolbar, click on the ActiveSheets Wizard button.

   The **Logon** screen displays.

2. Select the appropriate server from the list, then enter your login information.

   The first page of the ActiveSheets Wizard displays, as well as its Office Assistant (if you have enabled the Assistant).

3. Click Next.

   The next page of the Wizard displays.

The ActiveSheets Wizard provides you with a browser that helps you find the data source you need. Select the view that you would like to use for exploring the Information catalog. You can view by:

- Application Area—Application areas defined in the R/3 system
- Business Processes—Common business processes
- Business Objects—R/3 business objects
- R/3 Open Information Warehouse Reports—Data sources defined in the SAP R/3 Open Information Catalog
- Custom Reports Only—Your company's custom reports

You can also search the R/3 system for subjects, reports, and fields matching the text you enter. The ActiveSheets Wizard will display the search results in the order of the best-matched results.

◆   **To select a report:**

1. Select Browse reports by application area.

2. Open the Sales and Distribution folder.

   Subjects related to Sales and Distribution display.

3. Open the Sales Order subject.

   Data sources related to Sales Order display.

4. Select the Sales organization data source and click Next.

   The next page of the Wizard displays.

Each SAP data source contains a number of fields. The ActiveSheets Wizard displays a list of all available fields in the selected data source. Select the fields containing the data that you want to insert as columns into your worksheet.

◆ **To select fields:**

1. Select Distribution channel Text from the Available fields column.

2. Click on the Info button.

   The Info button provides you with additional information on the chosen field.

3. Close the Info window.

Add Column
button

4. Click on the Add Column button.

   The field is moved to the Selected field column.

5. Select and add the Net orders 1 and Sold-to party Text fields.

6. Click Sold-to party Text, then click the Move Up button twice.

   The field moves to the top of the list, and will be the first column in the worksheet.

7. Click Next.

   The next page of the Wizard displays.

The Available selection criteria listbox lists the criteria available to be used as constraining factors for your report. Selection criteria constrain the data in your report by certain type of value. Choose the desired criteria field from the available selection criteria, then specify the properties (placement and value) for the item.

◆   **To specify criteria:**

1. Select the Sales organization ID criteria and click on the Add
   Column button.

   The **Criteria Properties** dialog box displays. Here you can
   specify the criteria placement and value properties.

2. Click cell B2 on your worksheet.

   The cell you selected is recorded in the Location textbox.

3. Click in the Value textbox and press arrow to the right.

   A list of possible criteria values displays.

 *If the selection list is enabled in the ActiveSheets **Options**
dialog (General tab), you can retrieve a list of criteria values
from your R/3 system. The selection list can be used to find and
define specific criteria. Click on the arrow to the right of the
text box to view a drop-down list of all criteria values for the
selected item.*

4. Select 1000 Frankfurt Germany for the value.

5. Click OK.

   The sales organization ID is listed with a green check mark,
   indicating that its properties have been specified. The
   ActiveSheets Wizard places the criteria on your worksheet.

6. Click Next.

7. The next screen of the Wizard displays.

 *To give a more polished look to your worksheet, you can select
any of the ActiveSheets Wizard's built-in formats. You can see
what each format looks like in the Preview window.*

◆   **To select formatting:**

1. Select the Name the results area checkbox.

   ActiveSheets provides a default name, SalesOrganization, for your results area. When working with your report later, you can quickly select the results area by choosing this name from the Excel name box (located to the left of the formula bar).

2. Click Automatically format the results.

   The format list is enabled.

3. Select any format from the list and click Finish.

   The **Select Results Area** dialog box displays.

4. Click OK to accept the default values.

   The ActiveSheets Wizard places the report into your worksheet.

 You now have a complete report with an active link to R/3. Another great thing about ActiveSheets is that the report and chart need only be created once. You can email the workbook to other R/3 users, who can update the report if they have an R/3 information user profile.

Part IV:
Reference

Appendix A:
R/3 Configuration

This section details the activities that must be completed in order to enable users of ActiveSheets to access information from the R/3 system.

To perform the tasks in this section, you must:

- Have access to the R/3 system from which users will display data using ActiveSheets
- Know how to run transactions in R/3
- Have a basic understanding of R/3 info systems
- Have the appropriate system authorizations for modifying master data in R/3
- Have a basic understanding of ActiveSheets

Overview of Tasks

To configure ActiveSheets access to R/3, you need to:

- Configure the OIW (Open Information Warehouse) catalog. The OIW catalog contains references to the characteristics and values that users select from the ActiveSheets Wizard.
- Configure user authorizations. Consult with your system administration about configuring users with proper authorizations that conform to the security policy at your site.

Maintaining the OIW Info Catalog

ActiveSheets uses the Open Information Warehouse to access the SAP Logistics Information System (LIS). The LIS includes a variety of R/3 reporting tools, such as the Sales Information System and the Shop Floor Information System. (ActiveSheets also uses the Business Object Repository to retrieve business object reports in R/3.)

You need to configure the OIW catalog to supply the ActiveSheets Wizard with the reporting information—or metadata—it uses to insert reporting information into an Excel workbook. The OIW catalog is created from the LIS information structures defined in your system. In this way, the OIW information catalog provides the link between the reporting fields in the LIS info structure and your ActiveSheets workbook.

LIS information structures define the fields used for reporting within a specific R/3 application area. For example, the sales office information structure specifies the reporting fields used in ordering activities for a branch office or district, such as the gross and net order value and the quantities returned.

You can configure the OIW to:

- Access standard OIW info structures that are preinstalled with the R/3 system
- Access OIW reports custom-built for your company's R/3 system

---

Note: The steps for maintaining the OIW catalog are defined in the R/3 Implementation Guide (IMG). To view the steps in the IMG, first display the Enterprise IMG. Then select Open Information Warehouse under the chapter "Open Information Warehouse."

The system management at your site needs to perform certain customizing activities to make the OIW catalog available to users of ActiveSheets.

◆ **To enable access to the OIW catalog:**

1. Run transaction /nmcka (enter mcka in the command line).

   The maintain OIW metadata screen appears.

2. Select the metadata to maintain.

   If you need to access cost center accounting information, check the "Cost Center Accounting" box.

   For logistics data, select the "Standard info structures" checkbox. If your company has created its own info structures, enter the name of the infostructure or a range of info structures in the "Info structure" field.

   If you need to access Personnel Administration information, select the "Personnel Administration" or the "Recruitment" checkbox.

3. Press F8 to generate the metadata.

   The system generates all metadata description for the OIW Information Catalog. This catalog is displayed in the ActiveSheets Report Builder.

4. To display the metadata that will be used to build the catalog in the Report Builder, click on the Display button.

5. To delete the metadata, click on the Delete button.

Maintaining the OIW Catalog for Your Company

You can create an OIW Catalog specific to the needs of your company. The Information Catalog contains your company-specific data and displays it in the ActiveSheets Wizard.

◆ **To create a specific Information Catalog:**

1. Run transaction mck6 (enter /nmck6 in the command line).

2. If you want to make modifications only to the standard catalog, copy the standard OIW Catalog into your catalog. To copy the standard catalog, select "Copy standard info catalog" from the OIW catalog menu.

3. To create a new node, or entry, in the hierarchy, position the cursor on the node you want to modify. Select **Create nodes** from the **Edit** menu. Enter the name of the new node.

   The new node will contain the information objects from which users can select data in the ActiveSheets Wizard.

4. Assign information objects to the node.

Note: The information objects reference the characteristics and values for the data that users select from the ActiveSheets Wizard. "Material" is an example of an information object.

---

5. Position the cursor on the node to which you want to add information objects.

6. From the **Edit** menu select **Info Obj. Create**.

7. Select the source for the info object you want to add to your information catalog.

8. You can do this by:

- Copying information objects from an R/3 data source. A data source is a collection of characteristics and values that are continually updated by R/3. These are the standard data sources delivered with R/3. For example, the "Customer" data source contains all relevant information about customers in R/3, such as the amount a customer has ordered and the products ordered.
- Selecting from a list of standard information objects. Choose this option if you want to select specific info objects from the total set of information objects in R/3.
- Creating info objects from a selection version in R/3. A selection version contains a list of info objects. For example, a selection version might include all information objects for producing a report with the first quarter turnover for a customer.

9. Edit the nodes, deleting or changing them in the Information Catalog as needed.

10. Position the cursor on the selection, then choose **Delete** or **Rename** from the **Edit** menu.

11. To save your work, choose **Save** from the **Information Catalog** menu.

Authorizations for ActiveSheets

ActiveSheets uses R/3 security to restrict access to company information. This section describes the R/3 authorizations required for users of ActiveSheets. Your system administration requires this information before it grants ActiveSheets users the appropriate permissions for accessing data in R/3.

Note: This section specifies the minimum set of values for authorizations. Please note that users may need additional authorizations, depending upon the type of reporting information that they need to access. This is especially true of the ActiveSheets Wizard, since it allows access to a wide range of information that may be sensitive to your organization.

Standard Profiles

You can use the following standard user profile as a guide for creating new R/3 users for ActiveSheets. You can also use these profiles to extend permissions of existing users to include access to R/3 data via ActiveSheets.

- See profile M_OIW_ALL.

Tip: If you want to grant ActiveSheets users access to all reporting data in the ActiveSheets Wizard, assign the users the standard display profile ANZEIGE This profile grants display privileges in all application areas.

Authorization Details

If desired, you can restrict access to specific information. The following represents the minimum authorizations required for ActiveSheets.

◆ **For ActiveSheets:**

M_OIW_META Activity = *

Tip: For users who need only access ActiveSheets, create a user with the user type "information user." You do this by selecting "measurement data" when editing or creating the user master.

Appendix B:
Reference Help

Here you will find reference help for all ActiveSheets features and functions. This appendix provides information for the following items:

- ActiveSheets Toolbar
- ActiveSheets Menu Items
- Loading the Add-ins

ActiveSheets Toolbar

    Log on to the R/3 system

OR

Log off from R/3

Start the ActiveSheets Wizard

Recalculate your current worksheet using data from R/3

Copy the worksheet using current values only (breaks active link to R/3)

Display the online Help file

ActiveSheets Menu Items

The following items are located on the **ActiveSheets** menu in Excel. For more information, see ActiveSheets Functions in Chapter 5.

R/3 Connection: Connects or disconnects from R/3, and provides connection information:

> **Logon:** Initiates a connection to R/3.
>
> **Logoff:** Closes your connection to R/3.
>
> **Connection Information:** Displays system administration information on your R/3 connection.

ActiveSheets Wizard: Activates the ActiveSheets Wizard and logs on to R/3.

Auto Recalculation: Recalculates formulas whenever you change any of the formula precedents.

Recalculate Sheet: Recalculates all the formulas on the active worksheet from R/3.

Copy as Values Only: Eliminates the active connection between the displayed data and the formulas.

Options: Contains the following four tabs—Prompts, General, Local Catalog, and Advanced—which will customize your ActiveSheets reports as required.

ActiveSheets Help: Displays the online Help file.

About ActiveSheets: Displays version information on the ActiveSheets add-in.

Loading the Add-ins

ActiveSheets includes add-ins that will need to be installed into your Microsoft Excel program. If the setup process was executed successfully, the ActiveSheets add-ins have already been installed into Excel.

Note: Before you can use an add-in, you must install it on your computer and then load it into Microsoft Excel. Loading an add-in makes the ActiveSheets feature available in Microsoft Excel and adds certain commands to the appropriate menus. By default, add-ins (*.xla files) are installed in the library folder within the Microsoft Excel folder. However, the ActiveSheets add-in is installed in the ActiveSheets folder.

◆ **To Load the ActiveSheets add-in:**

1. Start Microsoft Excel.

2. Choose **Add-ins** from the **Tools** menu.

   The **Add-ins** dialog opens.

3. Scroll through the list and see if ActiveSheets appears in the list.

4. If it does, simply make sure that the checkbox next to it is selected and click OK to close the **Add-ins** dialog. If ActiveSheets does not appear in the list, continue with the following steps.

5. Click on the Browse button in the **Add-ins** dialog.

   The **Browse** dialog opens.

6. Navigate to the directory in which you have installed ActiveSheets and click on ActShts.xla.

7. Click OK to close the **Browse** dialog.

8. Click OK to close the **Add-ins** dialog.

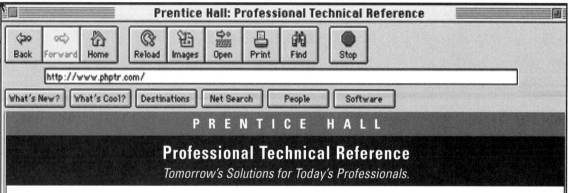

LICENSE AGREEMENT AND LIMITED WARRANTY

READ THE FOLLOWING TERMS AND CONDITIONS CAREFULLY BEFORE OPENING THIS SOFTWARE MEDIA PACKAGE. THIS LEGAL DOCUMENT IS AN AGREEMENT BETWEEN YOU AND PRENTICE-HALL, INC. (THE "COMPANY"). BY OPENING THIS SEALED SOFTWARE MEDIA PACKAGE, YOU ARE AGREEING TO BE BOUND BY THESE TERMS AND CONDITIONS. IF YOU DO NOT AGREE WITH THESE TERMS AND CONDITIONS, DO NOT OPEN THE SOFTWARE MEDIA PACKAGE. PROMPTLY RETURN THE UNOPENED SOFTWARE MEDIA PACKAGE AND ALL ACCOMPANYING ITEMS TO THE PLACE YOU OBTAINED THEM FOR A FULL REFUND OF ANY SUMS YOU HAVE PAID.

1.   **GRANT OF LICENSE:** In consideration of your payment of the license fee, which is part of the price you paid for this product, and your agreement to abide by the terms and conditions of this Agreement, the Company grants to you a nonexclusive right to use and display the copy of the enclosed software program (hereinafter the "SOFTWARE") on a single computer (i.e., with a single CPU) at a single location so long as you comply with the terms of this Agreement. The Company reserves all rights not expressly granted to you under this Agreement.

2.   **OWNERSHIP OF SOFTWARE:** You own only the magnetic or physical media (the enclosed software media) on which the SOFTWARE is recorded or fixed, but the Company retains all the rights, title, and ownership to the SOFTWARE recorded on the original software media copy(ies) and all subsequent copies of the SOFTWARE, regardless of the form or media on which the original or other copies may exist. This license is not a sale of the original SOFTWARE or any copy to you.

3.   **COPY RESTRICTIONS:** This SOFTWARE and the accompanying printed materials and user manual (the "Documentation") are the subject of copyright. You may not copy the Documentation or the SOFTWARE, except that you may make a single copy of the SOFTWARE for backup or archival purposes only. You may be held legally responsible for any copying or copyright infringement which is caused or encouraged by your failure to abide by the terms of this restriction.

4.   **USE RESTRICTIONS:** You may not network the SOFTWARE or otherwise use it on more than one computer or computer terminal at the same time. You may physically transfer the SOFTWARE from one computer to another provided that the SOFTWARE is used on only one computer at a time. You may not distribute copies of the SOFTWARE or Documentation to others. You may not reverse engineer, disassemble, decompile, modify, adapt, translate, or create derivative works based on the SOFTWARE or the Documentation without the prior written consent of the Company.

5.   **TRANSFER RESTRICTIONS:** The enclosed SOFTWARE is licensed only to you and may not be transferred to any one else without the prior written consent of the Company. Any unauthorized transfer of the SOFTWARE shall result in the immediate termination of this Agreement.

6.   **TERMINATION:** This license is effective until terminated. This license will terminate automatically without notice from the Company and become null and void if you fail to comply with any provisions or limitations of this license. Upon termination, you shall destroy the Documentation and all copies of the SOFTWARE. All provisions of this Agreement as to warranties, limitation of liability, remedies or damages, and our ownership rights shall survive termination.

7.   **MISCELLANEOUS:** This Agreement shall be construed in accordance with the laws of the United States of America and the State of New York and shall benefit the Company, its affiliates, and assignees.

8.   **LIMITED WARRANTY AND DISCLAIMER OF WARRANTY:** The Company warrants that the SOFTWARE, when properly used in accordance with the Documentation, will operate in substantial conformity with the description of the SOFTWARE set forth in the Documentation. The Company does not warrant that the SOFTWARE will meet your requirements or that the operation of the SOFTWARE will be uninterrupted or error-free. The Company warrants that the media on which the SOFTWARE is delivered shall be free from defects in materials and workmanship under normal use for a period of thirty (30) days from the date of your purchase. Your only remedy and the Company's only obligation under these limited warranties is, at the Company's option, return of the warranted item for a refund of any amounts paid by you or replacement of the item. Any replacement of SOFTWARE or media under the warranties shall not extend the original warranty period. The limited warranty set forth above shall not apply to any SOFTWARE which the Company determines in good faith has been subject to misuse, neglect, improper installation, repair, alteration, or dam-

age by you. EXCEPT FOR THE EXPRESSED WARRANTIES SET FORTH ABOVE, THE COMPANY DISCLAIMS ALL WARRANTIES, EXPRESS OR IMPLIED, INCLUDING WITHOUT LIMITATION, THE IMPLIED WARRANTIES OF MERCHANTABILITY AND FITNESS FOR A PARTICULAR PURPOSE. EXCEPT FOR THE EXPRESS WARRANTY SET FORTH ABOVE, THE COMPANY DOES NOT WARRANT, GUARANTEE, OR MAKE ANY REPRESENTATION REGARDING THE USE OR THE RESULTS OF THE USE OF THE SOFTWARE IN TERMS OF ITS CORRECTNESS, ACCURACY, RELIABILITY, CURRENTNESS, OR OTHERWISE.

IN NO EVENT, SHALL THE COMPANY OR ITS EMPLOYEES, AGENTS, SUPPLIERS, OR CONTRACTORS BE LIABLE FOR ANY INCIDENTAL, INDIRECT, SPECIAL, OR CONSEQUENTIAL DAMAGES ARISING OUT OF OR IN CONNECTION WITH THE LICENSE GRANTED UNDER THIS AGREEMENT, OR FOR LOSS OF USE, LOSS OF DATA, LOSS OF INCOME OR PROFIT, OR OTHER LOSSES, SUSTAINED AS A RESULT OF INJURY TO ANY PERSON, OR LOSS OF OR DAMAGE TO PROPERTY, OR CLAIMS OF THIRD PARTIES, EVEN IF THE COMPANY OR AN AUTHORIZED REPRESENTATIVE OF THE COMPANY HAS BEEN ADVISED OF THE POSSIBILITY OF SUCH DAMAGES. IN NO EVENT SHALL LIABILITY OF THE COMPANY FOR DAMAGES WITH RESPECT TO THE SOFTWARE EXCEED THE AMOUNTS ACTUALLY PAID BY YOU, IF ANY, FOR THE SOFTWARE.

SOME JURISDICTIONS DO NOT ALLOW THE LIMITATION OF IMPLIED WARRANTIES OR LIABILITY FOR INCIDENTAL, INDIRECT, SPECIAL, OR CONSEQUENTIAL DAMAGES, SO THE ABOVE LIMITATIONS MAY NOT ALWAYS APPLY. THE WARRANTIES IN THIS AGREEMENT GIVE YOU SPECIFIC LEGAL RIGHTS AND YOU MAY ALSO HAVE OTHER RIGHTS WHICH VARY IN ACCORDANCE WITH LOCAL LAW.

ACKNOWLEDGMENT

YOU ACKNOWLEDGE THAT YOU HAVE READ THIS AGREEMENT, UNDERSTAND IT, AND AGREE TO BE BOUND BY ITS TERMS AND CONDITIONS. YOU ALSO AGREE THAT THIS AGREEMENT IS THE COMPLETE AND EXCLUSIVE STATEMENT OF THE AGREEMENT BETWEEN YOU AND THE COMPANY AND SUPERSEDES ALL PROPOSALS OR PRIOR AGREEMENTS, ORAL, OR WRITTEN, AND ANY OTHER COMMUNICATIONS BETWEEN YOU AND THE COMPANY OR ANY REPRESENTATIVE OF THE COMPANY RELATING TO THE SUBJECT MATTER OF THIS AGREEMENT.

Should you have any questions concerning this Agreement or if you wish to contact the Company for any reason, please contact in writing at the address below.

Robin Short
Prentice Hall PTR
One Lake Street
Upper Saddle River, New Jersey 07458

ABOUT THE CD

This CD contains the ActiveSheets program. Just follow the instructions that follow after you insert the disk.

Installation

ActiveSheets is only installed on a client machine. The back-end R/3™ services can run on any type of machine that supports R/3™. ActiveSheets requires Windows 95 or Windows NT (Service Pack 3), and requires Microsoft Excel 97 with Service Release 1 or 2.

Security

ActiveSheets uses exactly the same security model as the R/3™ SAPGUI. Users must logon with the same information they would use for logging on to the SAPGUI. A user can see a piece of data in ActiveSheets if and only if they can see it in SAPGUI.

Modules

ActiveSheets works with all modules of SAP™ R/3™ that have corresponding information structures. This includes Sales and Distribution, Materials Management, Production Planning, etc. In short, if there is an entry in some "Information System" group (e.g., Logistics Information System), then that information is available through ActiveSheets. ActiveSheets can also access FI/CO information through Report Writer Reports with some restrictions (see OSS note 82836).

Documentation

The documentation found in the back of this book contains the complete documentation for the ActiveSheets software. The documentation will help you get up and running in a short amount of time. You will learn the basic features of ActiveSheets, and how to use the software to build R/3™ reports.

Technical Support

Prentice Hall does not offer technical support for this software. However, if there is a problem with the media, you may obtain a replacement copy by e-mailing us with your problem at: disc_exchange@prenhall.com